AUSTRALIA

ANTHONY TROLLOPE

AUSTRALIA

VOLUME I

ALAN SUTTON · Gloucester
HIPPOCRENE BOOKS, INC. · New York
1987

First Published 1873

Copyright © in this edition 1987
Alan Sutton Publishing Limited

This edition first published in Great Britain 1987
 Alan Sutton Publishing Limited
 30 Brunswick Road
 Gloucester GL1 1JJ

British Library Cataloguing in Publication Data

Trollope, Anthony
 Australia.
 1. Australia—Description and
 travel—1851–1900
 I. Title
 919.4′.0431   DU102

ISBN 0–86299–321–0

This edition first published in the U.S.A. 1987
 Hippocrene Books, Inc.
 171 Madison Avenue
 New York, N.Y. 10016

ISBN 0–87052–390–2

Cover picture: detail from Hobart *by George Rowe*
Photograph: courtesy of Cheltenham Museum and Art Gallery

Typesetting and origination by
Alan Sutton Publishing Limited.
Photoset Bembo 9/10
Printed in Great Britain
by The Guernsey Press Company Limited,
Guernsey, Channel Islands.

CONTENTS

VICTORIA

NEW SOUTH WALES

TASMANIA

BIOGRAPHICAL NOTE

In his *Autobiography*, Trollope explains how he spent the early years of his life 'in a world altogether outside the world of my material life.' In this world nothing impossibly fantastic happened, but stories developed in a serial way over months and even years. Although nothing was written down, these imaginings obviously provided the foundation for Trollope's later prolific creativity. He finally found a release from the drudgery and boredom of clerical work in 1841, when he was accepted as a post office surveyor's clerk at Banagher, in King's County, Ireland.

'This', remarked Trollope of his Irish posting, 'was the first good fortune of my life.' He started to make a success of his job as inspector and investigator of the local postal service, in spite of, or perhaps because of, his brusque manner; he developed a taste for hunting and mixing with the Irish gentry; he married, and his English wife, Rose, bore him two sons. Most importantly, he started writing. The first four pieces of work published were not best-sellers, by any means, but two, *The Macdermots of Ballycloran* (1847) and *The Kellys and the O'Kellys* (1848), received some critical acclaim and showed the author's potential.

Trollope's first successful novel, *The Warden* (1855), was not finished until he was once again in Ireland, having completed an assignment in the South West of England reorganizing the postal system. It was while there, that he conceived the idea of Barsetshire. In 1857 *Barchester Towers* was published, and Trollope's reputation was further established with the appearance of *The Three Clerks* a year later. 1858 also saw the publication of *Doctor Thorne* and the completion of *The Bertrams* (published 1859). Thenceforth Trollope's output was considerable – two or three books appearing every year until 1883. He wrote well over forty novels, various collections of short stories, travel books, a translation of Caesar's Commentaries, a life of Cicero, an appreciation of Thackeray, and an autobiography.

Trollope's approach to his art was extremely disciplined. He would write a set number of pages before breakfast every day, no matter where he was. *Lady Anna* (1874), for example, was written on a voyage out to Australia. Of his technique he said he went to work 'just like a shoemaker on a shoe, only taking care to make honest stitches.' But another admission reveals that, in spite of his disciplined approach, he was totally involved in his characters: 'I have wandered alone among the woods and rocks, crying at their grief, laughing at their absurdities and thoroughly enjoying their joy.'

The Post Office was indirectly responsible for Trollope's first travel book, because after a successful mission to Egypt in 1858, he was sent to review the postal services of the Caribbean Islands and Central America. This voyage gave rise to *The West Indies and the Spanish Main*, an immediately successful travelogue. Trollope later wrote about the other continents he visited, producing *North America* in 1862, *Australia and New Zealand* in 1873, when he travelled out for the marriage of his farming son, and *South Africa* in 1878.

It was during the sixties that Trollope's most famous works appeared: *Framley Parsonage* (1861), *Orley Farm* (1862), *The Small House at Allington* (1864) *The Last Chronicle of Barset* (1867). After his trip to the Caribbean, he had been appointed Surveyor of the Eastern District of England, and he had bought a house in Waltham cross. His new proximity to London allowed him to mix with the literati of England for the first time. He very soon became a popular member of the Garrick Club, the Athenaeum, and the Cosmopolitan, and he must have been stimulated by his new cultural environment. He admired and became friends with both Thackeray and George Eliot (at whose house he met many famous writers of the day including Turgenev). He was also a close friend of John Everett Millais, who illustrated *Framley Parsonage*, *Orley Farm*, and other novels. He visited his brother and mother in Italy several times, and there he met the Brownings and also a young American, Kate Field, whom he saw irregularly and with whom he corresponded until his death.

When he was fifty-two, in 1867, Trollope resigned from the Post Office and relied on his literary output for finance. He became editor of the new *St. Paul's Magazine*, but he did not enjoy the work and gave it up after three years. During that time he had political aspirations, as is reflected in the writing of the Palliser novels, but his attempt to stand as Parliamentary candidate for Beverley in 1868 was a failure.

Earlier in that same year, he had been in America, and had written *The Vicar of Bulhampton* while in New York. He thought that the story, which was about a prostitute, might be found distasteful, and therefore included an explanatory preface, but *The Times* commented: '. . . the general safeness of the story will make Bulhampton Vicarage welcome to all well-regulated families.' On the other hand, *Lady Anna*, written six years later caused considerable disturbance. The *Saturday Review* warned their readers against it, so that they 'may not betray into reading what will probably leave a disagreeable impression'. Many people, however, did read the novel, and some wrote to Trollope expressing their objections. Apparently the idea of an Earl's daughter honourably marrying a tailor was too extreme a notion for the class-bound Victorian society.

In 1870 Trollope sold Waltham House and moved into London, to Montagu Square. He gave up hunting, but kept his horses and often rode in London. During the seventies he wrote prolifically and travelled widely. His fame was past its peak, but in 1873 he was featured in the popular weekly, *Vanity Fair*, with a cartoon and text, which included: '. . . He is a correct painter of the small things of our small modern English life . . . His manners are a little rough, as is his voice, but he is nevertheless extremely popular among his personal friends . . .' The character outline is complemented and extended by J.R. Lowell's description: '. . . Anthony Trollope, a big red-faced rather underbred Englishman of the bald-with-spectacles type . . . A good roaring fellow who deafened me'; and by G.A. Sala's: 'Crusty, quarrelsome, wrongheaded, prejudiced, obstinate, kind-hearted and thoroughly honest old Tony Tollope.'

All his life Trollope was subject to depression because of what Escott, his biographer, explains as an 'almost feminine sensibility to the opinions of others, a self-consciousness altogether abnormal in a sensible and practical man of the world, as well as a strong love of approbation, whether from stranger or friend.'

By the end of the decade, Trollope was a familiar figure at literary gatherings in London, and in the country. He was a guest both at Lord Carnarvon's home at Highclere, Hampshire, and at Waddesdon Manor, the home of Baron Rothschild. But his health was declining and in 1880 he moved from London to the more salubrious area of the South Downs. He bought The Grange at South Harting in Hampshire, and there he wrote his last novels. These reflected his pessimistic outlook, and two of them concentrated on problems of growing older: *Mr. Scarborough's Family* and *An Old Man's Love*, the first a study of eccentricity, and the second a story of an older man's love for a younger woman. In 1882 he started his final novel, *The Landleaguers*, which was, like his first novel, set in Ireland. He made two trips to Ireland during that year to collect material which probably contributed to a rapid deterioration in his health and in the October of that year he moved up to London for the Winter. He suffered a stroke in November, and died five weeks later on 6 December 1882. He was buried in Kensal Green Cemetery. 'He was removed in a lusty majority, and before decay had begun to cripple his indefatigable industry or dull the brightness of his versatile fancy' (from his obituary in *The Times*).

SHEILA MICHELL

VICTORIA

CHAPTER I

SEPARATION

I propose in this chapter to say a few words as to the treatment which the Australian colonies generally have received and are receiving from the mother country. In the next I will endeavour to trace very shortly the early history of the most populous and most important in the group, and in doing so I will take my facts from a pamphlet lately published by Mr. G. W. Rusden, of Melbourne; – than whom I have found no one better informed on the affairs of Australia generally, and whose information, conveyed in a small compass, is the latest that has been given to us, – bearing the date September, 1871.

It may perhaps be right that I should state that Mr. Rusden's pamphlet is dedicated to myself, lest they who are disposed to think that I am here repaying one compliment by another may claim to have 'found me out' should they ever happen to have the two books in their hands at the same time. I find it also convenient to allude to the circumstance, in order that I may take this occasion of expressing an opinion as to the future destiny of our Australian colonies, which is specially evoked by a certain passage in Mr. Rusden's dedication. He, a colonist, seems to regard the colonies as an element in England's future glory, – to look upon Victoria, for instance, as one of the gems by which that glory is to be maintained and consummated. I, on the other hand, who am an Englishman, look upon the colonies as an element, and a very material element, in the future happiness of Englishmen, – or of men and women of English origin, – thinking that England's glory should be left altogether out of the question in any consideration of the matter. Mr. Rusden speaks of the revolt of the American colonies having been brought about by the 'wicked folly of Grenville and North,' as though the effects of that revolt were still to be deplored, and implies that any act

tending to the separation of the Australian colonies from the
mother country would be tainted with the same folly and
partake of the same wickedness. It is most remarkable that this
should be the aspect in which the future of these Australian
colonies is regarded by all the best minds among the colonists.
One hardly meets with an exception among educated men of
British origin. The few of this class who entertain feelings and
opinions of an opposite tendency are generally Irishmen,
whose immigration has been of a comparatively late date.

I hope that I am not myself dead to England's glory. I am
indeed well aware that my own feeling on the matter – my
own belief in my own country's pre-excellence, – is so near to
self- praise, that it should be checked rather than enforced. But
I cannot believe that the homes of millions of human beings
around the world are to be made subject to any special form of
government, or that their mode of living is to be regulated in
any special fashion, because such may be the form of
government and such the fashion of living adopted by the
country from which those millions have sprung, and whose
language those millions speak. This form of government and
this fashion of living may be the best the world has yet
known. I, with my English idiosyncrasies, do believe that
they are so. I believe further, – that we at home, with the
honest, high-spirited, high-handed, blundering philanthropy
which is peculiar to us, have, in spite of all the abuse which we
have lavished upon ourselves in the matter, done nearly the
best that we could have done with these colonies. But not on
that account can I bring myself to look forward to their being
kept as 'gems' in England's 'diadem.' As long as the national
prosperity of the colonies can be advanced by their dependence on England, that dependence England is bound, both
morally and politically, to maintain. When the time shall come
in which the colonies can serve themselves better by
separation than by prolonged adherence, England, I think,
should let them go. The difficulty will consist in fixing the
time; – but this question of time is one which must be solved
mainly by the colonies themselves. It will be for them to
declare, as it was for the United States, when that time shall
have come. It will be for us to take care that, when the time
does come, the work of separation may be effected, not only

without hostility, but without acerbating roughness.

'Here is a continent secured,' says Mr. Rusden, 'as never was continent secured by the genius of one man, for his countrymen to occupy.' The one man is Mr. Pitt, to whose policy and firmness in opposing the attempts which were being made at the same time and with the same object by the French government Mr. Rusden attributes the final acquisition by England of Australia. 'On the soil of Victoria there stand between seven and eight hundred thousand persons where twenty years ago there stood some seventy thousand. Thus fresh from their native land, are they not bone of their bone and flesh of their flesh to all living Englishmen as fully as if they still stood on English soil? Must it not be the shabbiest of statesmanship either in England or in the colony which would fret away the ties that bind the one to the other?'

Of course it is matter of pride to us Englishmen that there should be so many of our people in Victoria, – and matter of higher pride that there should be some forty millions speaking our language, and living almost entirely by our laws, and in accordance with our fashions, on the continent of North America. We may probably take the language spoken as the truest indication of the influence of nationality and the justest source of national pride. From our little island we have sent forth a people speaking English who are spreading themselves over all the world. It is a much greater boast than that of ruling dependencies on which the sun never sets. Though none of the English-speaking nations on the farther side of the globe should any longer acknowledge themselves to be dependent on England, it would matter nothing to the happiness of the race, and nothing to the true glory of the nationality, – so long as the numbers increased, and the material prosperity of those numbers. We are very proud of Victoria, – very proud of having colonised a country rich in gold and rich in flocks, and fitted by nature not only to support but to maintain and to increase the energy which is the gift of our race. We hope that the seven or eight hundred thousand may, as years run on, be quickly raised to millions. That they should have increased so rapidly, and been so prosperous in their increase, is to all of us a matter of self-congratulation. Though individually we at home may be less conversant than we ought with Australian affairs, we keep a sufficiently accurate record in our minds of her rising condition among the communities of the world. We know that the Australians are bone of our bone and flesh of our flesh, as fully as though they still stood on English soil. And we know the same of the Americans of the United States, – in spite of the 'Alabama' and indirect claims; in spite of rows about the 'Trent'; in spite of existing political differences; in spite of hostilities, should there be hostilities; and in spite even of war, should there be war. The grandchildren of our grandfathers are living there in prosperity and freedom, worshipping the God whom we worship, speaking the language which we speak, obeying the laws which we obey, and animated by that resolve to rule themselves, and to be free from the rule of individuals, which they took from our shores, and which is as strong with us as it is with them.

I deny, therefore, altogether the shabbiness of the statesmanship, whether in England or in the colonies, which would, – not fret away, – but gradually dissolve the ties which bind the one to the other. Such statesmanship, – when it exists, for as yet I am not aware that it has existed, – may be wrong, may be premature, may be one-sided, may indeed possibly be shabby. Of what matter open to statesmanship may not the same be said? But to declare that the statesmanship must be shabby that shall have the object of allowing the colonies to start themselves as a separate people at some future time, is to pronounce an opinion, – that indeed may be excused by the warm love of country which it indicates, – but which can never stand an argument.

I am not aware that any British statesman has as yet entertained the idea of dividing the mother country from her Australian colonies, – has ever thought that the time has now come in which he himself might go to work and arrange the terms of separation. But I imagine that no British statesman ever employs himself in the affairs of these colonies without a conviction that, in all that he does, he should have before his eyes the fact that separation will come at some future day. It is impossible that any statesman, or any speculator, that any philosopher should foresee the time. It must depend on the increasing wealth and the increasing population of the country. Any invention, – if such invention be within the bounds of natural possibility, – which should save the wheat crops of the South Australian colonies from the disease called Red Rust, would greatly accelerate separation, because it would at once increase the population and the wealth of the colonies. Iron has been found, but iron mines have never yet been properly worked. If this could be done to any great extent, it would accelerate separation. Increased supplies of copper and gold will do so; – the finding of tin will do so; – success in making sugar will do so; – and the exportation of fresh uncooked meat to Europe, when such exportation becomes practicable, will do so very materially. Does anybody believe that a population of twenty millions in Australia would remain subject to a population of forty millions in the British Isles? And the former numbers may be reached as quickly as the latter.

There is very much to be done before the question of separation can be regarded as one that is imminent, or fit for the immediate manipulations of statesmanship. Australia must be one whole before she can settle herself and take a place among the nations. There must be some federation of the different colonies before separation can be considered. The states must bind themselves together with the united object of making themselves a nation, and the men who now pride themselves on being Victorians, or South Australians, or Queenslanders, must learn to pride themselves on being Australians. At present they are very far from entertaining any such pride. The inhabitant of Melbourne thinks himself to be very much higher than the inhabitant of Sydney, and looks down from a great eminence upon the Tasmanian. In New South Wales there is a desire to maintain the distance between itself and Victoria, – as though a gulf between the two, which could not be passed, would be for its good. Queensland, the youngest daughter of New South Wales, has but little respect for her parent. South Australia thinks herself better than her neighbours because she has never received a convict. There is, no doubt, something of similar jealousy between different groups of states in the American Union; – but there they have learned the strength of union and have preserved it. As Australia becomes older, and as the number of her leading children who are Australian-born becomes greater, as the tendency to lean upon the mother country becomes slighter, the feeling for the newer patriotism will grow up; and with the feeling of Australian pride will grow the conviction that Australia, to be great and strong, should be one.

The first step towards federation will be the union of the colonies for purposes of general taxation. At present the two great sources of public revenue are the customs duties and the sale and lease of public lands. Let the union be as close as it may, the use of the public lands will probably remain in each colony, – to be applied as may best suit its own wants, – but the customs duties, from which by far the greater proportion of the public revenue is derived, may, and no doubt will, be collected under one tariff, by one arrangement, for the joint purposes of the whole group. At present these colonies all stand towards each other as though they were various nations, with varied interests, and endeavour each to rise on the commercial injuries inflicted on the others by hostile tariffs. They charge duties on each other's produce, and are towards each other as were England and France before Mr. Cobden had made his treaty. I do not purpose here to fight the battle of the border duties, – but here, and again hereafter, I must repeat the opinion, expressed by me in speaking of the other colonies, that at the present moment the creation of a customs union should be the first duty of any statesman to whom the interests and well-being of the colonies may be entrusted.

I look first to a customs union, then to federation, and then after some interval, – the duration of which I will not attempt to indicate, – to Separation and Self-control. In this idea as to the future of the colonies I cannot think that I am guilty of any shabbiness as an Englishman. And yet the expression of the accusation in Australia is by no means confined to the gentleman whose words I have quoted. Had it been so, – had I not found it general among those whom I describe as possessing the best minds in the colonies, – I should probably have contented myself in endeavouring to defend myself from the charge with the eager arguments to which private intercourse is open. But I have heard on all sides accusations of the littleness of England, – and worse than littleness, of the weakness and infanticide of which England is guilty, in her desire to repudiate and put away from her her own children. I

have heard it in details and in generals. England will not pay
for this statue, or subscribe for that building; she will not give
cannons and cannon-balls gratis; she has not left the vestige of
a company of soldiers in any one of the colonies; she charges a
price for whatever she supplies, and does not always supply
the best articles; when asked for selected emigrants she selects
the dregs of the workhouses. There are these and a hundred
other details which show the heart of a stepmother rather than
of a parent. But the great general accusation is stronger still.
Her statesmen, – or at least some of the chief among them, –
have declared their opinion that the links should be broken
which bind Australia to the mother country. In regard to the
details the answer is easy enough. The daughter has had her
dowry given to her, – and should now pay her own way, and
is able to do so. It often seems to be forgotten, in the colonies,
that British statesmen cannot give away English property out
of their own munificence. The colonies have agreed, with
willingness, to certain terms, which certainly for them have
not been unprofitable, and should not now ask for further
small gifts. When our boys and girls are young we expect
them to assail us for half-crowns, and rather like putting our
hands in our pockets, even when we affect to rebuke the
frequency of the solicitation; but when our girls are married
and have had their fortunes, or when our sons have been set up
in business by considerable self-sacrifice on the part of us their
fathers, we do not like then to be told that we ought to pay for
new carpets or cases of champagne. As to that general
accusation, I think it is founded not on any words spoken or
acts done tending to immediate Separation, but on words and
acts preparatory to Separation when it shall come.

The mistake I think is in this, – that the colonists allow
themselves to believe that the mother country is repudiating
them because the statesmen want to save themselves trouble,
and because her people desire to avoid expense, – whereas at
home we feel, not a wish to repudiate the colonies, but a
conviction that after a while they will repudiate us, and that
we are bound by our duty to them and to ourselves to be ready
for the time when that repudiation shall come. We are called
upon to rule them, – as far as we do rule them, – not for our
glory, but for their happiness. If we keep them, we should

keep them, – not because they add prestige to the name of Great Britain, not because they are gems in our diadem, not in order that we may boast that the sun never sets on our dependencies, but because by keeping them we may best assist them in developing their own resources. And when we part with them, as part with them we shall, let us do so with neither smothered jealousy nor open hostility, but with a proud feeling that we are sending a son out into the world able to take his place among men. That is the halcyon view which I entertain of the closing days of the connection between England and Australia; and I think that it is one which is tainted with no shabbiness, and which should make me subject to no reproof from any colonist.

CHAPTER II

EARLY HISTORY OF PORT PHILLIP

'The Discovery, Survey, and Settlement of Port Phillip,' is the name of the pamphlet to which I have alluded, and to which I shall mainly trust for the facts to be stated in this chapter. In the lines which I shall quote between inverted commas in the early part of this chapter, the reader will understand that I am quoting the words of the author, Mr. Rusden.

In the year 1802, fourteen years after the first actual occupation by the English of New South Wales, the inland sea which we now know as Port Phillip was first discovered by Lieutenant Murray, who had come out from England under Captain Grant in 'The Nelson' with the special object of prosecuting Australian discoveries. The name was given by Captain King, the then governor of New South Wales, in honour of Colonel Phillip, the first governor. Captain Flinders, who, in regard to this period of Australian discovery, is Mr. Rusden's great hero, followed Lieutenant Murray after an interval of ten weeks. The French, in their exploration of the southern coast of New Holland, conducted by Captain Baudin, had sailed past the narrow entrance of Port Phillip without noticing it, and had called the whole region in those parts Terre Napoléon. Indeed they afterwards gave an appellation of their own to the harbour, but did not subsequently attempt to establish it. Captain Flinders, whose name is now perhaps better known from the street in Melbourne which bears it than from the deeds which he did and the sufferings which he bore in these discoveries, is the first who has left us any record of his having landed on the country which we now call Victoria. 'At day dawn,' – says Captain Flinders, as reported by Mr. Rusden, – 'I set off with three of the boat's crew for the highest part of the back hills, called Station Peak. Our way was over a low plain where the water appeared frequently to lodge; it was covered with small-bladed grass, but almost destitute of wood, and the soil was clayey and shallow. I left the ship's name on a scroll of paper deposited on a small pile of stones upon the top of the peak; and at three in the afternoon, – 1st May (1802), – reached the tent much fatigued, having walked more than twenty miles without finding a drop of water. No runs of fresh water were seen in my excursion; but Mr. Charles Grimes, surveyor-general of New South Wales, afterwards found several, and in particular a small river falling into the northern head of the port.' This small river was the Yarra Yarra, on which the city of Melbourne is now built, – and such was, in truth, the first discovery of Victoria.

In 1803 Colonel Collins landed at Port Phillip to form a penal settlement, intended as a supplemental offshoot to that then fully established at Port Jackson, – which the world used to call Botany Bay, – on the eastern shore of the continent; but he seems to have chosen his site badly, and to have kept his men close down upon the sea-shore where there was no fresh water. This attempt at a settlement was made at Point Nepean, the eastern headland at the mouth of Port Phillip, and was soon abandoned. The depôt was removed thence to the mouth of the Derwent, on the opposite island, and was the commencement of the great penal depôt which afterwards flourished in Van Diemen's Land, – if an establishment for the custody of convicts may under any circumstances be said to flourish. From the settlement at Point Nepean some of the convicts escaped, and one of them was neither retaken, nor did he return, nor did he perish. This man, named Buckley, lived thirty-two years among the blacks, forgot his own language, and became as one of them. In 1835 he reappeared, and was found by a party of white men who then landed at Port Phillip from Van Diemen's Land.

'No effort was made to colonise Port Phillip for many years after 1803.' But during all those years explorations from Sydney as a centre were being made into the continent. 'In 1817 Oxley, the surveyor-general of New South Wales, had traced the Lachlan River nearly to its junction with the Murrumbidgee, and had therefore nearly approached the present boundary of Victoria, being within 240 miles of the site of Melbourne.' In 1824 an expedition was formed under the auspices of Sir Thomas Brisbane, the governor, the object of which was to penetrate through from the known parts of New South Wales, across the rivers and over the mountains, to the southern coast. This expedition was entrusted to Mr. Hamilton Hume, who was joined by Mr. Hovell, two men whose names are well known among those of Australian discoverers. Both these gentlemen were still alive when I was in the colony, and I will not take upon myself to give either of them the greater credit in the matter, but will content myself with stating that Mr. Rusden is a strong advocate of Mr. Hume's claims. The great Australian river which we know as the Murray was crossed, and was called the Hume, which name it still bears in its upper waters. After many sufferings and great dangers, Hume and Hovell reached Port Phillip overland. It will be understood that hitherto this district had only been touched from the sea-board, and that the very scanty knowledge possessed by Hume and Hovell as to Port Phillip and Western Port was simply that which had resulted from the maritime discoveries of Murray and Flinders. At any rate they had reached the southern coast of that 'Terre Napoléon,' of which as yet no real possession had been taken on behalf of the British government. Another expedition was then made by sea to Western Port, under Governor Darling's instructions, apparently with the double object of opening a subsidiary convict establishment, and of confirming the claim made by Great Britain to the possession of the country. This was commanded by Captain Wright, accompanied by Mr. Hovell, – and was made in 1826, – at which time also another convict offshoot of the centre establishment at Port Jackson was sent under Major Lockyer to King George's Sound, – the southern part of that colony which we now call Western Australia. This seems also to have been made with the double object of disposing of convicts, and taking possession of the land as against French claims. Major Lockyer had some success, but Captain Wright had none. 'The fears of French colonisation evaporated, and Western Port was abandoned, its shores being described as "scrubby".'

'At this period,' says Mr. Rusden, 'John Batman must be introduced upon the scene. Now Mr. John Batman is a very interesting person, and was certainly the first coloniser of the ground on which Melbourne stands. On the 11th of January, 1827, he, conjointly with another energetic settler, addressed the following letter to Governor Darling, from Launceston, in Van Diemen's Land, to which place he had betaken himself from Paramatta, near Sydney, where he was born:–

'SIR, – Understanding that it is your Excellency's intention to establish a permanent settlement at Western Point, and to afford encourage-ment to respectable persons to settle there, we beg leave most respectfully to solicit at the hands of your Excellency a grant of land at that place proportionable to the property which we intend to embark. We are in possession of some flocks of sheep highly improved, some of the Merino breed, and some of the pure South Devon; of some pure South Devon cattle imported from England; and also of a fine breed of horses. We propose to ship from this place 1,500 to 2,000 sheep; 30 head of superior cows, oxen, horses, &c., &c, to the value of from £4,000 to £5,000, the whole to be under the personal direction of Mr. Batman, who is a native of New South Wales, who will constantly reside there for the protection of the establishment. Under these circumstances, we are induced to hope your Excellency will be pleased to grant us a tract of land proportionable to the sum of money we propose to expend, and also to afford us every encouragement in carrying the proposed object into effect.

                                                    T.J. GELLIBRAND.
                                                    JOHN BATMAN.'

This letter is a clear indication of the manner in which it was then presumed that grants of land in the Australian colonies would be made to those who brought with them the means of occupying the land, and that the grants should be made in some proportion to the capital invested. On this application Governor Darling wrote the following curt memorandum, and we may presume that the answer was in accordance with it: –

'Acknowledge; and inform them that no determination having been come to with respect to the settlement of Western Port, it is not in my power to comply with their request. March 17 (1827.) R.D.'

Mr. Batman was rebuffed, and for a time silenced, but his idea of embarking all his fortunes for Port Phillip was never abandoned. Mr. Rusden goes on to describe how South Australia was founded in 1834, owing its birth to the enterprise of Captain Sturt. Of South Australia I shall speak elsewhere. But it may be well to notice here that although the discovery of Port Phillip was very much antecedent to that of the land on which Adelaide now stands, though Victoria had been crossed from north to south before any attempt at exploration had been made in the sister colony farther west, South Australia was an established province, with a company to regulate her proceedings, with a governor and recognised officers of her own, when the first real atttempt was being made by any man to earn his bread or to push his fortunes in Victoria. Mr. Batman had meditated the attempt in 1827, but, as we have seen, had been rebuffed. In 1834, however, Mr. Henty, also a settler in the neighbourhood of Launceston, on the opposite island, determined to make a venture, and this he did, – no doubt having heard of John Batman's failure, – without any reference to the government. 'Mr. Henty,' says Rusden, 'shipped off building materials, agricultural implements, and live stock. On 19th of November, 1834, having lost fifteen head of stock on the voyage, the adventurers reached Portland Bay, and on the 6th December ploughing was commenced; and thus the first unbroken colonisation of Victorian soil dates from the enterprise of Mr. Henty. In a very short time his few head of stock increased to some 7,000 sheep, and 247 cattle, and 25 horses, and continued intercourse was kept up with Launceston.' As it happened, Mr. Henty had made good his footing, guided as we must suppose, only by chance on the happiest point on all the southern shore. Portland, and Warnambool, to the east of Portland, are the harbours of that western district of Australia, which was once called Austraiia Felix, and which is in many respects the fairest region of the whole continent. There Mr. Henty lived and prospered, – and there he still lives and, as I believe, still prospers; but no great town sprang up on the site which he had chosen, and therefore his name has not become conspicuous, as perhaps it ought to have done, among the founders of his country.

We will now return to Mr. Batman, who did become conspicuous. His mind was still full of that opposite shore, respecting which he had, with a wide ambition but humble language, made his unavailing petition to the Governor of New South Wales. 'Provoked beyond endurance, Batman would no longer be debarred from the downs of Iramoo, so temptingly described by Hume and mapped by Sturt. He determined to carve out his own way. South Australia was being occupied, and the occupation was called laudable in the preamble of an Act of Parliament. Henty had gone to Portland Bay, and no man had stayed him. Batman would go to Port Phillip; and as the New South Wales governor had not recognised his right to go there, Batman would make a convention with the rightful and natural "lords of the soil".

Batman did go over, and did make a convention with the natives. He landed on Indented Head, on the western side of the harbour, and tracked out a large district of country, including the site on which the town of Geelong now stands, including the Iramoo Downs and the country called Dutigalla by the natives; and on a spot a mile or two north of the present city of Melbourne, he made a treaty with them, by which he pledged himself to protect them and to pay them some annual tribute, and by which they undertook to surrender to him the country which he proposed thus to purchase. Batman had with him the chart of the country, as drawn by Captain Flinders, and published by the subsequent explorer, Captain Sturt, and did not himself profess, as Mr. Rusden points out, to discover, but simply to occupy the country. But he prepared, or had prepared for him, a chart of his proposed purchase, which he sent to the Governor of Van Diemen's Land, from whom he first endeavoured to obtain government sanction for what he had done. 'The limits of the land purchased by me,' he said, 'are defined in the chart, which I have the honour of transmitting, taken from personal inquiry.' In this chart, of which Mr. Rusden has published a copy, the land – not on which Melbourne proper now stands, but which is occupied by Emerald Hill, Sandridge, and other suburbs of the city, – is marked as 'reserved for the township, and other public purposes'. The site of the city itself is a part of the tract intended to be used by Batman for pastoral purposes.

The treaty is a marvellous document, – as being intended to make good a purchase of land from the aboriginal savages, in a country as to which Batman had already shown, by his petition to the Governor of New South Wales, that he was well aware that the British Crown claimed the ownership of it. He must have known that it could not have been operative either on his side or that of the aborigines. It seems that he landed with the treaty in his pocket, – with the places for the names and distances left blank, to be filled by him. When so completed it stipulated that we, 'Jaga Jaga, and others,' – the black chiefs of the tribes, – 'do, for ourselves, our heirs and successors, give, grant, enfeoff, and confirm unto the said John Batman, his heirs and assigns, all that tract of country situate and being in Port Phillip, running from the branch of the river at the top of the Port, about seven miles from the mouth of the river, forty miles N.E., and from thence west forty miles across Iramoo Downs, and from thence S.S.W. across Vilumanata to Geelong harbour at the head of the same, and containing about 500,000 acres, more or less.' So that Mr. Batman was determined to obtain a goodly estate, if in this way it might be obtained. It would probably be difficult to ascertain how many millions of pounds the land so defined is now worth. This treaty was made in June, 1835. Batman probably never thought that he should be allowed to take possession of the land, but did think, and with just ground, that he would not be expelled from it without compensation, and that by his occupation of it he would obtain some recognised position. By asking much he would get something, especially when he adopted a mode of asking so much more likely to obtain serious attention than that which he adopted when he wrote to Governor Darling. Batman, having so far carried out his scheme, returned to Van Diemen's Land, and applied to the governor there for his sanction, sending a chart of his new estate. But the Governor of Van Diemen's Land had no sanction to give. Port Phillip was not within his jurisdiction, but was within the jurisdiction of the Governor-General of New South Wales. And the Governor of Van Diemen's Land also remarked, that the recognition of Batman's treaty 'would appear to me a departure from the principle upon which a parliamentary sanction, without reference to the aborigines, has been given to the settlement of South Australia, as part of the possessions of the

Crown.' There could be no doubt about it. The British
Crown had decided that it owned all Australia, that consequently the aborigines had nothing to sell, and that, consequently again, Mr. Batman could purchase nothing from them.
Had Mr. Batman's claim to purchase from the blacks been
allowed, very many such purchases would have been made, –
and some of the purchasers would have been even less
scrupulous in their dimensions than was Mr. Batman. But
Mr. Batman did not stop here. He also applied to the
authorities at home, and expressed a hope that the Crown
would 'relinquish any legal point of constructive right to the
land in question.' But the Crown, or rather Lord Glenelg,
who was then Secretary of State for Colonial Affairs,
informed him 'that the territory was part of the colony of
New South Wales, and that no title to lands could be acquired
there, except upon the terms presented in Sir R. Bourke's
commission and instruction from the Queen.' At this time Sir
R. Bourke was Governor of New South Wales, and was also
Governor-in-Chief over the Governor of Tasmania.

Mr. Batman, though he was the moving spirit in the whole
matter, was only one of an association in regard to the capital
invested. This association at last wound itself up by selling
whatever interests it had to two of its own members; and the
government allowed to these two gentlemen a sum of £7,000,
in liquidation of so much money expended on a legal purchase
of lands; and this was done, as is expressed, in consideration
'of expenses incurred by them in the first formation of the
settlement'.

I cannot complete this short record of Mr. Batman's
adventures without alluding to Mr. Fawkner, on whose behalf
many have claimed the honour of having founded Melbourne,
– and who, I believe, was declared to claim it for himself. Mr.
Batman had been busy with Jaga Jaga, the native chief, in
June, 1835. In October, 1835, Mr. Fawkner landed at Port
Phillip, – also from Van Diemen's Land, whence came all the
early settlers of Victoria, so that the leading Australian colony
may be said to be an offshoot from that island, rather than
from New South Wales, – but the party with which he was
connected seem to have made their way across in July. They
encountered some of Batman's followers, and after trying

various places for a settlement, made their way up Port Phillip, and at last pitched on the present site of Melbourne, and seem to have settled there, not quite in unity with the Batman party, but without direct hostility. Their feuds, such as they were, will hardly interest the reader, – but it is interesting to learn that the situation of the city, and consequently the origin of the colony, was due to the enterprise of these two men, Batman and Fawkner, and of the associations with which their names are connected. In 1836 there arrived H.M.S. 'Rattlesnake,' bringing with her, as the official head of the new settlement, Captain Lonsdale, – after whom one of the main streets of Melbourne is now named. This seems to have been the first official recognition of the place; and at that time the town, – or rather settlement, – had been called by the inhabitants, Glenelg, after the Colonial Secretary, whom we, who are old, remember as Charles Grant. It was not till the next year that it was named Melbourne, after the then Prime Minister in England.

This was the beginning of Port Phillip; but Victoria did not even then exist. From its very earliest commencement Port Phillip was a success. It must be remembered that in those days there was no gold, and that this new settlement was not bolstered up by money from home, as was the case with the convict establishment at Sydney, in Van Diemen's Land, and at Moreton Bay. It seems that from the first agriculture, joined with the growth of wool, – not the growth of wool only, – had been the purpose of those who migrated from Launceston to Port Phillip. We are told as regards the first comers that after so many days, – within five days or within six days of their arrival, – the plough had passed through the soil, and that the seed was sown. Australian colonists had become discontented with themselves in that they had not as yet produced wheat for their own use. In New South Wales the effort to do so had failed. In South Australia it was already succeeding. In Victoria the attempt was at once made, and it has progressed with moderate success. The colony has not as yet been able to feed itself. In 1838 the young settlement had all the healthy roughness of youth. Melbourne consisted of a few wooden huts, and, as we are told, looked like an Indian village. There was a wooden church with a bell suspended from a tree. There

were two little wooden public-houses. Kangaroos were eaten
because mutton was still scarce. Mr. Fawkner, of whom I
have spoken, established a newspaper, but it was a newspaper
in manuscript, of which I will speak further in a future
chapter. In one of these papers there is an advertisement for a
ferry between Melbourne and Williamstown, which is now
the port of Melbourne. 'Parties from Melbourne are requested
to raise a smoke and the boat will be at their service as soon as
practicable.' The stumps of trees still stood in the one or two
streets which were already in course of formation. That such
should have been the condition of a young town is by no
means remarkable; but that it should so lately have been the
condition of a city so great as Melbourne now is, I regard as
very remarkable. This was in 1838, – a period which to some
of us does not seem to be very remote; and now Melbourne is
one of the most successful cities on the face of the earth.

'The Port Phillip settlement was not five years old when its
inhabitants began to call for separation from New South
Wales, and for its establishment as a distinct colony, with
equal privileges to those conferred upon Van Diemen's Land
in the south and South Australia in the west. A partial answer
to their demand was made by the political reform of 1842,
which gave a larger area and political institution to the district,
and allowed it to send six delegates of its own to the
Legislative Council at Sydney.'* But such representation as
this by no means satisfied the aspiring political idea of the new
settlers. It did not suit them to send delegates to Sydney,
which they regarded as a place subject altogether to government authority, – slow, conservative, and down-trodden.
Such has ever been and still is the idea held in Melbourne and
Victoria generally of Sydney and its surroundings. It seems
that from the very beginning of its life Melbourne resolved
that she would not be subject to Sydney. The agitation was
continued down to 1850, taking at last the form of a demand
for absolute separation. In those days, – though they are but
the other day, – such requests were not granted easily, as they
are now. It was thought wise then to grant slowly and with
seeming reluctance. But in 1850 the request was granted, and

* 'The Story of Our Colonies', by Fox Bourne.

an Act of Parliament was passed making Port Phillip a separate colony. The arrangement commenced on 1st July, 1851, and its present name, Victoria, is said to have been selected by the Queen herself. On that date Victoria became a separate colony, the fifth in chronological order of those which we know together as Australia. New South Wales had been the first, Van Diemen's Land, – now Tasmania, – the second, Western Australia the third, South Australia the fourth, and now Victoria, soon to become by far the most important, was the youngest.

But its importance did not come from that wealth of pasture and wealth of corn-bearing soil to which the Hentys, Batmans, and Fawkners had looked when they passed over into the land from Tasmania. What might have been the future of Victoria had her success depended on those simple products of the soil, it is useless now to speculate. In growing wheat she could not have competed with South Australia, as her climate is less favourable for the product. In producing wool she could not have competed with New South Wales, as her borders are narrower and her limits confined. In regard to fruits and vegetables she is infinitely inferior to her despised mother, Tasmania. She has no special gifts of fine harbours, an advantage bestowed by nature, which will sometimes compensate evil qualities in other directions. Port Jackson, Hobart Town, and King George's Sound are infinitely better ports than Hobson's Bay, the roadstead at the top of Port Phillip, into which the Yarra River runs, and which forms the port of Williamstown and the harbour of Melbourne, – for in reaching this haven vessels have to pass the Rip, which bubbles and eddies between the heads which guard the entrance forty miles down from Melbourne. Luckily for the new settlement, they who had founded it had been men of energy, fit for the work in hand, not expecting too much, anxious of course to thrive, but not looking for instant fortunes, prone to work themselves and capable of making others work; by no means gentlemen in the ordinary sense of the word, but as good a set of colonists as ever were landed on the shores of a new country. Within fifteen years from their start, if we count from the foundation of Melbourne, – or within sixteen from the date of Mr. Henty's arrival at

Portland, – they had already caused themselves to be classed as a separate colony, with a governor of their own, – and a parliament of their own, though not a parliament so thoroughly radical in its construction as that which they now possess. There can be but little doubt that without other chances in its favour a colony so founded would not have been the last in the race. But other fortune did attend it, so rich, so attractive, and so magnificent that it has become the very first on the list. No single British colony has ever enjoyed prosperity so great and so rapid as has fallen to the lot of Victoria.

In 1851 gold was struck at Ballaarat or the neighbourhood. It was soon apparent that the entire condition of the colony was changed by the success of the gold-finders, and that Victoria, as she is now and has been since we first began to talk about Melbourne at home as one of the great cities of the earth, was made out of gold. Gold made Melbourne. Gold made the other cities of Victoria. Gold made her railways; gold brought to her the population which demanded and obtained that democratic form of government which is her pride. Gold gave its special value to her soil, – not only or chiefly from its own intrinsic value, not only or chiefly to that soil which contains it, – but to surrounding districts, far and wide, by the increased demand for its product and the increasing population which required it for their homes.

But this success was achieved by no means without a struggle, nor did the good things come without bringing for awhile many ill things in their train. There is this peculiarity in gold, as an object of industry, that the quest of it disturbs all other adjacent industries. It is natural of course that men should seek that work in which they can earn the best wages, and that any new calling offering high pay will to a certain degree derange the supply of labour ordinarily forthcoming for ordinary occupations. But in all other trades than that of gold-seeking, the customary working of commerce soon brings matters to a level. Wages rise a little on one side and fall a little on the other. Skill, and power, and intelligence hold their own, and the disruptions that occur are those of a passing storm. But gold upheaves everything, and its disruptions are those of an earthquake. The workman rushes away from his old allotted task, not to higher wages, not to 3s. a day instead of 2s., or 6s. instead of 5s., but to untold wealth and unlimited splendour, – to an unknown, fabulous, but not the less credited realm of riches. All that he has seen of worldly grandeur, hitherto removed high as the heavens above his head, may with success be his. All that he has dreamed of the luxurious happiness of those whom he has envied seems to be brought within his reach. It seems to him that the affairs of the world generally are to be turned over and reversed, and that thus at last justice is to be done to him who has hitherto been kept cruelly too near the bottom of the wheel. His imagination is on fire, and he is unable any longer to listen to reason. He is no longer capable of doing a plain day's work for a plain day's wages. There is gold to be had by lifting it from the earth, and he will be one of the happy ones to lift it. The presence of gold is a fact. All the corollaries of the fact might be plain to him also, if he would open his ears to them, – but, in regard to himself, he is deaf as an adder to them. That all the world around him is rushing to the diggings, he can see, – and he knows that there are not princely fortunes for them all. In some rough way he knows that, were there fortunes for them all, the fortunes would cease to be princely. But 'something tells him,' – as he explains to the friend of his bosom, – 'something tells him' that he is to be the lucky man. There is a something telling the same lie to every man in that toil-worn crowd, as with sore feet and heavy burden on his shoulders he hurries on to the diggings. In truth he has become a gambler, – and from this time forth a gambler he will live; though his true industry, the sweat of his brow, which will be really productive for the world's good, will save him from those worst curses which attend a gambler's career.

Thus it was that men from all this colony and all the colonies, and that men in crowds from the old mother country and from other countries, hurried off to Victoria. The effect upon South Australia, to the west, was so great, that for a time it was feared that the young settlement would be depopulated. Farms were abandoned, and sold for a trifle. Tradesmen shut up their shops. When their customers had gone to the diggings, what could they do but follow? Shepherds from the recently stocked pastures of the Riverina and the Darling rushed down over the Murray. And worse still, the shearers who should have shorn the flocks were gone when the fleeces were ready for the shears. All these were welcomed by the young colony. There was no jealousy of new-comers as long as those who came bore characters as honest men, – or had at least had no brands upon the forehead. But the convicts from Tasmania broke loose and swelled the crowd. Barriers which had sufficed to retain the unexcited felon availed nothing when the imagination of the wretch had been inflamed by tidings of gold. They also swarmed over from the island and joined the crowd, to the loudly expressed disgust of a colony which was perhaps somewhat Pharisaical by reason of her own comparative purity.

Then there arose such a turmoil of circumstances, such a hurly-burly of social and material wants, as men were sure not to have anticipated, though in looking back upon the facts every one now can see well that they were unavoidable. How was the crowd to feed itself, to shelter itself, and to clothe itself? With such business as that on which they were engaged, deficiencies in respect of house accommodation could be endured. The smallest and the roughest tents sufficed. Boots, trousers, and a flannel shirt completed the wardrobe of many a high-born digger, and as long as the articles would hold together men working for gold would be content. But there must be food; and the feeding of 20,000 men, brought together as though by magic, requires almost miraculous energy. All things in the neighbourhood of the diggings became extravagantly dear, – so dear that the absolute value of the article seemed hardly to bear at all on the price fixed. And in response to this, or rather as an encouragement to it, the diggers themselves, with newly found gold in their hands, indifferent as they were to comforts, seemed hardly to care what they paid for those luxuries of which they had dreamed. To such a one it was nothing to give an ounce of gold for a bottle of so-called champagne, though the champagne had cost in Melbourne perhaps 3s. 6d., and the gold was worth certainly more than £3 10s.

But who was to supply the wants of diggers when every one was himself a digger? Or, if there were some steady enough to resist the temptations and to cling to haunts which were comparatively old, how were they to obtain that assistance in their work of living, which in this complex world we all render one to another? Who was to cook his dinner for the unfortunate lawyer who had lately settled in the rising town of Melbourne, when every young woman had rushed off to the diggings, to get whatever wages she chose to ask, even if she could not do better for herself by getting a digger as a husband? Or, whoever was to sell him a mutton chop to be cooked, when the half-dozen butchers of the rising metropolis had gone away to the diggings, either themselves to dig or else to follow the much more profitable occupation of supplying the diggers? For it was soon found that this first El Dorado had brought a second with it. There was already a double set of gold-seekers. It was a grand thing to drink champagne at an ounce of gold the bottle; but it was a much better thing, if not a grander, to sell champagne at that price. It was fine to get a nugget, – only that nuggets were so uncertain. But there were nuggets found daily by some happy diggers, and those who found were always ready to buy everything that was offered to them. That second El Dorado was more certain though less glorious than the first.

There was, indeed, an earthquake which at first it seemed impossible that the community as a whole should withstand. Everything was disordered and out of place. All that had been at the bottom was at the top. That which had been at the top was at the bottom. How were these men to be governed, who by the very nature of their calling want much of that protection which we call government? Something of the same kind occurred in the early days of California, – but not to the same extent; and there Lynch law had prevailed. They who saw those times in California declare that society there was preserved by Lynch law, – that, bad as it must necessarily be, unjust, tyrannical, cruel, conducive as it must be to a reign of terror and unlimited power in the hands of some few utterly unfit to use it, it was infinitely better than the no-law which would otherwise have prevailed. But California had then been very distant from any recognised seat of power, whereas Ballaarat was no more than 100 miles from Melbourne. The government was bound to govern, – to send magistrates, commissioners, inspectors, constables, and the like. But you cannot make a man be a constable, nor even a magistrate,

against his will. When the men to be watched were finding
nuggets of gold before noon, and nuggets in the afternoon,
and nuggets at night, at what rate per annum and per week
were you to pay your magistrates and your constables?

The reader will not, I think, fail to understand that there
was much of what we call rough work in the colony at that
time. There arose one turmoil so loud that soldiers were called
on to fight the miners, and that miners entrenched themselves
within palisades, intending to fight the soldiers. This, too,
occurred at Ballaarat, and I shall say perhaps a word of that
affair when speaking of Victoria's mining capital. My present
object is to show the conditions through which the colony has
passed, and the causes which have made it what it is.
Gradually things settle themselves into the old grooves, and
the earthquake died out. Its rumblings were still heard, – but
at last it rumbled only, and did not frighten. And when it had
passed away the causes which had created it had filled the land
with wealth. Many had been ruined. Many a youth, who in
his own country had enjoyed all that love and education could
do for him, had come out to perish miserably in the mud of an
Australian gully. There had been terrible suffering, crushing
disappointment, – all the agonies of toil, at first hopeful, but at
last utterly unremunerative, of which no history can ever be
written. There had been broken hopes, wasted energies, the
ague-fit after the fever. But a people had been established, and
a land had been enriched. This, I take it, is all that need be said
of the early history of Victoria.

CHAPTER III

MELBOURNE

Melbourne has certainly made a great name for itself, and is the undoubted capital, not only of Victoria but of all Australia. It contains, together with her suburbs, 206,000 souls, and of these so-called suburbs the most populous are as much a part of Melbourne as Southwark is of London; – or were I to say as Marylebone is of London, my description would be true, as there is no line of demarcation traceable by any eyes but those of town-councillors and the collectors of borough rates. There are very many cities in the world with larger populations, – so many that the number does not strike one with surprise. But I believe that no city has ever attained so great a size with such rapidity. Forty years ago from the present date (1873), the foot of no white man had trodden the ground on which Melbourne now stands, unless it was the foot of Buckley the escaped convict, who lived for thirty years with a tribe of native savages.

Melbourne is not a city beautiful to the eye from the charms of the landscape surrounding it, as are Edinburgh and Bath with us, and as are Sydney and Hobart Town in Australia, and Dunedin in New Zealand. Though it stands on a river which has in itself many qualities of prettiness in streams, – a tortuous, rapid little river with varied banks, – the Yarra Yarra by name, it seems to have but little to do with the city. It furnishes the means of rowing to young men, and waters the Botanical Gardens. But it is not 'a joy for ever' to the Melbournites, as the Seine is to the people of Paris, or the Inn to the people of Innsbruck. You might live in Melbourne all your life and hardly know that the Yarra Yarra was running by your door. Nor is Melbourne made graceful with neighbouring hills. It stands indeed itself on two hills, and on the valley which separates them; and these afford rising ground sufficient to cause considerable delay to the obese and middle-aged pedestrian when the hot winds are blowing, – as hot winds do blow at summer-time in Melbourne. But there are no hills to produce scenery, or scenic effect.

Nevertheless the internal appearance of the city is certainly magnificent. The city proper, – that Melbourne itself which is subject to the municipal control of the mayor, and which in regard to all its municipal regulations is distinct from its suburbs, – is built on the Philadelphian, rectangular, parallelogrammic plan. Every street runs straight, and every other street runs either parallel to it or at right angles with it. The principal streets run east and west, – Great Flinders Street, then Collins Street, – which is the High Street of the city, and its Regent Street and Bond Street; then Bourke Street, – which is its Oxford Street and Cheapside; and then beyond them Latrobe Street, Lonsdale Street, and others. Second class streets, but streets which do not admit themselves to be second class, run at right angles to these; Russell Street, Swanston Street, – a street which by no means thinks itself second class; Elizabeth Street, – also a proud street; Queen Street, William Street, and King Street. And then between all these streets, – which are busy streets, – there run little streets calling themselves lanes, and assuming generally the name of their big brother. Thus there are Flinders Lane and Collins Lane, and so on. But they are all regular, all rectangular, and all parallelogrammic.

It is the width of the streets chiefly which gives to the city its appearance of magnificence; – that, and the devotion of very large spaces within the city to public gardens. These gardens are not in themselves well kept. They are not lovely, as are those of Sydney in a super-excellent degree. Some of them are profusely ornamented with bad statues. None of them, whatever may be their botanical value, are good gardens. But they are large and numerous, and give an air of wholesomeness and space to the whole city. They afford green walks to the citizens, and bring much of the health and some of the pleasures of the country home to them all.

One cannot walk about Melbourne without being struck by all that has been done for the welfare of the people generally. There is no squalor to be seen, – though there are quarters of the town in which the people no doubt are squalid. In every great congregation of men there will be a residuum of poverty and filth, let humanity do what it will to prevent it. In Melbourne there is an Irish quarter, and there is a Chinese quarter, as to both of which I was told that the visitor who visited them aright might see much of the worst side of life. But he who would see such misery in Melbourne must search for it especially. It will not meet his eye by chance as it does in London, in Paris, and now also in New York. The time will come no doubt when it will do so also in Melbourne, but at present the city, in all the pride of youthful power, looks as though she were boasting to herself hourly that she is not as are other cities.

And she certainly does utter many such boasts. I do not think that I said a pleasant word about the town to any inhabitant of it during my sojourn there, driven into silence on the subject by the calls which were made upon me for praise. 'We like to be cracked up, sir,' says the American. I never heard an American say so, but such are the words which we put into his mouth, and they are true as to his character. They are equally true as to the Australian generally, as to the Victorian specially, and as to the citizen of Melbourne in a more especial degree. He likes to be 'cracked up,' and he does not hesitate to ask you to 'crack him up.' He does not proceed to gouging or bowie knives if you decline, and therefore I never did crack him up.

I suppose that a young people falls naturally into the fault of self-adulation. I must say somewhere, and may as well say here as elsewhere, that the wonders performed in the way of riding, driving, fighting, walking, working, drinking, love-making, and speech-making, which men and women in Australia told me of themselves, would have been worth recording in a separate volume had they been related by any but the heroes and heroines themselves. But, reaching one as they did always in the first person, these stories were soon received as works of a fine art much cultivated in the colonies, for which the colonial phrase of 'blowing' has been created. When a gentleman sounds his own trumpet he 'blows'. The art is perfectly understood and appreciated among the people who practise it. Such a gentleman or such a lady was only 'blowing'! You hear it and hear of it every day. They blow a good deal in Queensland, – a good deal in South Australia. They blow even in poor Tasmania. They blow loudly in New South Wales, and very loudly in New Zealand. But the blast of the trumpet as heard in Victoria is louder than all the blasts, – and the Melbourne blast beats all the other blowing of that proud colony. My first, my constant, my parting advice to my Australian cousins is contained in two words – 'Don't blow.'

But if a man must blow it is well that he should have something to blow about beyond his own prowess, and I do not know that a man can have a more rational source of pride than the well-being of the city in which he lives. It is impossible for a man to walk the length of Collins Street up by the churches and the club to the Treasury Chambers, and then round by the Houses of Parliament away into Victoria Parade, without being struck by the grandeur of the dimensions of the town. It is the work of half a morning for an old man to walk the length of some of the streets, and to a man who cannot walk well the distances of Melbourne soon become very great indeed. There seems to be this drawback upon noble streets, and large spaces, and houses with comfortable dimensions, that as the city grows the distances become immense. They are now far longer in Melbourne with its 200,000 inhabitants clustered together than in Glasgow with 500,000; and as the population increases and houses are added to houses, it will become impossible for pedestrians to communicate unless they devote the entire day to travelling. There will, no doubt, be railways about the town, as there are about London, but it seems strange that half a million of people should not be able to live together within reach of each other.

The city, I have said, is magnificent, – and yet no street in it is finished. Even in Collins Street the houses stand in gaps. Here and there are grand edifices, – in the first place banks, as to which it seems that in these days grandeur pays as in old days did that quiet, almost funereal, deportment which was the characteristic of Lombard Street, and is still maintained by one or two highly respectable London firms. The banks in Melbourne are pre-eminent, and next to them the warehouses of ambitious retail dealers. And there are some very handsome churches, – not always built with close attention to the properties of church architecture as recognised by us, but nevertheless handsome. Here and there is a grand public building, – the Post Office and the Town Hall being very grand. There are institutions of various kinds, all having domiciles more or less magnificent. A few private houses have been built with architectural pretensions, and in this way there is enough of detailed splendour to give a character to the streets. But no street is as yet splendid throughout. In speaking of the outward appearance of Melbourne, I must not forget the gutters, which in rainy weather run down each side of the street like little rivers. These are now bridged over so constantly and so well that they offer practically but little impediment to the walker. In hot weather they often flow with water from the reservoir, and help to cool the town. But in the old days, – when the bridges were few and far between, or when there were no bridges at all, – it used to be a work of danger to get about. It was then no uncommon thing to hear that 'another child' had been drowned in Melbourne that morning.

Though the suburbs of Melbourne, – such specially as Collingwood, Fitzroy, and Richmond, – are in fact parts of the town, they seem to have been built on separate plans, and each to have had a ceremonial act of founding or settlement on its own part, – being in this respect unlike suburbs, which are usually excrescences upon a town, arising at haphazard as houses are wanted. But these subsidiary towns are all rect-angular and parallelogrammic on their own bottom, though not rectangular and parallelogrammic in regard to Melbourne, If the streets of the one run from north to south, and from east to west, the streets of the other run from north-east to south-west, and from south-east to north-west. This seems to have been of importance, – and equally so that they should have separate mayors, separate town-councils, and above all separate town-halls. Collingwood has over 18,000 inhabitants; Emerald Hill over 17,000; Richmond over 16,000; and Fitzroy over 15,000 inhabitants; but to the world at large these places are parts of Melbourne.

But the magnificence of Melbourne is not only external. The city is very proud of its institutions, and is justified in its pride. Foremost among these, as being very excellent in the mode of its administration, is the public Library. In the first place it is open gratuitously to all the world, six days a week, from ten in the morning till ten in the evening. In the second place, whatever the library possesses can be got by any reader without trouble. It contained indeed, in 1870, no more than 60,000 volumes, which to those who are accustomed to wander among the shelves of the British Museum, or of the Oxford and Cambridge libraries, does not seem to be a large number. But the books have been selected for the uses of the people, and in such a library multiplied editions are hardly necessary. And the too vast multiplication of volumes leads to infinite difficulty in the manipulation of them. Here at Melbourne any man who is decent in his dress and behaviour can have books, shelter, warmth, chair, table, and light up to ten at night, day after day, night after night, year after year, – and all for nothing. For women, who choose to be alone, – and in the colonies as in the United States it is always presumed that women will choose to be alone, – a separate room is provided. This is only beaten at Boston, Massachusetts, where the inhabitants of the city are allowed to take the books home with them.

Melbourne also has its University, – which has hardly as yet been as successful as its Library; though for it, as for that at Sydney, I do not doubt that success will be forthcoming. It is at present richer in the possession of council, of senate, of doctors of law and medicine, and in masters of arts, than it is in students. In 1870 seven gentlemen took degrees as bachelors of arts, the average of ten years having been five in each year. In 1870, 122 students, in all, attended lectures, – a number which is poor for a university with a chancellor, a vice-chancellor, a senate, four professors, and nine other lecturers. In 1870 the government paid £9,000 towards the expenses of the University, the college fees amounting to no more than £2,793, – a pecuniary result which must be acknowledged to be poor in so rich a community. But in considering all this the nature of the community must be borne in mind, and the fact, that though education generally is more desired by such a people than it is in an old country such as ours, education of a high order is by no means equally in demand. People even who are rich are unwilling to pay the expenses of procuring it for their children, – an expense which is not at all in proportion with their previous experience of the cost of education. It will probably be acknowledged that a government, in such circumstances, is right to support a university among its people till the time shall come in which a class shall have grown up willing to support it for themselves.

The University itself is a modest, pretty quadrangular building, of which three sides are completed, containing simply the lecture-rooms and library, and the residences of the professors. The fourth side will be added as funds are found. The University itself does not profess to provide accommodation for the residence of scholars. Attached to it, however, is an affiliated institution called Trinity College, – got up in the interests of the Church of England, and I believe I shall be correct in saying, chiefly by the energy of that most excellent of men, the present bishop. No salary is here provided by government for a fainéant Head of the House, as I found to be the case at Sydney. When I visited the Melbourne University in 1872, there was Trinity College,* but as yet there were no collegians. The building had been erected and furnished, and was ready to take in twenty students, at 30s. a week for board and lodging. Here, it was hoped, might the future young pastors of the Church of England in the colony receive their learning. Seeing how much had been done by how good a man, I give the new college all my best wishes. Behind the University, and in the grounds belonging to it, stands the Museum, which is open to the public gratuitously. I am not, myself, qualified to speak of the value of museums, but this one seems to have the special and somewhat unusual merit of being so arranged that its contents are intelligible to ordinary capacities.

I have spoken of the gardens of Melbourne generally as contributing largely to the spacious dimensions of the town; but I must not omit to make special mention of the Botanical Gardens, and of their learned curator, Dr. Von Mueller. Dr. Von Mueller, who is also a baron, a fellow of half the learned societies in Europe, and a Commander of the Order of St. Jago, has made these gardens a perfect paradise of science for those who are given to botany rather than to beauty. I am told that the gardens and the gardener, the botany and the baron, rank very highly indeed in the estimation of those who have

---

* I have since been much pleased at learning that the affiliated college was nearly full.

devoted themselves to the study of trees, and that Melbourne should consider herself to be rich in having such a man. But the gardens though spacious are not charming, and the lessons which they teach are out of the reach of ninety-nine in every hundred. The baron has sacrificed beauty to science, and the charm of flowers to the production of scarce shrubs, till the higher authorities have interfered. When I was at Melbourne there had arisen a question whether there should not be some second and, alas! rival head-gardener, so that the people of Melbourne might get some gratification for their money. The quarrel was running high when I was there. I can only hope that flowers may carry the day against the shrubs.

There are no poor-laws in the colonies, and consequently no poor-rates. Destitute men and women are not entitled by law to be fed and housed at the public expense, as they are in England. As far as the law is concerned any man who cannot feed himself may lay down and die. But such is not the result of things as they exist. Poor and destitute there are, though they are very few in number as compared with those among us at home. Work is more plentiful. Wages are higher. Food is cheaper. In his personal condition the working man does not stand always near to the edge of the precipice of destitution, as he too frequently does in Europe. But there are poor, – both men and women, – and for them shelter and food are found, and very many of the comforts of life. These are provided in buildings called Benevolent Asylums, of which there are five in Victoria, – the largest establishment being in Melbourne. Here, in Melbourne, about 12,000 poor are relieved in the course of the year, some using it as a temporary refuge and some living in it altogether. No one is ever turned out; nor does there seem to be any great difficulty in getting in if the applicant be really destitute. It is worthy of remark that a very small proportion of those who apply for relief are colonial born. The growth of the colony, and the fact that most of the aged in the country have been immigrants, will account for this in some degree. But though Victoria is still growing the colonies are old enough to have produced destitution of their own. In 1870 there were 11,739 persons in the Victorian Benevolent Asylums, of which but little more than a tenth were born in the colony. This I attribute to the fact that the generation born in the colonies drinks less and is more careful of its means than they who go thither from Europe. The theory of these asylums is that they should be supported by voluntary contribution with aid from government. The fact is that they are supported by government with some little aid from voluntary contribution, – and with something made by the work of the inmates. In 1870 the asylum at Melbourne cost £18, 856, of which £15,000 were paid by the government, and but £2,000 by private contributions. In Victoria government pays for everything; and, why should the benevolent contribute when the thing is provided in a different way? I have said that there were no poor-rates; – but perhaps it may be thought that the same thing is effected when the parliament makes a grant out of the general taxes of the country. Could a pauper be suddenly removed out of an English union workhouse into the Melbourne Benevolent Asylum, he might probably think that he had migrated to Buckingham Palace.

When giving a catalogue of the peculiar institutions of Melbourne, I must not omit 'The Verandah'. Not that there is anything beautiful or grand about the Verandah, or that it is an institution of which Melbourne is inclined to boast. It is one, however, which she uses perhaps with more thorough devotion than all the others put together. The opportunities offered by it are never neglected; and they who have once tasted its charms, seldom fail to return to them. 'The Verandah' is a morsel of pavement in Collins Street, on which men congregate under a balcony, and there buy and sell gold shares. It is a small Bourse or 'Capel Court', held out of doors, the operations of which are conducted with all the broad daylight of the public street upon them, – but not on that account conducted with any peculiar formality or reticence. I shall, however, be under the necessity of speaking of 'The Verandah' again when describing the gold-fields of the colony and the operations which they have produced.

I visited the Lunatic Asylum at Yarra Bend, – or rather the two lunatic asylums, for there is an old and a new establishment on opposite sides of the river Yarra, – and other hospitals, and the penal establishment at Pentridge and other gaols. I could tell how many inmates there were in each, and how much each inmate cost, – no doubt with all that inaccuracy which a confidence in statistics customarily produces. But I doubt

whether I should serve or interest any one by doing so. But it
may be well to express the general conviction left on my mind
by all these visitings, – not only in reference to Melbourne and
Victoria, but as regards the colonies generally, –that a care for
public things predominates in them all. However greedy
individuals may be after the wealth of each other, whatever
fallings off there may be in individual morality and honesty,
whatever lapses in individual honour, the care of public things
is maintained throughout with an unsparing expenditure. In
nothing is this more conspicuous than in the protection given
to the afflicted by the State. Let the cost be what it may, the
poor are to be taught, the needy sheltered and fed, and the
afflicted, whether in mind or body, relieved as far as outward
appliances may relieve them.

Melbourne is the centre of a series of railways of which I
shall speak in another chapter, as they belong to the colony
generally rather then to the town; but the city has the
advantage of a local line, –belonging to a private company and
not worked by the government as are the colonial lines
generally, – which passes from St. Kilda and Emerald Hill on
one side, through Melbourne to Richmond, Prahran,
Brighton, and other suburbs on the other side, which is so
generally used that Melbourne itself is nearly as hollow as
London. I may almost say that no one lives in Melbourne. Of
this, one consequence is disagreeable. When you dine out you
are generally under the necessity of returning by railway, –
which is an abomination. But in other respects the railway is a
great blessing. People even of moderate means live in the
country air and have gardens and pleasant houses. On two
sides, south and east, Melbourne is surrounded for miles by
villa residences.

There is now being built, very close to the town, a new
Government House, which is intended to be very magnificent. The governors who occupy it will probably find it by
far too much so. The present house, which is four miles out of
town, is very much abused as being inadequate to its purpose.
It certainly is much less grand than those at Sydney, at Hobart
Town, – which is first among government houses, – or even
at Perth in poor Western Australia. Nevertheless I was present
there at a public ball, at which all Melbourne was entertained

with true vice-royal munificence. Were I appointed governor of a colony, I should deprecate very much a too palatial residence. I think it may be admitted as a rule that governors find it hard to live upon the salaries allotted to them, and generally do not do so. Men used to accept bishopricks and governorships with a view to making fortunes. It is beginning to be admitted now that men with private means are wanted for both.

There is perhaps no town in the world in which an ordinary working man can do better for himself and for his family with his work than he can at Melbourne. There may be places at which wages are higher, but then at those places the necessaries of life are dearer and the comforts of life less easily attainable. There are others undoubtedly at which living is cheaper; – but there also are wages lower, and the means of living less salutary and commodious. When I left Melbourne in July, 1872, flour was cheaper than in England. The price of wheat was then 6s.8d. a bushel in the Melbourne markets. Meat had risen greatly during the last twelve months in consequence of the increased exportation and the rise in the price of wool, and then ranged in the city from 4d. to 6d. the pound. Butter varied from 6d. to 1s.9d the pound, potatoes from, £3 to £4 the ton; eggs from 10d. to 2s. the dozen; tea from 1s. 6d. to 2s. 6d. the pound; coffee from 1s. to 1s. 10d. a pound; coals from 28s. to 35s. a ton. The price of clothes, taken all round, is I think about 20 per cent. dearer than in London. A working man in Melbourne no doubt pays more for his house or for his lodgings than he would in London; but then in Melbourne the labourer or artisan enjoys a home of a better sort than would be within the reach of his brother in London doing work of the same nature, and in regard to house-rent gets more for his money than he would do at home. In Melbourne the wages of artisans and mechanics generally are 10s. a day. Such is stated by the registrar of the colony to have been the customary payment to blacksmiths, carpenters, masons, and bricklayers in 1870, and I am assured that there has been no reduction since that date. Gardeners receive from 50s. to 60s. a week, and common labourers about 36s. a week. These men, so paid, are supposed to be employed without diet, – or rations, as is the colonial phrase. A cook will earn from £35 to £45 a year; laundresses from £30 to £40; other maid-servants from £20 to £30. The ordinary wages of a housemaid, who of course lives in the house, are 10s. a week. Men-servants, in the house, earn from £40 to £55 per annum.

There can I think be little doubt that the artisan with £3 a week, paying 4d. a pound for his meat and 7d. for a 4-lb loaf, may live very plentifully. He probably pays about 1s. a week for the schooling of each of his children, but such is the comfort of his condition that he can do this without difficulty. I would not say to every artisan in London that he should save his money and pack up all that he has, and come out to Melbourne. Too often he cannot save any money. Frequently he is unfit to emigrate. It is, too generally, the case that the man who thus seeks new fortunes has to undergo some hardship before he can find his feet in the country of his adoption. I would not have any one believe that he can enter in upon the good things of the new world, without doubt, and without delay. Many a poor fellow burdened with wife and family, the best of whose strength has gone from him amidst the hardships of labour at home, has been tempted to go out, and when there has been unable to bear the roughness of beginning and has fallen in the struggle. But when the first struggle is over, and when the first battle has been won, the life of the artisan there is certainly a better life than he can find at home. He not only lives better, with more comfortable appurtenances around him, but he fills a higher position in reference to those around him, and has greater consideration paid to him, than would have fallen to his lot at home. He gets a better education for his children than he can in England, and may have a more assured hope of seeing them rise above himself, and has less cause to fear that they shall fall infinitely lower. Therefore I would say to any young man whose courage is high and whose intelligence is not below par, that he should not be satisfied to remain at home; but should come out, – to Melbourne, if that destination will in other respects suit him; and try to win a higher lot and a better fortune than the old country can afford to give him.

But if he take my advice and then turn recreant, – if he become idle or self-indulgent, or take to drink and vicious courses of pleasure, – then will woe betide him. For the fate of such a one in the colonies is worse even than it is at home.

CHAPTER IV

BALLAARAT

Ballarat, the gold-field city, – or Ballaarat as the conscientious orthographists of the district insist on spelling it, – deserves a separate chapter to itself. Not that the two towns of that name, – Ballaarat and Ballaarat East, – with their vicinities comprise now – A.D. 1873 – the most productive gold-fields of Australia, as they are beaten by those of Sandhurst; but that the place has been more noticeable than any other in the history of Australian gold, and more productive, taking its history back to the time when gold was first discovered there in 1851.

That was the great year of the discovery of Australian gold. I am not going into the deeply discussed question of the merits of this or that discoverer, – as to which jealousy is still rife both in New South Wales and Victoria. Taking the belief which I now find to be the most common in the colonies, I may say that Sir Roderick Murchison and Count Strzelecki both foretold the finding of Australian gold, basing their opinion on the geographical condition of the country; that Hargreaves, acting with others, first struck gold at Ophir in New South Wales; and that gold was first discovered, in Victoria, at Clunes, some few miles from the present city of Ballaarat. I will not venture to say who was the first discoverer, but a miner named Esmond was rewarded for the discovery. In New South Wales gold was declared to be found in April, 1851, and at Clunes in July, 1851, so that the interval between the two colonies was very small.

But, in regard to the discovery at Clunes, I think it is not to be doubted that gold was in fact found there eighteen months before it was declared. The date usually given as that of Esmond's discovery is July, 1851, – that being the very month in which the government of the new colony of Victoria commenced.

Both Hargreaves and Esmond had been gold-seekers in California, and were led to their discoveries by observation rather than by chance. There is, I believe, no doubt that gold had been found by chance previous to the discoveries of Hargreaves and Esmond, – but the finding of it had not led to great public results. Both Hargreaves and Esmond were rewarded.

Clunes is about 16 miles from Ballaarat, but the richness of the Ballaarat gold-fields soon followed the first discovery at Clunes. I am aware that I shall tread on very dangerous ground indeed if I assign either names or dates to the first movement of the soil at Golden Point, which is now built over by the present town, – Ballaarat East. But before the end of 1851 the rush to Ballaarat was an established thing, and whole streets of canvas tents were covering crowds of miners. We are told that men flocked to the place at the rate of 500 a day, – for whom no preparation had been made, no shelter built, no food brought together, no local laws enacted, no powers to enforce the laws existing. Its too great prosperity, its prospect of immediate and apparently unlimited wealth, was for a time more than the colony could bear. The minds of men were so disturbed that no man would remain at any old employment. Servants were out of the question. Shearers would not shear sheep unless they could earn their £6 or £7 a day. Gold commissioners with their clerks, police magistrates and policemen, were indispensable; but who would be a clerk, or a policeman, – who even a magistrate or a commissioner, – when gold could be washed out of the dirt at the rate of ten ounces a day to each happy miner? Food rose to incredible prices, – but then it was almost matter of indifference to a man whether he gave a shilling or a sovereign for his meal. The young government was almost beside itself, – and letters full of frantic questions, eager fears, ambitious hopes, and almost despair, must have reached our Colonial Office at home by every mail. To whom did the gold belong? If to the Crown, how should the Crown use and how protect its rights? In what way might this new wealth be turned to account, so that the colony at large might enjoy the prosperity? Might any man dig where he pleased, – and if so, how should he be protected in his digging? What should be his rights, and what his limits, and how should he be made to pay for the now to him inestimable blessing of protection?

It was at first decreed that a miner should pay a fee of 30s. a month for a licence to dig. This was very shortly raised to £3 a month, though that amount was in truth never collected. The idea of charging a miner £36 a year for the privilege of digging arose from the desire to prevent all the labour of the colony from throwing itself into the one employment. But the outcry was so great that it was again fixed at 30s. In October, 1854, the charge for a miner's licence was £2 for three months. In the colony of Victoria the licence now costs 5s. a year. But the system of licensing – of charging diggers even £18 per annum for the privilege of mining – was not received with ready submission, and the money was collected with infinite difficulty. Recusant diggers were hunted down by armed police; men refused to pay; indignation meetings were held; – and at length something like war broke out at Ballaarat. This was in December, 1854, – when Sir Charles Hotham was governor, and about twelve months before his death. The diggers entrenched themselves on the gold-fields in a place that was called the Eureka Stockade. Here they were attacked by night, and thirty of them were killed. The ringleaders were afterwards tried and acquitted, – and so the war was brought to an end. But in those days there was certainly much difficulty in governing the colony, and in bringing into order a new state of things. It seemed for a time as though the very wealth of the soil would prove the ruin of the country.

Now it might be difficult to find a more quiet town than Ballaarat, as it certainly would be to find one of the same age better built and more lavishly provided with all the appurtenances which municipalities require. It is certainly a most remarkable town. It struck me with more surprise than any other city in Australia. It is not only its youth, for Melbourne also is very young; nor is it the population of Ballaarat which amazes, for it does not exceed a quarter of that of Melbourne; but that a town so well built, so well ordered, endowed with present advantages so great in the way of schools, hospitals, libraries, hotels, public gardens and the like, should have sprung up so quickly with no internal advantages of its own other than that of gold. The town is very pleasant to the sight, which is, perhaps, more than can be said for any other 'provincial' town in the Australian colonies. When the year

1851 commenced, Ballaarat was an unknown name except perhaps here and there to a few shepherds. These words are written in the house of Messrs. Learmonth, – younger men than I, and therefore not old men to me, – who were the first pioneers in the country, and who ran the sheep which they brought with them from Van Dieman's Land over the hills adjacent to Ballaarat. They have given way to the gold-seekers, and, establishing themselves far enough from mines for rural serenity and pastoral comfort, are regarded as the territorial aristocrats of the district. Breathing their air and listening to their ideas, one feels as one does in the almost feudal establishment of some great English squire, who watches with a regret he cannot quite repress the daily encroachments made upon his life by the approaching hordes of some large neighbouring town. Ballaarat has no navigable river. It is seventy or eighty miles from any possibility of sea-carriage. The land immediately around it is not fertile. It is high above the sea-level, and runs in gentle hills which twenty years since were thinly covered with gum-trees; and here wandered the flocks of a few patriarch pioneers. Then came first one or two rough seekers after gold, then half-a-dozen, then a score, then a rush, – and Ballaarat was established as one among the few great golden cities of the young world. I do not think that there is any city equal to it that has sprung from gold alone.

I myself believe in cities, – even though there should be place in them for dishonest ambition, short-sighted policy, and rowdiness. The dishonesty, the folly, and the rowdiness are but the overboiling of the pot without which cannot be had the hot water which is so necessary to our well-being. I heard much abuse of Ballaarat from Ballaaratters. There are three towns conjoined, Ballaarat, Ballaarat East, and Sebastopol, with three town-halls, three municipalities, and the like. The smaller towns will not consent to merge themselves. There are in them men of obstruction, and things cannot be done as they should be done. Money is wasted; municipal funds are expended foolishly, – perhaps fraudu-lently on an occasion. If this class would only see with the eyes of that class, what a paradise it might be! But they see with quite other eyes, – and what a pandemonium it is becoming.

So say the men of Ballaarat. Trade is going to the dogs, because there is not sufficient protection, – or else because a tariff of 20 per cent. on all imported goods, levied in accordance with the wisdom of certain ministers is destroying all trade by raising the price of bad goods and driving serviceable goods out of the market. No words which can here be used are strong enough to describe the iniquity which some MacEvoy attributes to some O'Brien, or some Murphy to some Jones or Smith. Population is falling off, so that shortly Ballaarat will be as a city of the dead. Such are the accounts a stranger hears either from this side or from that. One gentleman, who certainly was very much in the dark as to the statistics of his town, assured me that 20,000 people had gone out of Ballaarat in two years. Another was angry with me because I hesitated to believe that the place was ruined. I was assured that I might hire 1,500 vacant houses at an hour's notice if I wanted them. As for gold at Ballaarat, everybody knew that the game had been played out!

Such were the records of some men. As far as the eye went, I saw nothing but prosperity. Here I found that most of the mines were worked by companies at wages paid to the men, – and that a miner's wages averaged from 40s. to 48s. a week, – the man working eight hours a day, and thus reaching the acme of the workman's bliss –

> 'Eight hours for work, and eight for play,
> Eight for sleep, and eight shillings a day.'

And the necessaries of life, and the comforts, are at any rate as cheap at Ballaarat as they are in England, in spite of protective duties. Meat was about 2½d. a pound, and for nothing did the workmen of Ballaarat pay more than his brother in England, unless it be for clothes, for house-rent, – and strong drinks, if he be that way given. Wages for all work are high in proportion. In rural labour in the neighbourhood the farmer pays 20s. a week and rations, and at harvest-time must pay double that amount. Female servants in houses get 12s. a week, – or above £30 per annum.

Houses no doubt have been built too quickly, – as is always found to be the case when some check comes to the rising population of young towns. Such check had reached Ballaarat when I was there, – the rush for the time being to the gold-fields of Sandhurst, and newly built houses were to be seen empty. 'There's a "spec" that won't answer,' said a gentleman to me, pointing to a row of houses just finished, but which from end to end showed no sign of habitation. In two years' time some great quartz-crushing operation will probably have been commenced; and the then owner of the row, – for the unfortunate first speculator will no doubt have been sold out by his assignees, – will be making 30 per cent. on his money.

There may be rowdiness, dishonesty and all other civic sins in the manipulation of the municipal powers of Ballaarat and other Australian cities; – but as a rule the things which a city requires are there. At Ballaarat this is conspicuously the case. The hospital has more wards than it uses, and more funds than it needs. As regards internal cleanliness and sweetness, and external prettiness, it is perfect. The Benevolent Institution, – which does the work that a poor-house does with us, – gives out-door relief or in-door shelter and sustenance to all who cannot support themselves. Such sustenance in Ballaarat – as indeed at all such institutions in Victoria – includes a thoroughly good dinner of meat and vegetables every day, with tea for breakfast and tea for 'tea'. It includes a bed perfectly clean, sitting-room, books, newspapers, comfortable clothes, and a garden to walk in infinitely superior to that enjoyed by many comfortable folk at home. Ballaarat has a public library. free to all the city, – and a mechanics' institute, with newspapers and privileges, at £1 a head. It has indeed every municipal luxury that can be named, including a public garden full of shrubs and flowers, and a lake of its own, – Lake Wendouree, – with a steamer and row-boats and regattas. It has a cricket-ground, and athletic games; and it has omnibuses and cabs, which by their cleanliness and general excellence make a Londoner blush. For the privilege of seeing all these things with ease and comfort, and for much steady information, without exaggeration either on one side or the other, I have to thank that best of all mayors, Mr. R. Lewes, who reigned at Ballaarat at the time of my visit.

But as yet I have said nothing of the gold-mines which have made Ballaarat what it is. Among Victorian gold-fields it is famous for alluvial dirt to be washed, – not for quartz to be crushed, as is the case with its rival town of Sandhurst, of which I shall speak in the next chapter. But the reader must not therefore suppose that Ballaarat is a place of mere surface scratching, an agglomeration of gullies from which the mud is shovelled into cradles, a congregation of 'fossickers' – men who search about, picking and washing a bit of earth here and a bit there, or upper-air miners who know nothing of large operations. The alluvial dirt which produces the greater portion of the wealth of Ballaarat has not only to be brought up many hundred feet from under the surface, but it has to be sought for through underground passages thousands of feet in length, and has to be followed up by geological deductions which too often fail in their promises.

I went down one such mine called 'Winter's Freehold', descending 450 feet in an iron cage. I was then taken 4,000 feet along an underground tramway in a truck drawn by a horse. At the end of that journey I was called upon to mount a perpendicular ladder about 20 feet high, and was then led along another tramway running apparently at right angles to the first. From this opened out the cross passages in which the miners were at work. Here we saw the loose alluvial grit, so loose that a penknife would remove it, lying on the solid rock, – on it and under it, – to the breadth I was told of some four feet; for though I saw the bottom of the grit, where it lay on its bed, I could not see the top where it was covered. Here and there among the grit, with candle held up, and some experienced miner directing my eye, I could see the minute specs of gold, in search of which these vast subterranean tunnels had been made. It seemed to be but a speck here and there, – so inconsiderable as to be altogether unworth the search. But the mining men who were with us, the manager, deputy-manager, or shareholders, – for on such occasions one hardly knows who are the friends who accompany one, – expressed themselves highly satisfied.

I was told that £150,000 had been expended on this single mine up to the present time, and that the machinery was the finest in the colony. Perhaps the finest machinery in the colony may be seen at more than one mine in the colony. But I was informed that hitherto the results had not been magnificent. There was, however, a good time coming, and all the money

expended would certainly come back with copious interest. I
hope that it may be so. We were two hours in seeing the mine,
– and I must say that as regards immediate enjoyment the two
hours were not well spent. The place was wet and dirty and
dark, the progress was tedious, and the result to the eye very
poor. But such is the result to all amateur inspectors of mines.
When we had extricated ourselves from the bowels of the
earth we ascended to a platform on the top of the machinery,
to which the wash–dirt is carried that it may there be puddled
and the gold extracted. The height enables the water and mud
to run off. The dirt is placed in a round flat receptacle or
trough, into which water runs, and an instrument somewhat
like a harrow is worked through it. The water and mud are
amalgamated, and the height enables them to run off together.
The gold by its own weight falls to the bottom mixed with
stones or shingle. This is afterwards sent down to an open
spout below, through which water runs, a man the while
working it with a fork prepared for the purpose. Again the
stones and mud pass off with the water, and again the gold
remains behind, sinking to the bottom by its own weight.
When all has escaped that will escape, and the stones that will
not fall have been thrown out, then the specks of gold are seen
lying thick, collected in the little furrows which are marked on
the bottom of the spout. To the uninitiated eye the product of
all this costly labour still seems to be small.

   After all this the gold is smelted into bars and sold to the
merchants or bankers. We went to the offices of another
company, – the Band of Hope and Albion Consols, – to see
the smelting. In this operation there is nothing wonderful.
The small gold, – for it is all small in comparison with the
nuggets of which we have heard so much and which are now
very rare in Australia – is poured into an earthen pot, is
melted, is poured out into moulds, is then washed so that it
may have a clean face, and is straightway sent to the bank. At
present the greater part of the gold found at Ballaarat when
thus prepared is worth something over £4 an ounce. At this
Band of Hope mine they raise about 3,000 ounces of gold a
month, at an expense of about half its value. The other half is
divided among the shareholders, and gives an average interest
of £12 15s. per cent. on the capital expended on the work.

This, in a business subject to great risk, with bank interest at 8 and 9 per cent. does not seem to be a very rich result.

We also saw a quartz-crushing machine at work, – for quartz is raised at Ballaarat, though in much less quantity than the wash-dirt. The nature of a quartz-crusher I have described in speaking of Gympie, the great Queensland gold-field. In Victoria, as I have said, Sandhurst is the great quartz district; – but there are sanguine people who predict a vast wealth of quartz reefs at Ballaarat after the wash-dirt has been all extracted.

CHAPTER V

BENDIGO OR SANDHURST

Having thus described Ballaarat, which in point of architectural excellence and general civilized city comfort is at present certainly the metropolis of the Australian gold-fields, I should lay myself open to charges of gross partiality if I omitted to give some account of Sandhurst, – which intends to surpass Ballaarat, and to become mightier and more world-famous than that very mighty and world famous place. I do not pretend to say what may be the result of the race.

My readers have, no doubt, heard of the Bendigo gold-fields. I think it by no means improbable that some of them, – in England, – may never have heard the name of Sandhurst as connected with gold. I had not done so when I first landed in Australia, though I had been often told of Bendigo, having some hazy idea that the place had called itself after a prize-fighter, and therefore must be a very rowdy place indeed. I imagine that some such feeling must have been predominant with the people of the place when Bendigo, as a name, was dropped, and Sandhurst, – which is not only euphonious, but which carries with it also a certain mixed idea of youthful energy and military discipline, – was chosen in its stead. Sandhurst means to go ahead, and become a great city. In regard to the production of gold it has gone very much ahead. As a city, when I was there, it was neither handsome nor commodious. It had the appearance, which is common to all new mining towns, of having been scratched up violently out of the body of the earth by the rake of some great infernal deity, who had left everything behind him dirty, uncouth, barren, and disorderly! Any one who has seen the mining towns as they rose in Cornwall and Glamorganshire must have observed the same ugliness. At Sandhurst you see heaps of upturned dry soil here and there, dislocated whims, rows of humble houses built just as they were wanted, shops with gewgaw fronts put up at a moment's notice, drinking-bars in abundance, here and there an attempt at architecture, made almost invariably by some banking company eager to push itself into large operations, – but with it all a look of eager, keen energy which would redeem to the mind the hideous objects which meet the eye, were it not that the mind becomes conscious of the too-speculative nature of the work done, – of the gambling propensities of the people around, – and is driven to feeling that the buying and selling of mining shares cannot be done by yea, yea, and nay, nay.

In Melbourne there is the 'verandah'; – in Sandhurst there is a 'verandah;' in Ballaarat there is a 'verandah'. The verandah is a kind of open exchange, – some place on the street pavement apparently selected by chance, on which the dealers in mining shares do congregate. What they do, or how they carry on their business when there, I am unable to explain. But to the stranger, or the passer- by, they do not look lovely. He almost trembles lest his eyes should be picked out of his head as he goes. He has no business there, and soon learns to walk on the other side of the road. And he hears strange tales which make him feel that the innocence of the dove would not befriend him at all were he to attempt to trade in those parts. I think there is a racing phrase as to 'getting a tip'. The happy man who gets a tip learns something special as to the competence or incompetence of a horse. There are a great many tips in gold mines which fall into the fortunate hands of those who attend most closely, and perhaps with most unscrupulous fidelity, to the business of the verandahs. The knowing ones know that a certain claim is going to give gold. The man who has the tip sells out at a low price, sells out a certain number of shares, probably to a friend who holds the tip with him, The price is quoted on the share list, and the unfortunate non-tipped sell out also, and the fortunate tipped one buys up all. A claim is not going to give gold, – and the reverse happens. Or a claim is salted, – gold is surreptitiously introduced, is then taken out, and made the base of a fictitious prosperity. The tipped ones sell, and the untipped buy. It is easy to see that the game is very pretty, but then it is dangerous. It has certainly become very popular. One is told at Melbourne that all are

playing it, – clergymen, judges, ladies, old ladies and young,
married ladies and single, – old men and boys, fathers
unknown to their sons, and sons unknown to their fathers,
mothers unknown to their daughters, daughters unknown to
their mothers, – masters and servants, tradesmen and their
apprentices. 'You shall go from one end of Collins Street to
another,' a man said to me, 'and you will hardly meet one who
has not owned a share or a part of a share.' Gold-mining in
Victoria is as was to us the railway mania some twenty-four
years ago. Melbourne no doubt is the centre of the trade in
shares, but low beneath the surface in the mines of Sandhurst
lie the hearts of the gold-gamblers.

At Ballaarat the chief produce of gold is still obtained from
alluvial dirt, – from dirt which is indeed extracted by deep
working out of the bowels of the earth, and not, as at first,
from the channels of rivers and the crevices of mountain
gullies, – but still from alluvial dirt, which, when extracted, is
washed. The gold remains after the washing and then the
operation is at an end. At Sandhurst the gold is got by
quartz-crushing. The gold-bearing rock is brought up in great
masses, – thousands and thousands of tons of stone, which is
called quartz. This is crushed by huge machinery, and the gold
is separated from the dirt by the use of quicksilver and water.
The washing of alluvial soil is the readier way of getting gold,
but the quartz-crushing is the more important. Of the alluvial
dirt there must, or at any rate there may, soon be an end. The
geologists say that the crushers of quartz may eat up whole
mountains, and still go on finding stone that will give gold.
Looking at a table now before me as to quartz crushed at
Sandhurst in 1871, I find that 2 oz. 14 dwt. to the ton of quartz
was the highest amount extracted, and that 4 dwt. to the ton is
the lowest quantity there quoted. The proportion that will pay
depends of course on the amount of outlay. Some of the
gold-bearing stone is brought up 800 feet, and some only 100.
In some mines the levels and cross-cuts and underground
passages are worked for long distances, perhaps for a mile,
without gold. In others the gold is struck at once. It is
impossible, therefore, to say what proportion will pay, but it
is certain that in many mines half an ounce, or two sovereigns,
to a ton of rock will pay well. It is on record that 250 oz. of

gold were extracted on the Bendigo goldfields from one ton of stone, – fifteen years ago. But the great glory of Sandhurst was reached, when an average of 9 oz. per ton was extracted from 264 tons of quartz, taken from 'The Great Extended Hustler's mine'.

I venture to extract a quotation from a published 'Digest of the Dividend-Paying Companies of the Bendigo Gold-Fields', which is now before me, – given in the shape of a note, – because it purports to be a record of the greatest event of the year 1871.

'NOTE. – On October 18th, the greatest event of the year's quartz-mining occurred. For some days previously the gathering of the Extended Hustler's Tribute amalgam created much interest in mining circles; 6,400 oz. aggregate of amalgam was reached when the company proceeded to retort, and betting, except with those intimately acquainted with the nature of the stone, was in favour of over 3,000 oz., of gold. A little after 7 p.m. of the 18th the Oriental Bank solved all doubts by exhibiting the Tribute Company's cake of 2,564 oz., and shortly afterwards the Great Extended Hustler's Tribute declared the largest dividend ever paid on Sandhurst, 6s. 6d. per share, equal to £9,100. The yield was obtained from 264 tons, reef 18 feet thick, average 9 oz. per ton.'

I saw this interesting cake at the Oriental Bank in Melbourne, on which occasion the manager kindly offered to give it to me on condition that I should carry it away.

All prosperous trades have a slang of their own, – certain terms used to keep outsiders at a distance, and to create that feeling of esoteric privilege which we all like to have in regard to matters which we think we understand. A man who only uses horses can never talk in professional language to a man who breeds them and deals in them and lives with them. A layman in politics, let him be ever so anxious for his country, is all abroad when conversing with a member of parliament about bills and acts, about notices of motion and 'the previous question'. It is very much so with mining. Everything is told to the visiting stranger, but I don't think he is intended to understand anything. What with tributes and claims, with leads and lodes, with shafts and levels and cross-cuts and veins, with reefs and gullies, with quartz, amalgam, tailings, and mullock, – I am by no means sure of the spelling of that last word, – he is made to feel that he is an outsider, and that he cannot learn mining in a day. At Sandhurst I felt this very strongly, – and my reader will probably feel as I did.

He will simply acknowledge to himself the fact that a cake of gold containing 2,564 oz., – and worth about £10,000, – is a very large cake indeed.

The names selected by various companies at the Sandhurst gold-fields deserve attention. Sandhurst, which now aspires to be the leading Australian gold-field, and which certainly turns out more gold than any other, boasts at present no less than 1,200 different companies. I should say that there were 1,200 in the early part of 1872. The number will probably be very greatly increased before these words are published. The names chosen for these companies are certainly very quaint. There are not less than fourteen 'New Chum' Companies, and there are three or four 'Old Chum' Companies. There are the Peg Leg, the Perfect Cure, the Who can Tell, the Great Extended Who can Tell, the Sons of Freedom, the Sir Walter Scott, the Sailor Prince, the Royal Louisa, the Lord Byron, the Little Chum, the Jonadab, the Hand and Band, the Happy Day, the Happy-go-Lucky, the Great Extended South Golden Pyke, the Go by Gold, the Charles Gavan Duffy, the Gladstone, – indeed there are five or six Gladstone Companies, – and, to be fair, I must add that there is a Disraeli Company; I do not, however, find it quoted among those that are paying dividends. But, among all names at Sandhurst, the greatest name, the most thriving, the best known, and the name in highest repute, is – 'Hustler.' Whence came the appellation I do not distinctly know, but I believe that there once was, – perhaps still is, – a happy Hustler. If so, even the Marquis of Granby among publicans has not been a more prolific godfather than has Mr. Hustler among Sandhurst miners. What with original Hustler Companies and Tribute Hustler Companies, with simple Hustlers, and extended Hustlers, and Great Extended Hustlers, with North Hustlers, and South Hustlers, and with Extended North and South Hustlers, the companies who claim the happy name are difficult to count. There are at any rate two dozen of them, and all, or nearly all, are doing well.

Of these 1,200 different companies, about one-third are, so called, Tribute Companies. The parent company – for instance the parent Great Extended Hustlers, – lets off a piece of land, or a claim, to a set of men, generally working miners, having performed a certain portion of the preliminary work, –

having opened the shaft and put up machinery, and probably shown that gold is to be had for the labour. The claim is let on a certain tribute, – the tributers or sub-company agreeing to pay a fixed proportion of the gold extracted to the original company. The miners are very fond of going into this kind of speculation, as it opens up to them the chance of making a fortune. But on the other hand it opens up to them also the chance – and very often the reality – of working for nothing. The expenses of the mine and the tribute which is exacted will not infrequently consume all the gold produced; or, – worse than that, – the expense of the mine will go on, and there will be no produce. The tributer will not only be working for nothing, but will also be called on to pay towards the continuance of the enterprise. He must live the while, – and would thus seem to be debarred from such speculation unless he is possessed of capital. But in fact such is not the case. A miner at Sandhurst, when I was there, could earn from £2 10s. to £3 a week, and could live well on 20s. Two men, or more, would form a partnership, of which the one half would work for wages, and the other half on a tribute claim. The wages would suffice to support the whole, and even to pay up a certain amount of 'calls'. Should the speculation turn out well, the profits would be divided among the lot. The speculation often does turn out well, and men become suddenly enriched. It often turns out badly, – and in such cases the miners have worked barely for a subsistence. At such places as Sandhurst it is said that in this way a grand spirit of commercial enterprise is created and fostered. Men without capital are enabled to enter in upon the joys of commercial speculation. There is, however, another way of looking at it; and many no doubt will think that the commercial speculation is simple gambling on a great scale. I have no doubt myself that the miners who work simply for wages are in the long run more prosperous than they who work on tribute. A man's wages represent to him with clear and well-defined reality the very sweat of his brow. If there be enough for him to save something, and if he be given to saving, he will save the surplus of money so earned. But that which comes to him in a lump, from some happy chance, from some pocket of gold found in the bowels of the earth, from some rich crushing of quartz with which it

has been his lot to become connected, exalts him suddenly,
upsets his head, – and is apt to disappear as rapidly as it came.
All this of course is old-world teaching and grandmother's
tales. I feel as I write it that it is too trite to be written. But I
feel at the same time that it is impossible to write of
gold-mining in Australia without repeating the old lesson. No
doubt instances may be adduced of men who have made and
have kept splendid fortunes by gold-mining, – of men who
have done so without capital, by small speculations at first,
and by extended operations as the means have come to them. I
have heard of men so blessed, – and could name one or two.
But I have heard of no case in which the man so blessed was
represented to me as living after a blessed fashion. I have,
however, heard of cases by the score in which the questionable
blessing has never been achieved, – as to which I have been
told, frequently by the speculators themselves, that had they
stopped here or had they stopped there, they would have
made two, four, six, ten, or twenty thousand pounds as the
case may have been. There has been a shake of the head, and a
soft regret; and I always felt that I liked the man the better in
that he had lost it all, than I should have done had he become
permanently successful

As regards the working miners, including all those who
manage the works and overlook the machinery, I am bound to
say that they are a fine body of able and industrious men. This
is so on all the large gold-fields, and nowhere more noticeably
than at Sandhurst. They are intelligent, manly, and independent, – altogether free from that subservience which the
domination of capital too often produces in most fields of
labour. I have spoken, perhaps as strongly as I know how to
speak, of the gambling propensities of the population of a
gold-mining town. I should be wrong if I did not speak as
strongly of the efforts which are made by such communities, –
which in Australia are always made when the communities
become large and apparently fixed, – to ameliorate the condition of the people. The hospitals are excellent, the provision
for the indigent is so good as almost to promote indigence, the
schools are well conducted and well filled, the churches are
sufficient, and the clergymen are supported. The money
comes freely and is freely expended. And in no community are

the manners of the people more courteous or their conduct more decent. Of course there is drinking. The idle men drink, – would-be gentlemen, who are trying to speculate, without apparent means of livelihood, drink, – miners who are not mining, having what they call a spell, or holiday, will drink. But the working miner is a sober man, with a sober family; and of such the bulk of the mining population is made up. In England working men drink, – work by day, and drink by night, – till the thing soon comes to an end. In Australia, as a rule, the working man does not drink while he works. The shearer does not drink; the shepherd and boundary-rider do not drink; the reaper and ploughman do not drink; nor does the miner drink. Let them be idle for a while; let them take their wages and go away for a 'spell;' – then they will drink as no Englishman ever drinks, drink down in a fortnight the earnings of a year. But there is less of this with miners than with shearers or ploughmen. The miner gambles, – and is so saved from the worse vice of drinking.

And the gambling of the miner has about it a certain redeeming manliness which is altogether wanting to the denizen of the race-course or of the roulette-table. Though he gambles, he works and produces. The gambling is but an excrescence on his genuine industry. The Sandhurst regular miner works in shifts, of eight hours each shift, throughout the day and night. The gold is being sought and found, dug out and dragged up, and crushed out of its matrix, the quartz, for four-and- twenty hours a day, during six days of the week. And the skilled miner, by eight hours' work a day, may earn at least 9s. a day in a country in which he and his wife and children may live comfortably, – and as regards food with absolute plenty, – for 4s. a day. The gold-miner at Sandhurst who keeps himself simply to his work, and takes no part in New Extended Great Chum Tributes, has, as work goes on in the world, by no means an unhappy lot.

I went down the shaft of one mine, – the Great Extended Hustler, I think it was called, – 600 feet below the surface, and was received with the greatest courtesy. I am bound to say that I saw nothing that was worth seeing, and that I understood nothing of all that was told me. This is an almost disgraceful declaration to make, after one has pretended to understand all that was said. But it was so with me, and is so I take it with all travellers. The experienced and good-natured professional miners who conduct the strangers are anxious that everything should be made plain. To them everything is plain. But the very A B C of their necessary knowledge is probably Hebrew to the listener, who is too grateful for the attention paid to him to tell the kind teacher how utterly unintelligible to him is the whole matter in question. It was so with me, – but this I saw, and could have seen as well above the earth as by going below, – that tons of grey stone were dragged up, that the grey stone was all stamped and crushed into powder by machinery, and that out of the powder gold was got in certain proportions, – so many ounces, or more probably so many pennyweights, to the ton of stone, – and that, as the result was good or bad, dividends were divided or were not divided among the speculators.

CHAPTER VI

GIPPSLAND, WALHALLA AND WOODS POINT

I went by coach from Melbourne to Gippsland with a friend, partly with a view of visiting that district generally, and partly that I might see the eastern gold-fields of the colony. I had indeed become very tired of gold, – which to a traveller who enjoys none of the excitement arising from the hope of acquiring it, is but a wearisome object. I did not desire to go down more mines, and yet I felt that I should not be strong-minded enough to save myself from further descents. I think I should have taken the Gippsland gold-fields on credit, had I not been told that the scenery around them was peculiarly beautiful. I was specially desired not to miss Woods Point, – which indeed is not in Gippsland, but which could be visited from Gippsland by any one who would trust himself among the mountains on horseback. From Woods Point I could return to Melbourne by a direct road, so as to avoid the disagreeable task of retracing my steps over the same path. As far as scenery was concerned, I was certainly repaid for the labour of a somewhat laborious journey. Gippsland is in the south-eastern district of Victoria. It has I believe lately been divided into counties, – or rather, a portion of it has been so far civilized. It is separated from the Murray district of Victoria by spurs of the so-called Australian Alps, among which lie the eastern gold-fields.

We started by one of Cobb's coaches at one o'clock in the day, and reached the little town of Rosedale in Gippsland at ten the next morning. Cobb's coaches have the name of being very rough, – and more than once I have been warned against travelling by them. They were not fit, I was told, for an effeminate Englishman of my time of life. The idea that Englishmen, – that is, new-chums, or Englishmen just come from home, – are made of paste, whereas the Australian native or thoroughly acclimatized, is steel all through, I found to be universal. On hearing such an opinion as to his own person, a man is bound to sacrifice himself, and to act contrary to the advice given, even though he perish in doing so. This journey I made and did not perish at all, – and on arriving at Rosedale had made up my mind that twenty hours on a Cobb's coach through the bush in Australia does not inflict so severe a martyrdom as did in the old days a journey of equal duration on one of the time-famous, much-regretted old English mails. More space is allowed you for stretching your legs on the seat, and more time for stretching your legs at the stages. The road of course is rough, – generally altogether unmade, – but the roughness lends an interest to the occasion, and when the coach is stuck in a swamp, – as happens daily, – it is pleasant to remember that the horses do finally succeed, every day, in pulling it out again. On this road there is a place called the Glue Pot, extending perhaps for a furlong, as to which the gratified traveller feels that now, at any rate, the real perils of travel have been attained. But the horses, rolling up to their bellies in the mud, do pull the coach through. This happens in the darkness of night, in the thick forest, – and the English traveller in his enthusiasm tells the coachman that no English whip would have looked at such a place even by daylight. The man is gratified, lights his pipe, ands rushes headlong into the next gully.

The land between Melbourne and Gippsland, through the county of Mornington, is very poor; as it is also for some distance in Gippsland itself. Then the timber becomes less thick and the grasses rich. When first taken up the country was used for sheep, – but it was not found to be good for wool, and the sheep now have given place to cattle. A large proportion of the beef with which Melbourne is fed is fattened on the Gippsland runs. Here, as throughout Victoria, all the best of the soil has been already purchased, and is for the most part in the hand of large owners, – of men whose successors will be lords of vast territorial properties, and not of small free-selecters or farmers. Throughout the colony it is impossible not to see how futile have been the efforts of legislation to prevent the accumulation of large domains in the hands of successful men. It has been thought by one ministry after another to be wise, – or, at any rate, to be expedient, – to break up the holdings of the great squatters, so that there should be no territorial magnates. The law has done all that it could be made to do, compatibly with justice, – sometimes perhaps more than it could do with that condition, – to make the colony a paradise for small landowners, and a purgatory for wealthy men who should attempt to accumulate acres. Politicians ambitious of being statesmen, who can reach power only by the aid of universal suffrage, are prone to look for popularity, and popularity in Victoria has much dependence on adherence to the interests of the free-selecter. As I have said elsewhere, the interests of the small buyer of land are entitled to warmer sympathy than those of the would-be territorial magnates. One still dreams of a happy land in which every man with his wife and children shall live happily and honestly on his own acres, – owing neither rent nor submission to any lord. It may be that this feeling has been stronger with Victorian politicians than the love of political power. It is at any rate the feeling by which they claim to have been actuated, and they have worked hard to carry out their theory. But the wages of commerce and the enterprise of the intelligent have been stronger than any bonds which statesmen or legislators could forge. Wealth has been accumulated by a few, and wealth has procured the land in spite of the laws. Though cabinet ministers and land commissioners have had the land in their hands to sell under such laws as they have pleased to pass, though they have had a power entrusted to them as managers and agents greater than any confided by us to our ministers at home, though it has been declared by politicians that there should be no land magnates in Victoria, the rich have bought the land; and now vast territories are possessed by individuals which more than rival in area, – and in course of time will rival in value, – the possessions of great families at home. This is hardly so in the United States, – is not so certainly to the same extent. These men seek to build up wealth in the cities rather than in the country, and prefer shares and scrip and commercial speculation to land. Why there should be this difference in the same race, when settled away from home in different regions, some one some day no doubt will tell us.

To fatten cattle is the present business of the Gippsland squire. Cattle, no doubt, are bred there, but it seemed to be more usual to buy them young from some other district, and have them driven up over long distances to the Gippsland pastures. I do not pride myself on having a good eye for a bullock, – but those I saw seemed to be very big and fat, very tame and very stupid. Why a bullock who has a paddock of seven or eight thousand acres in which to roam should make so little of himself as these beasts do in Australia I cannot understand. At home I think they are more troublesome and have higher hearts. I went out one morning at four A.M. to see a lot drafted out of a herd for sale. 'Cutting out' is the proper name for this operation. Two or three men on horseback, of whom I considered myself to be by far the most active, drove some hundreds of them into a selected corner of the paddock called a 'camp.' There was no enclosure, no hurdles, no gates, no flogging, very little hallooing, and very little work. This camp happened to be in a corner; but camps for cattle generally are in the centre of the field, a bare spot, – made bare by its repeated use for this purpose, – to which the bullocks go when they are told, and on which they stand quietly till the operation of cutting out is over. On the occasion on which I was assisting, the owner himself was the 'cutter out'. He rode in among the herd, and selecting with his eye some animal sufficiently obese for market purposes, signified to the doomed one that he should leave the herd. There was a stock-rider to assist him, and the stock-rider also signified his intention. It seemed to be done altogether by the eye. The beast went out and stood apart, till he was joined by a second selected one and then by a third. On this occasion some thirty or forty were selected, – either as many as were fit or as the owner desired to sell. These were at once driven off on the way to Melbourne, and the others were allowed to go back to their grazing. I had looked for racing, and cracking of stock-whips, and horses falling, and some wild work among the forest trees. I would not knowingly have left my bed at four o'clock to see so tame a performance. At least for half its distance the road up to Melbourne is not fenced off from the timber, and consists of devious forest tracts; but these tame brutes never make their way out into the woods on the journey, as they might do.

My friend and I bought two horses and two saddles, and started from Rosedale on our journey to the mines. We had met some influential gentlemen of the district, – a judge, a resident magistrate, and an inspector of police, – who were united in their assurance that if we went without a guide we should certainly be lost in the bush. Now my friend was a man of mark, whose loss would have been severely felt by the community, and for his security we were furnished with a mounted trooper, or policeman, to show us our way, and generally take care of us on our expedition. We certainly needed him, and, as I believe, would have been sleeping now in some Gippsland gully but for his assistance. Our first day's march was to Walhalla, a mining town of great wealth to which there is literally no road. Our journey was one of about forty miles, – for the latter half of it, continuously through forests, and as continuously up and down mountains. These were so steep that it was often impossible to sit on horseback. As the weather was very hot our toil was great, and I shall never forget the welcome with which I greeted the beer-shop on the Thompson River. The scenery through these mountains is magnificent, – when it can be seen. But such is the continuity and contiguity of the trees, that it becomes impossible for miles together to see either the hill-tops or the depths of the valleys. Going down to the Thompson River, and again down into Walhalla, we found it to be impossible to ride; and yet we knew that immense masses of machinery had been taken down by bullocks for the use of the miners. We were told that very many bullocks had been destroyed at the work. I could not have believed that there had been such a traffic across the mountains and through the forests, had I not afterwards seen the things at Walhalla.

At last we got to the place, very tired and very footsore, and had bedrooms allocated to us in the hotel close to the quartz-crushing machine, which goes on day and night eating up the rock which is dragged forth from the bowels of the earth. The noisy monster continued his voracious meal without cessation for a moment, so that sleep was out of the question. To the residents of the inn the effect was simply somniferous. Their complaint was that from twelve o'clock on Saturday night when the monster begins to keep his Sabbath, to twelve o'clock on Sunday night when his religious observances are over, the air is so burdened by silence that they can neither talk by day nor sleep by night.

The mining town which has been dignified by the name of
Walhalla lies at the bottom of a gully from which the wooded
sides rise steeply. Through it meanders a stream which is now,
of course, contaminated by the diggings and pumpings, and
gold-washing and quartz-crushing, which have befallen the
locality. Nevertheless it has a peculiar beauty of its own, and a
picturesque interest arising in part from the wooded hills which
so closely overhang it, – but partly also from the quaintness of a
town so placed. The buildings, consisting of banks, churches,
schools, hotels, managers' houses, and miners' cottages, lie
along the stream, or are perched up on low altitudes among the
trees. There is something like a winding street through it,
which is nearly a mile long, – though indeed it is difficult
sometimes to distinguish between the river and the street; but
there is no road to it from any place in the world, – and even the
tracks by which it is to be left are not easy of discovery. We
went down to it by the 'Little Joe', the Little Joe being a
hillside, and I hope I may never have to go down the Little Joe
again with a tired horse behind me. We left it by a path as steep
and so hidden that we should never have found it without a
guide. As it was, the mayor conducted us out of Walhalla with
some solemnity.

And yet in this singular place there are, or seem to be,
congregated all the necessaries and most of the luxuries of life.
There was a pianoforte in the hotel sitting-room, and framed
pictures hanging on the wall, – just as there might be in
Birmingham. And there was a billiard-table, – at which
unwashed earth-soiled diggers were playing, and playing, too,
very well. At what cost must the pianoforte and the billiard-
table have been brought down the mountain track! Nevertheless the charge for billiards was no more than sixpence a game;
and no charge whatever was made for the piano!

The great mine at Walhalla when I was there was the Long
Tunnel. Shares in the Long Tunnel were hardly to be had for
money; but, bought even at most exaggerated prices, gave
almost endless interest. I went down the Long Tunnel, – and
came up again. As usual I found below a dirty grubbing world.
Men were earning between £2 and £3 a week, living hardly, –
though always plenteously; and speculating in gold with their
savings. But here, as elsewhere, they were courteous and kind.

Their children are all educated, and if churches and meeting-houses may be taken as proof of religion they are religious. I was told that the place contained about 15,000 inhabitants. I cannot repeat too often that I have never met more courteous men than the gold miners of Australia.

We stayed but one night, and then proceeded on our journey, still taking our mounted guide, and for the first ten miles were under the special guardianship of the mayor, – who was to be looked upon, I was told, as a deputation from the town in honour of my friend. A very pleasant fellow we found the Mayor of Walhalla, and we parted from him in great kindness, even though he did lose the way in the forest, and take us, all for nothing, up and down one mountain side. When he parted from us our trusty trooper was a safer guide. This man was, I believe, no more than an ordinary policeman. The rural policemen of the colonies, who have to pass over wide districts, are all mounted. But they carry themselves higher, and stand much higher among their fellow-citizens, than do the men of the same class with us. We are apt to separate men into two classes, – and define each man by saying that he is or that he is not a gentleman. This man was a private policeman. Had I not known the fact, I should have taken him for a gentleman. Even as it is I rather think that I regard him in that light. He was a fine, powerful fellow, well mannered, able to talk on all subjects, extremely courteous, – and he amused us greatly by explaining to us why it was that a policeman must be always more than a match for at any rate two rogues. He was an Irishman, – of course. In the colonies those who make money are generally Scotchmen, and those who do not are mostly Irishmen. He had probably come out because his family could do nothing for him at home. I hope that he may live to be General-in-Chief of the Victorian police. He took us through the mountains to an old and apparently worn-out diggings called Edwards' Reef, – a miserable, melancholy place, surrounded by interminable forests, in which unhappy diggers had sunk holes here and there, so that one wondered that the children did not all perish by falling into them. But even at Edwards' Reef there was an hotel, though I was at a loss to imagine by whom it could be supported. It was a large wooden building, now nearly falling to the ground; though doubtless it had once been alive with the sound of miners' voices in the days when there was gold in those quarters.

From Edwards' Reef we went on to Woods Point, having changed our policeman. It seems that the magistrates had ordered that we should be taken in safety as far as the latter place. We passed another day in traversing endless forests, and in ascending and descending ravines. Here and there, in the densest parts of the forests , we came on the old tracks of miners, finding the holes which they had dug in search of gold. How many a heart must have been broken, – how many a back nearly broken, among these mountains! The ascents and descents here were very steep, and on one occasion we submitted to be pulled up, hanging on to our horses' tails, – an operation which I had not seen since I hunted, many years ago, in Carmarthenshire. On this journey we had an adventure. At an inn among the mountains, – for here and there one comes upon an inn, though there are no roads, – we found two girls who were desirous of going to a wedding which was to be held in a neighbouring gully. Luckily, or perhaps unluckily, the mounted mailman came up, driving two spare horses before him. So the girls at once borrowed the horses, and the inn afforded one side-saddle. The girl who mounted without the side- saddle rode well, and might have reached the wedding triumphantly; but the other was somewhat at fault, even with the side-saddle. She was bold enough, but had probably never been on horseback before. We had gone on during the trouble of the saddle as there appeared to be some bashfulness in completing the arrangement; but before long the poor maiden's steed was after us. He had run away with her, and for a moment or two I thought she must have perished among the trees, – but as the beast passed us he shied, and deposited his burden close at the feet of the horse I was riding. She was shaken, for awhile speechless, soiled and wretched; but before long she proclaimed her intention of walking to the wedding. The distance was not above six miles through the woods. The other girl like a true friend dismounted, that she might walk with her companion, and the mailman with his spare horses proceeded on with us to Jericho.

Jericho was another digging town, down in a gully, at which men were grubbing for gold, scooping out great holes in and near the bed of the river. The great forests rose steep on each side, and the place was grandly picturesque. We were told that Jericho not long since had been a prosperous place for gold-seekers. Thence we ascended a hill to Matlock, another gold-digging town, very high up, very bleak, and the most wretched place I ever saw. Some one there declared that Matlock was the highest inhabited spot in Victoria. This was in February, a summer month, – but even then the cold was intense. There is no gold now at Matlock, and I could not understand what induced the few unfortunate inhabitants to remain there. Though it is a difficult thing to establish a town or village, it is still more difficult to disestablish it. But Matlock will soon disestablish itself under the effect of the winds of heaven. From Matlock we descended four miles into Woods Point.

Woods Point is a gold-field of great importance, – of very great importance indeed in the estimation of the Woods-Pointers. It has been very rich and is still producing gold in remunerating quantities. But I met nowhere gold-seekers so wedded to gold as were the heroes of Woods Point. I was allowed the privilege of dining with some of the great men of the place, and I thought that I should hardly have been permitted to leave the room alive, because I expressed an opinion that wool was of more importance to the colonies generally than the precious metal, which I found to be so well loved at this place. Oh, men of Woods Point, if ever these words should meet your ears, know how utterly unconvinced I was by your oratory, though in arguments I was unable to stand up against the fervour of your eloquence! At Woods Point I inspected a mine, but contented myself with inspecting it from the surface. Every opportunity, however, was given me to go below, had I chosen to avail myself of the courtesy of my conductors.

Woods Point, like Walhalla, is a gully or ravine, – though less singular than Walhalla, because there is a coach-road running through it. The scenery around it is very lovely, – so much so as to inspire a feeling of sorrow that so much beauty should be desecrated by miners. Altogether the beauty of the country through which we had passed, and through which we did pass on our way back to Melbourne, contradicted the too general assertion that Australia is destitute of lovely scenery.

Three days more, with a pleasant rest at a friend's house on the road, – as to which I have spoken in another chapter, referring to the Yering wine, – brought us back to Melbourne. On the way down we passed through a country now well known for its enormous trees, – all gum-trees of various sorts, or Eucalypti as they are called by the learned.

At the land office in Melbourne I heard tidings of one enormous tree which had lately been discovered in this region, prostrate over a river-bed, and of which the remaining portion, – for the head had been broken off in the fall, – measured 435 ft. in length. The gentleman by whom this monster was found had been sent out by the commissioners of the lands to inspect the timber in the ranges of the watershed of the Watts River, and a copy of his report was published in one of the Melbourne newspapers. It is, I believe, now admitted that the gum-trees of this district are the highest trees yet found in the world, surpassing altogether those world-famous productions of California, which have for a while been regarded as the kings of the forest. I believe I am right in asserting that no other measured trunk has been found equal in length to that above recorded.

At Melbourne I sold my horse and saddle for £3 10s. less than I had given for them, and I thought that I had made my journey with sufficient economy.

CHAPTER VII

LAND

I will now speak of the disposition of waste or crown lands in Victoria. In doing so it will be my chief object to explain the terms on which land can at present be bought, or hired, from the local authorities who represent the Crown generally in the colonies. The still unalienated lands of Australia, – by which term is included the great bulk of the Australian continent, – did belong to the British Crown till the period at which the colonies commenced the task of self-government. Then each colony took possession of its own land, relieving the Crown, – or in other words the taxpayers of Great Britain, – of the expense of colonial government in return for that concession. From that time the existing governments of the day have administered the land as trustees for the people of the colonies in conformity, – or, as some allege, not always in conformity, – with the land laws as passed by the different colonial parliaments.

That is, I think, after a rough fashion a correct statement of the manner in which the question of the disposition of Australian lands has been treated. But the subject is one full of complications, and for its thorough understanding demands the close study of some British Acts of Parliament, and of very many colonial land laws. I am aware of no general British Act of Parliament regulating the sale of waste lands in Australia, prior to that passed on June 22nd, 1842. By that Act the power of the Crown to alienate the lands was limited, or I might almost say abrogated. With certain exceptions made on behalf of the public service, 'the Crown shall not alienate these lands, unless by way of sale, nor unless such sales be conducted in the manner and according to the regulations hereinafter prescribed.' Previously to that date, grants had been made at the discretion of the Crown or of the governor, and sales had been

made either by auction, or at a fixed price, – generally 20s. an
acre, – in accordance with the same discretion. But long before
1842, a great interest had grown up in Australia, which, though
certainly dependent on the land, did not require its alienation, –
which was indeed in its effects altogether opposed to its
alienation. In 1803, Captain Macarthur, who had been
employed as a soldier in New South Wales, first proposed to
the government the importation of sheep and the growth of
wool. If the government would grant the land, then absolutely
useless, he would, at his own risk, import the sheep. Grants of
land were made to Macarthur, and his scheme was pre- emi-
nently successful. There may be a doubt whom we should
regard as the first discoverer of gold in Australia, but there is
no doubt that we are indebted to Captain Macarthur for the
great staple of that country, – for that which was its staple
before men had dreamed of Australian gold, – and for that
which probably will be its chief staple again, when gold shall
have either been worked out, or, as is more probable, shall
have become less valuable than wool. Captain Macarthur at
first asked, not for possession of land, but for 'permission to
occupy a sufficient tract of unoccupied lands to feed his flocks'.

   Mr. William Campbell, of the Legislative Council of Victoria, in an indignant protest published by him against the
legislation of his colony in regard of land, thus describes the
commencement of those pastoral leases by which squatters first
held their somewhat precarious property:

'Others,' he says, 'followed his', – Captain Macarthur's – 'example; the
lands were lying waste; the government very wisely encouraged their
occupation, and licensed any free and respectable person who desired to
occupy them. Commissioners were appointed to manage these waste
lands, and the occupants voluntarily paid an assessment to defray the
commissioners' expenses, and that of the police under their direction; so
that their occupation might not cost the government anything. But in
the course of time, when nearly all the lands within a penetrable
distance were occupied, great evils were experienced from the arbitrary
acts of these functionaries, who assumed great power in defining the
extent of runs by lessening one run in order to enlarge another. They
were accused of receiving bribes, and of acting very unfairly between
man and man. The occupants were powerless against the government,
as they had only an annual licence. They could not be otherwise than

dissatisfied. They required a better tenure to secure them against the irresponsible acts of an arbitrary governor and his needy subordinates. They agitated their grievances, and ultimately obtained an equitable title to a lease upon definite terms, – with a preferable right to purchase at a fair value. They obtained that title through an Act of Parliament', – an act, that is, of the Imperial Parliament, – 'and an Order of Her Majesty in Council. They were grateful for that boon granted to them, and were encouraged to improve their property under the fullest confidence that the promise of the Queen under the sanction of the Imperial Parliament would be held sacred. In this, however, they have been much disappointed; as her Majesty's representative in Victoria violated that promise, by refusing to give the occupant of crown lands the stipulated pre-emptive right, and otherwise illegally disposed of such lands to their prejudice.'

The work from which I quote was published as long ago as 1855, at which time Mr. Campbell represented very accurately the state of the Australian squatter's mind. That mind has been in no degree altered since. As Mr. Campbell and the squatters felt then, Mr. Campbell and the squatters feel now. In the above passage Mr. Campbell speaks of the squatting interest of the Australian continent generally. When the Order in Council above referred to was made, both Victoria and Queensland, – under the names of Port Phillip and Moreton Bay, – were parts of the great colony of New South Wales, and the order, therefore, was supposed to govern the pastoral interest of the whole territory now comprised in these three colonies. But the edge of Mr. Campbell's sword is specially sharpened against Mr. La Trobe, the first governor of Victoria, who was thought by him to have violated that Order in Council on behalf of the small farmers or free-selecters; and the swords of the Victorian squatters generally have been sharpened against the Victorian legislatures since Mr. La Trobe's days on the same ground, – under a biting, burning, overwhelming conviction, not only that their interests, but also that their rights, have been sacrificed to a thirst for popularity. As Mr. La Trobe was supposed, by the squatters, to have been unjust in order that he might propitiate the growing numbers of the agricultural interest as opposed to the pastoral interest, so succeeding legislators and succeeding cabinets have been supposed to be unjust in order that they might obtain the votes of the people. Indignation is the general tone of the Australian squatter's mind; indignation such as glowed in the bosom of the old Duke of Newcastle when he asked whether he might not do as he liked with his own; that indignation which the aristocrat feels all the world over when he dreads that his heels will be wounded by the clouted toe of the aggressive peasant. In the old country men are reticent, and the indignation is expressed only among peers in fortune and in misfortune. When doors are closed, and the claret circulates, and all the company are azure blue, men lapped in luxury, and so secure in their possessions that they are content to hold them though giving but two per cent. for their capital, mourn together painfully, and with feigned horrors speculate on the coming of an imaginary chaos. Among the squatters of Australia the spirit of men is the same, but the lamentations are loud and public. In both countries they who lament are the rich ones of the earth. In both countries real wealth has made itself secure, having the power which wealth always possesses of fortifying itself against aggression; and in both cases the basis of that wealth is the possession of land.

Mr. Campbell, I think, makes out his case, – as I intend to endeavour to explain. He and the other squatters were unjustly used, – were illegally deprived of their rights, I would say, were it not that the deprivation was effected by law. I conceive it to be impossible to examine the matter without coming to the conclusion that the squatters, at any rate in Victoria, were barred by the colonial government and colonial legislature from entering in upon certain privileges promised to them by a British Order in Council founded on an Act of the British Parliament, – in full confidence upon which promises they had expended their energies and their money. But a man may be defrauded of a portion of his gains and still have so much left to him as to induce an outside observer to think that the country in which he has been able to accumulate so much so quickly, and to conserve so vast a proportion of what he has accumulated, has been a blessed country to him. Such I conceive to be the condition of the Victorian squatter, – of the man who was a squatter but is now a huge territorial landowner. He has been injured. But he has been too great to be much affected by such injury; and in spite of governors, in spite of laws, in spite of would-be-popular cabinet ministers and tribes of voters, he rides triumphant on the top of the tide.

I have alluded to the law of 1842, passed by the British Parliament in reference to Australian lands, as barring the power of the Crown to give away the crown lands at its pleasure, or to sell them except in accordance with certain fixed rules. I have also alluded to a further Act of the Imperial Parliament and to an Order in Council founded upon it, as being the basis on which the Australian squatters generally, and especially those of Victoria, rested for that security which they think has been denied to them. This Act bears date 28th August, 1846, the Order in Council 9th March, 1847, – and they provide especially for the lease of lands in New South Wales. They state the terms on which squatters will be allowed to run their flocks on the public unalienated lands in that colony, which then included both the Victoria and the Queensland of the present day.

This order, which had and has all the strength of an Act of Parliament, having been issued in conformity with the express injunctions of an Act of Parliament, divides the public lands into three classes, – a settled district, an intermediate district, and an unsettled district, and it describes, as accurately as it can do, by the names of towns, counties, and rivers, the boundaries of each. Our concern at present is with the unsettled districts, over which, more extensively from year to year, the Australian wool-growers run their flocks of sheep. The settled districts consisted chiefly of lands lying contiguous to towns or townships, and did not much concern the squatter. The intermediate districts were wider, and did concern the squatter, – but as to them he makes no complaint. The Order in Council enacted that in using such land he should practically have no more than one years' tenure. If he chose to occupy such land with his sheep, – and these lands were so occupied almost exclusively, – he did so with the knowledge that any portion of them might be thrown open to sale at a year's notice. They were thrown open for sale, and have been purchased, chiefly by the squatters themselves. In regard to the unsettled districts it stipulates that the squatters shall have a lease of fourteen years, that they shall pay a rental calculated at the rate of £2 10s. per thousand sheep for such a number as the run may by survey be computed to be able to carry, that during their leases and at the end of their leases they shall have a pre-emptive right of purchase at some price not less than 20*s.* an acre, and that 'during the continuance of any lease of lands occupied as a run, the same shall not be open to purchase by any other person or persons except the lessee thereof'. The governor, however, has reserved to him the power of selling or otherwise disposing of any special portion of land, the sale of which, or alienation of which by other means, may be required for the public good. It can be sold, for instance, if wanted for a village, for a railway, for a church or school, for a mine, 'or for any other purpose of public defence, safety, utility, convenience, or enjoyment, or for otherwise facilitating the improvement and settlement of the colony'. 'Hinc illae lachrymae.' These words are very wide, – and from the extreme latitude given to them, or rather imposed on them, by governors, colonial cabinet ministers, and legislators have come the wailings and moanings of which Mr. Campbell eighteen years since was the eloquent expositor, and which are still heard at large through the colony.

I think that no man of common sense, who understands the ordinary meaning of words, can doubt that the Order in Council intended to defend the lands leased to the squatters from all sale except when special plots were required for special purposes. It was not intended that the land should be thrown open to sale generally, in order that the improvement and settlement of the colony might be facilitated by such proceeding. If so, why all these words? If so, why defend the squatters at all from aggression of purchasers by a special Act of Parliament and a special Order in Council? The Act of 1846, and the Order in Council founded on it, may have been injudicious in conferring privileges with too open a hand upon the squatters. I think myself that such was the case. But the favours were conferred; and in any further operations either of the imperial or colonial parliaments the rights so given should have been regarded as far as the vested interests of the existing holders were concerned. It was surely a quibble to say that any governor, – as long as the governors were the responsible agents, – or any land minister when the ministers were responsible, – could sell these lands without doing violence to the Order in Council, because they were empowered to do so by the clause in reference to the improvement and settlement of the colony.

But this was done. The lands were put up to sale, because, as was asserted, townships would be beneficial, and it was expedient that there should be land to be had for agricultural purposes in the neighbourhood of townships. My sympathies are all on behalf of the townships and the agricultural lands. But a bargain is a bargain, and a law is a law; and one's sense of justice is offended by any escape from a bargain or from a law by a verbal quibble. The nature of the quibble, and the ease with which an Act of Parliament may be thrown open to a coach and horses, is made ludicrously apparent by a legal opinion which the squatters got from our side of the water. They were much enraged, and determined to defend themselves, if there could be any defence, in the courts of law. So they sent home for an opinion to no less a person and no less a lawyer than our late Lord Chancellor, who was then Mr. Roundell Palmer. Probably the opinion of no English lawyer on such a subject would carry more confidence than his. Mr. Palmer's opinion was as follows:–

'I am of opinion that Mr. Forlonge' – Mr. Forlonge's case having been that which was chosen for reference, – 'has a clear and indisputable right to the leases; but inasmuch as they are to be granted by the authority of the governor, who represents the Crown, and no form of judicial proceeding against the governor is provided by the Act of Parliament, or the regulations, I do not think he has a specific remedy to compel the execution of such leases. At present, however, he has a complete equitable title, which the courts of justice in the colony would, I conceive, be bound and authorised to recognise, and to protest against any illegal encroachments, whether by the executive government or by private persons.

'I am clearly of opinion that neither of the sections referred to gives the governor power to withdraw any part of the runs in question – assuming, as I do, that no forfeiture has taken place – for the purposes of sale to private persons.

'I think Mr. Forlonge will be entitled to the right of pre-emption under sixth section.

'There is no course open for Mr. Forlonge, that I am aware of, except to appeal to the courts of justice in case of any illegal disturbance of his possessions.

ROUNDELL PALMER.
'Lincoln's Inn, 26th July, 1853.'

From this I think it will be manifest that, though Mr. Palmer had a strong opinion on Mr. Forlonge's rights, he was very far from being assured of Mr. Forlonge's power to enforce those rights. There can be be no doubt of Mr. Forlonge's rights, and as little that he was not able to enforce them.

Mr. Campbell quotes with evident glee another opinion equally in his favour, and that from an enemy, – and, as it happens, from a person almost as great in the world as our late Lord Chancellor, namely, from our late Chancellor of the Exchequer. But he appeals to Mr. Lowe as to an enemy, and shows what evidence he can adduce to support his own views even from a foe. Mr. Lowe, when a colonist, was supposed to be inimical to the views of the squatters, and disapproved of the passing of the Act of 1846 and the Order in Council founded upon it. From an address which he made in 1847, Mr. Campbell quotes the following passage: – 'Once grant these leases, and beyond the settled districts there will be no land to be sold. The lessees will have a right to hold these lands till some one will give £1 an acre for them. These leases cannot be sold, mortgaged, or sublet. Be the capabilities of these lands what they may, they are to be sheep-walks for ever.' It was clearly Mr. Lowe's opinion, when he spoke those words, that the squatters would be protected by the Order in Council against disturbance from purchasers, and that they would enjoy the right of pre-emption themselves if that order were made. But the opinions held by Mr. Lowe as a politician, and expressed by Mr. Roundell Palmer as a lawyer, have been of no avail. The Order in Council was disregarded, and the free-selecters were let in upon the lands of the squatters.

I doubt much whether it will now be worth the while of any ordinary English reader to trouble himself with these matters. The chief of the lands of Victoria have settled themselves down into the hands of undoubted owners, – and as to what remains, the present law, though it may be arbitrary, is clear. Mr. Campbell and his associate squatters cannot now gain anything, and are as little likely to lose anything, by the future doings of the colonial legislature. Lord Selborne's opinion and Mr. Lowe's oratory are equally inefficacious. The thing is a thing completed. But it is impossible to understand the completion without looking back to the manner in which it was accomplished. In the Australian colonies there is growing up a rich landed aristocracy, already surrounding itself with all the feelings which attach to land in the old country. Captain Macarthur, with his first importation of sheep, might be said to be the creator of this condition of things, were it not that it is a condition peculiarly conformable to the English mind in general, so that it was in truth created to hand before Captain Macarthur ever owned a sheep. It is clear that such feelings would be fostered and brought into prominence by a pastoral and therefore patriarchal life. Squatter added himself to squatter, often suffering much, sometimes going quite to the wall, struggling frequently with untoward circumstances, – with insufficient capital, with clever and greedy merchants, with insolent servants, with unforeseen causes of decay among his flocks, – sometimes with ill-conduct, idleness, profligacy, and extravagance on his own part; but his lot, on the whole, was a blessed lot, and he prospered marvellously. For a while it did seem as though the whole country would fall into his hands, and that the people of Australia would consist of squatters and their servants. Very much has been said, and is repeated from day to day, of what is due to the squatters as the pioneers of Australian civilisation. I do not think very much of the claim. When a man encounters danger manifestly for the sake of others, – that knowledge may grow and science progress, and the world be opened to new-comers, as did such men as Columbus and Cook, as many Australian explorers did, as Livingstone was doing till he died the other day in the doing of it, – he is entitled to public recognition and honour. But he can hardly with justice put forward the same claim because he seeks fortune for himself in stormy paths. He probably counts his chances, and, seeing personal security with ten per cent. at home, with forty per cent. and the not improbable annihilation at the hands of a savage at the Antipodes, chooses forty per cent, and Antipodes with his eyes open. I admire his courage, and applaud his decision. But I cannot admit his claim as a great public benefactor, because he has thriven and others have followed him. He has his reward. It is the reward which honest, energetic men should seek. But I have heard the Australian squatter, when discussing these matters, continually assert that he and his interests should be especially regarded, because he has been the pioneer of the country. He has been the pioneer of his own fortune; and I have been rejoiced to find how often that fortune has been noble and even princely.

The Order in Council, of which I have spoken, was clearly made in the interests of the squatters, and was therefore, of course, objectionable to the anti-squatting interests. In my opinion it was not judicious. If followed to the letter it would, as Mr, Lowe said, have barred the land against new-comers, and have perpetuated wool-growing upon soil adapted for purposes more beneficial to mankind at large. I do not think that there was any just claim at the time on the part of the squatters to such favours as were conferred upon them. The first object of the mother country, or of those to whose hands were confided for the time the duty of legislating for the colonies, was to prepare homes for the increasing hordes of colonists. The wool-growers had spread themselves over lands which did not belong to them, and which they occupied, – no doubt with proper sanction, – as waste lands. Three acres to a sheep, which sheep would produce annually about 54s. worth of wool, may be taken as a fair statement of the condition of their affairs. As long as land could be converted to no better purpose it was well that it should serve this purpose. As far as we can see at present, a very large proportion of the lands of Australia can be made to serve no better purpose. It is doubtless a fact that Australia first grew to prosperity by means of wool. At the present moment, in the very midst of the pride which she feels in her gold-fields, I put more confidence in her wool than I do in her gold. I look upon the wool-growers of Australia as her aristocracy, her gentry, her strong men, her backbone. But, in managing the affairs of this world, I do not like the theory of giving to those who have got much, and taking away from those who have got nothing. If in 1874 the general welfare of the colonists demanded that the lands of the colony should be thrown open to general sale, there was certainly nothing specially due to the squatters which should have interfered with such a policy.

It must be remembered that a system of leases to the squatters was quite compatible with a system of free-selection and open sale, that such a combination is now the law, with various modified circumstances, in the different Australian colonies, and that under it the squatters have grown rich and thriven, – unless when shut out from success by other circumstances such as want of capital. The free-selecter will not select land serviceable only for pastoral purposes, or will ruin himself at once if he does so. He selects patches of land, and leaves the wild boundless prairies to the squatter. No doubt in Victoria the land has been bought up very much more extensively than in the other colonies; but the history of these sales proves two points, both of which militate against the squatter's plaintive view of the matter. It shows that very much of the land was fit for higher than pastoral purposes, and that therefore the adapting of it to such higher purposes was proper. And it shows also that the prosperity of the squatters had not been seriously damaged, as they themselves have been the great purchasers of land from one end of the colony to the other.

The Act of Parliament of 1846, and the Order in Council of the following year, were surely issued in a spirit of unnecessary tenderness for the squatter. The result of this tenderness was disobedience to their spirit. The colony of Victoria, whether by its governor or subsequently by its own parliament, upset the Order in Council. Our great English lawyer declared very plainly the strength of Mr. Forlonge's undoubted legal rights. But Mr. Forlonge and his brethren did not get their legal rights. They only got what should have been their rights. That such a course has in the long run been greatly for the advantage of the squatters will hardly be doubted by a looker-on from a distance. No law can render permanent injustice endurable to a community. As it is the squatters hold their own, and can hold it with a tight hand. The public feeling that if they have had some favour shown them they have also had some disfavour, gives them strength. Nothing ruins so surely as uninterrupted and partial privileges. Nothing strengthens so healthily as bearable wrongs. The Victorian squatter has suffered no more than parental scourges.

But indeed the Victorian squatter has almost ceased to exist, – for the squatter, properly so called, is he who runs his flocks upon crown lands. The Victorian wool-grower has generally purchased his run and owns it in fee, – as does also the

Victorian grazier, who is as great a man as the wool-grower. Were I to attempt to describe the manner in which the lands of the colony have been purchased, I might devote a volume to the subject, and years to the study of it before I could write the volume. It seems to have been the object of the legislature to prevent the absorption of large tracts of land by great capitalists, and to create a yeomanry possessing freeholds. The result has been directly opposite to the intended purpose. The yeomanry, such as it is, can hardly as yet be regarded as a prosperous people. Their lands pass frequently from hand to hand. But, on the other hand, a strong race of territorial magnates has created itself, so wealthy and so extensive that the political power of the country is inefficacious against them. Laws have been passed with the express intention of keeping the lands out of the squatters' hands. Nevertheless the squatters have bought the lands. There have been subterfuges, chicanery, bribery, the driving of many coaches through many Acts of Parliament. The squatters no doubt have been subjected to cruel ill-usage by a tribe of land-sharks. Men have lived and made fortunes by threatening to bid for land against the squatters, unless paid exorbitantly for bidding on their behalf. The poor squatters have bled at all pores. But they have had the blood to give, and now they own the land.

I have said that the lands of Victoria have been for the most part sold. This, no doubt, is the case in regard to the colony at large, and the traveller as he travels through the better-known and better-cultivated parts of it, – especially those western regions which were at one time called Australia Felix, – will find that he passes from one property to another, much in the same fashion as he will do at home. But Victoria is a large place, and there is still very much land open for purchase from the government. The existing law under which land can be bought is as follows –

The intending purchaser, having selected his block of land, which must not exceed half a square mile, or 320 acres, applies for a licence to occupy it for three years as a tenant at a rent of 2s, an acre. The law states that this licence, may be granted by the governor, but in fact the power rests with a member of the cabinet, who is called the Commissioner of Lands. One half-year's rent must be paid in advance, and for the three years he continues to pay at the rate of 2s. an acre. At the end of the three years, provided the selecter shall then have fenced his land and have cultivated one-tenth of it, he can become the freeholder by paying 14s. an acre down, or he can continue to pay a rental for seven years at the rate of 2s. an acre, at the end of which time the land will be his. He thus, in fact, pays a rental of 2s. an acre for ten years, and then becomes the owner of the land without further purchase-money. The terms are very easy, and it is certain that there is still land to be bought in Victoria on those terms, which is worth much more than the money required for it. But there are two difficulties in the way of the free-selecter, – he may not know how to choose his land, and, when he has made his choice, his application may be unsuccessful.

That many men choose amiss in this colony and others is too true. They are in a hurry for possession. They do not know the circumstances of the country or district which affect the land, – such as the prevalence of drought, the prevalence of rust in the wheat, the difficulty of finding a market, the cost of labour, and the like. They have no friend capable of giving counsel, or, more probably, they have a friend who has some interest of his own in the transaction. One's heart bleeds at hearing of the unfortunate purchases sometimes made by new-comers, and one thinks of Cairo and Martin Chuzzlewit. As to that want of success in the application, I feel that I tread on somewhat delicate ground in alluding to it. One supposes naturally that if the applicant comply with all the required stipulations and have his money in his hands, he will be successful as a matter of course. Why not? And if he be not so, on what ground and in whose bosom shall rest the decision of granting this application and refusing that? I must say that if there be no other ground than that of fitness, – if nothing else than the character and means of the applicant be considered in granting and refusing these applications, – the minister of the day who happens to be Commissioner of Lands is at the same time the best and the worst abused man in the colony. It is asserted everywhere that the sales of land are effected with direct reference to political support, and that it would be impossible for a land minister to carry on his work in the colony on any other basis. This system of political corruption,

of using the patronage and discretion of the government to
bolster up the power of the government, from which we are
only now emerging at home, is in truth so rampant in Victoria
that honest men, – in no wise concerned in the matter, but who
have become used to it by daily observation, – have learned to
think that it is a necessary part of government. Remembering
how offices in England were given away in my own time, how
some are given still, solely on the score of political subserviency,
I do not feel justified in expressing great indignation at this
practice in the colonies. It will doubtless pass away. But the
wrongful exercise of patronage in a young colony is a smaller
fault than an unjust political manipulation in the distribution of
public lands.

It is especially stipulated by the Victorian land law that no one
person, either in his own name or that of another, shall select and
purchase above 320 acres, – the object being to prevent the
accumulation of large landed estates. But the clause has been
constantly set at nought. If I buy one section for myself, and nine
other adjacent sections through the friendly assistance of nine
'dummies', as they are called, how can a land commissioner,
with a whole colony on his hands, discern the fraud? And if I be
true to the party which have put him into office, why should he
wish to discern it? Without a doubt the squatters themselves,
who are loud against the lawlessness of Victorian legislation,
have been the most constant in evading the laws. Their success
makes it impossible for the stranger to condole with their
wrongs. At the end of this volume, as an appendix, will be
found a digest of the present land laws of Victoria, as far as they
refer to free-selection. This digest is taken from MacPhaile's
Australian Squatting Directory.

They who are still really squatters in Victoria, – who run their
sheep on public lands, and not on their own, – now pay a
pastoral rent of 8d. a sheep, or £33 6s. 8d. per thousand. The old
rental as fixed by the Order in Council in 1847 was £2 10s. per
thousand. The rental at present paid is four times higher than
that collected in either of the other Australian colonies. But the
bulk of the Victorian wool is grown by men who own the land
which produces it.

I found that the system of landlord and tenant – with which
we are so familiar at home as almost to have conceived the idea

that land cannot be occupied on any other system – does prevail in certain parts of Victoria. I visited a district in which large wheat farms were held by tenants, and I was told of rents varying from 5s. to 15s. an acre. But it did not appear that the tenant-farmers were a prosperous class, or that the letting of land was popular among landowners. In some instances a whole property is let with the stock upon it, and I have heard of as much as '10,000 a year being paid for a sheep-run with the use of the sheep on it; but in speaking of the letting of land of course I do not allude to such cases as this. The small tenant-farmer in the colonies is seldom a man of means. Did he possess capital he would buy his farm. Not possessing capital he cannot pay his rent when bad years come, – and it almost seemed that, as far as the produce of wheat went, bad years were as common as good years in Victoria. The ground produced enormously, – with most generous vigour, I must say, considering how little is restored to it. But the climate is uncertain, and the disease called the rust is pernicious. One gentleman, who owned a large tract of corn-bearing land, assured me that he much preferred selling portions of his property, even though the purchase-money were left on mortgage, to accepting a promise of yearly rent for the use of his land.

I have said that the public lands are alienated in fee for a rental of 2s. an acre for ten years, and that tenant-farmers pay rents varying from 5s. to 15s. an acre, – the payment of which for any number of years gives, of course, no title to possession. It is presumed that the reader will understand that the public, or crown, lands spoken of are uncultivated, unfenced, and probably covered with timber. The farm lands let for the higher rentals named have been brought into cultivation, have been farmed, and are supposed to be capable of bearing corn.

CHAPTER VIII

LADIES AND GENTLEMEN

A writer attempting to describe England, and capable of doing so, would fill those chapters with the strongest interest in which he painted the various forms of English country life. He would know, and he would teach his readers, that the English character, with its faults and virtues, its prejudices and steadfastness, can be better studied in the mansions of noblemen, in country-houses, in parsonages, in farms, and small meaningless towns, than in the great cities, devoted as is London to politics and gaiety, or as are Glasgow, Manchester, Birmingham, and others like them, to manufactures and commerce. I doubt whether this be so in any other country. France has many aspects, but the Parisian aspect is more French than any other. Italy is to be seen only in her cities. In the United States the towns altogether overrule and subdue the country, so that the traveller who visits America under the most favourable circumstances rarely sees aught of her cornfields and pastures, except in passing from one great centre of population to another. But the visitors to England who have not sojourned at a country-house, whether it be squire's, parson's, or farmer's, have not seen the most English phase of the country.

The same form and fashion of life is repeating itself in the Australian colonies. The race of farmers, such as are our own well-to-do farmers at home, does not, indeed, exist. The clergy are scattered at long distances, and hardly as yet form a distinctive social class, – probably never will do so as they do in England, and in England only. But the country gentlemen, almost all of whom were originally squatters, have fixed their homes about the colony, and have built their houses, – not exactly after the English fashion in regard to architecture, because the climate is of a different nature, – but with the

English appurtenances of substantial comfort, with many rooms, with gardens, outhouses, and lawns, and with sweeping roads leading through timbered parks to the retired abode of the rural magistrate who owns the property. The visitor to Australia, who goes there under favourable auspices, will as surely find himself pressed to make his home at such country houses, as will the stranger in the United States be asked to enjoy the luxurious hospitality of her rich citizens, either in city mansions or in suburban villas. And such a one, if he have time on his hands, and can dally with weeks in idleness, may pass from station to station, – from one gentleman's house to another, – till he will hardly know who has sent him on, or on what ground he bases his claim to the hospitality of his new friends.

There is perhaps more of this in Victoria than in the other colonies, because the country gentlemen have more thoroughly established their fortunes there than elsewhere; but the same feeling prevails throughout Australia, and the same mode of life. They who rise to the top of the tree, – or in other words, the gentry, if I may use such a phrase which is somewhat invidious but which will be better understood than any other, – seek to establish country houses for themselves; and homesteads of this class have sprung up with incredible rapidity. Nothing, I think, so clearly declares the wealth of the colony, – which is not yet forty years old, – as the solidity of her country life. When the stranger asks whence came these country gentlemen, whom he sees occasionally at the clubs and dinner-tables in Melbourne, exactly as he finds those in England up in London during the winter frosts, or in the month of May, he is invariably told that they or their fathers made their own fortunes. This man and that and the other came over perhaps from Tasmania, in the early days, joint owners of a small flock of sheep. They generally claim to have suffered every adversity with which Providence and unjust legislators could inflict a wretched victim; and, as the result, each owns so many thousand horned cattle, so many tens of thousand sheep, so many square miles of country, and so many thousands a year. Most of them have, I think, originally come out of Scotland. When you hear an absent acquaintance spoken of as 'Mac', you will not at all know who is meant, but you may safely conclude that it is some prosperous individual. Some were butchers, drovers, or shepherds themselves but a few years since. But they now form an established aristocracy, with very conservative feelings, and are quickly becoming as firm a country party as that which is formed by our squire-archy at home.

I have spoken of country life in New South Wales without reserve, because the small establishment which I described belongs to my own son. In Victoria I visited many houses of infinitely greater pretension, but I fear to speak of any one in particular lest I should commit that great sin, – not always avoided as scrupulously as it should be by travelling authors, – of putting some kind host into a book, with his wife, family, kitchen and cellars. And yet, if it be possible, I would fain let English readers know what these houses are, and of what nature is the life contained in them. They are generally less remote from towns than are the habitations of squatters in the other colonies, – the towns being more numerous, and the roads more formed. The buildings themselves are generally of two storeys, – always having the tropical addition of a verandah, but not erected in that straggling, many-roofed, one-storied fashion which is common in Queensland and New South Wales. They betoken a gradually increasing prosperity. The squatter builds first a wooden hut which ultimately becomes his kitchen, then a wooden sitting-room and bed-room near to it; then a bigger sitting-room with two small bedrooms, still of wood, – and so on. But when he has realised to himself the fact that he is a rich man he rushes into brick and mortar or stone, and erects a European country house, – with the addition of a wide verandah. This has been done now very generally by the landowners of Victoria. But still the place has rarely all the finished comfort, the easy grace, coming from long habit, which belong to our country seats at home. There is a roughness and a heaviness about it, a want of completion about the gardens, of neatness about the paths, and of close-shorn trimness about the plots and lawns, which strikes the beholder at once, and declares that though the likeness be there, it exists with a difference.

This difference is caused chiefly by the dearness of labour, a fact which influences not only the outside of the Victorian gentleman's house, but also every part of his establishment. Let his means be what they may, he never has the retinue of servants which is to be found in an ordinary English household. The high rate of wages and the difficulty of getting persons to accept these high rates for any considerable number of months together, cause even the wealthy to dispense with much of that attendance which is often considered indispensable at home even among families that are not wealthy. On the other hand, certain luxuries are common among Australian families, which few among us can enjoy without stint. He who has a carriage and horses at home is supposed to be a rich man. If a gentleman have daughters fond of riding, he will perhaps have one horse for two girls. Young men can hardly hunt unless their fathers be wealthy. But horses on an Australian station are as common as blackberries on English hedges, and the possession of a carriage and pair of horses is as much a matter of course as the possession of a pair of boots. But horses are cheap and servants are dear in Victoria.

I have spoken of sweeping roads through timbered parks. It must not, however, be conceived that I speak of parks such as those which are the glory of our English magnates. The Australian park is hitherto much as nature fashioned it. The trees are the gum-trees which the present resident or his father found there when he first drove his sheep on the pastures which had never yet known the foot of a white man. The grasses round his house he may gradually have changed, and have extirpated those indigenous to the soil by the use of English seeds. The road will probably be somewhat rough, and the fences which divide the paddocks still rougher. He is now a rich man, but he is rich because in all his expenditure he has thought more of a return for his capital than of the adornment of his place. He calls his park a paddock, and he has thought only of the welfare of his stock. But, nevertheless, there is that beauty about it which trees and grass, with the sky above them, always produce. And the territory is large and spacious, and all the magnificence of ownership is there. The man drives for miles through his own land. He has fortified himself on all sides against free-selecters. All those who frequent the place are his servants or guests, and of every stranger whom he may see within miles of his house he is entitled to ask why he is there. He exercises a wide hospitality to the poor and the rich, and he is an aristocrat.

I imagine that the life of the Victorian landowner is very much as was that of the English country gentleman a century or a century and a half ago. In those days roads in England were very bad, so that it was a work of trouble to get from one house to another, a distance of twenty miles. Country houses of pretension were not numerous as they are now, and they who owned the halls and granges scattered through the counties rarely moved from their homes. There was great plenty, but of that finished luxury which is now as common in the country as in the capital, there was but little. Roast beef, – or in winter powdered beef, – and October ale were the fare. The men were fond of sport, but they did not go far afield for it as they do now, hunting in the shires, shooting on the moors, and fishing on all lakes and rivers. They shot over their own lands, and hunted over their own land and that of a few neighbours who would join them. The ladies stayed at home and looked after the house, and much that is now trusted to domestics and stewards was done by the mistress and her daughters, or by the master and his sons. The owners of these country houses were Tories, aristocrats, proud gentlemen; but they were not fine gentlemen, nor, for the most part, were they gentlemen of fine tastes in art or literature. We know them very well from plays and novels, – and know something of them too from history, as history has of late been written. The ladies' dresses, the books, the equipages, the wines, the kitchens, which are now found in English country houses, were in those days known only in the metropolis, or at the castle of some almost royal nobleman. As were country houses and country life then in England, plentiful, proud, prejudiced, given to hospitality, impatient of contradiction, not highly lettered, healthy, industrious, careful of the main chance, thoughtful of the future, and, above all, conscious, – perhaps a little too conscious, – of their own importance, so now is the house and so is the life of the country gentleman in Australia. And as Justice Shallow in times still farther distant was ever anxious as to the price of a good yoke of bullocks or a score of ewes, so does the Australian country gentleman never omit his solicitude concerning those things which have made him what he is. The value of beef in the Melbourne market, and of wool at London, are continually in his thoughts, and as continually on his tongue, even though he may have reached that stage of prosperity which cannot be much affected by the transient rise or fall of prices. He has not at any rate reached that condition, – be it good or bad, – which enables the English country gentleman to drop all outward show of solicitude for the trade in which he is embarked, the trade namely of living upon his land, and to pursue the unruffled tenor of his way as though all the good things came to him and were sure to come to him like manna from heaven. The Victorian wool-grower or grazier will be sure to tell you, if you visit him in his own home, what has been his produce of wool, and what prices he has realised for it, – and will take you to his washpool, if he wash his sheep before shearing, and to his wool-shed; or he will show you his Durhams and Herefords, and boast how he has led the markets. Out of the full heart the mouth speaks. He has made himself what he is by his sheep and oxen, and the sheep and the oxen are still dear to him. His grandson or great-grandson will probably be as outwardly indifferent as an English country gentleman, who is no more given to talk of his rents than a banker is of his profits, and who is concerned wholly, perhaps with his hounds, perhaps with his library, perhaps with his politics, or perhaps with his cook.

Out-of-door sports do not form so prominent a part of country life in the colonies as they do at home, partly because there are not so many idle men, and partly because there has not been as yet so great an expenditure of money with the view of creating sport. As years pass on both these causes will vanish. The idle men will be forthcoming, and game, brought from England, Scotland, and Ireland, will be naturalised in the country. Hares in Victoria will be, I hope, not quite so plentiful as rabbits. There are deer already in the country, and they will soon abound with that prolific increase which seems to attend all animals brought from the old country to these colonies. Duck-shooting is much practised, and ducks abound. Pheasants are already more common in parts of New Zealand than in England, though not so plentiful, and will probably become equally common in Tasmania and Victoria. I despair, however, of fox-hunting. I think it is improbable that that most anomalous, most irrational, most exciting,

most delightful, and most beneficent sport should thrive
elsewhere on the world's surface than in the British Isles.
None but the British and Irish farmer will bear the invasion of
a troop of horsemen. None but the British or Irish sportsman
can have that tenderness in preserving and that stern per-
severance in killing a little vermin, which fox-hunting
requires. None but a British or an Irish gentleman can expend
thousands in furnishing amusement for an entire county.

The fault of a country home in the Australian colonies is
that it furnishes but little employment, and that its ordinary
life seems to be antagonistic to industry, at any rate on the part
of the visitor. The master of the house is or is not the working
manager of his property. If he be so, his time is fully occupied.
He is on horseback before breakfast, and seems never to
slacken his labours till the evening dews have long fallen. The
exclusive care of a large flock of sheep, – which includes
breeding, feeding, doctoring, shearing, selling and buying,
together with the hiring, feeding, inspection, and payment of
a great number of by no means subservient workmen, – taxes
a man's energies to the utmost. Cattle probably impose less
labour, but a man will have his hands fairly full who owns
three or four thousand head of cattle, who breeds them by his
own judgement, and himself selects them for market. But
very many squatters and graziers really manage their properties by deputy. Serviceable men have grown up in their
employment, and as years creep on the real work of the run is
allowed to fall from their own hands into those of superintendents and overseers. Then the country gentleman, though
he still talks of 'a score of ewes' as did Justice Shallow,
becomes an idle man. He comes down to breakfast at nine,
and is impatient for his dinner before six, thinking that the
clock must be losing time. The ladies no doubt look after their
houses, order lunch and dinner, and superintend the servants.
But they seem to be insufficiently provided with occupations
over and above these. There is a piano in every house. There
are always books, – enough for reading, though not enough
for literary luxury. There may be croquet out of doors. There
are horses to ride; and there is the unlimited bush, with its
magpies, its laughing jackasses, and its bell-birds, if you be
good at walking. But there is no provision made for the

passing of time. There is no period of the day at which books fall naturally into the hands of men and women. Loitering is common, and the hours too often become foes instead of friends. This is specially the case during the long evenings. I fancy that the same fault might have been found with country houses in England a hundred and fifty years ago.

Eating and drinking occupy so many of our thoughts, and contribute so much to the excitement and to the amusement of life, that I feel myself bound to say something of the Victorian country gentleman's taste. No table more plentiful or more hospitable was ever spread. Its chief distinctive feature is the similarity of the meals. The breakfast is nearly as substantial as the lunch and dinner, and between the lunch and dinner it was long before I could find out any difference. Two or three hot joints of meat and four or five dishes of vegetables, wine-decanters, and not uncommonly a teapot, are common to both of them. As regarded the time allowed, or the appetite, or that addition to appetite which greediness furnishes throughout the world, I could not ascertain that there was any distinction between the two. With us at home the cook never exerts herself, – or himself, – for lunch, and is not expected to do so. The Victorian cook is equally awake all the day long. At last I perceived that at luncheon there would never be more than two puddings. At dinner the number was not limited. As a rule, gentlemen in the colonies do not sit long over their wine; and, as a rule, also, – and rules, of course, have their exceptions, – the wine is not worth a long sitting.

But these little details of which I have spoken do but form the outside skin of society, whereas the bones, the muscles, the blood, and the flesh consist of the people themselves. Whether men and women dine at five or seven, whether they drive out regularly or irregularly, whether they hunt foxes or kangaroos, drink bad wine or good, matters little, in regard to social delights, in comparison with the character, the manners, and the gifts of the men and women themselves. In describing Victorians of the upper classes, and of the two sexes, I would say that both in their defects and their excellences they approach nearer to the American than to the British type. And in this respect the Victorian is distinct from the colonist of New South Wales, who retains more of the John-Bull attributes of the mother country than his younger and more energetic brother in the South. This is visible, I think, quite as much in the women as in the men. I am speaking now especially of those women whom on account of their education and position we should class as ladies; but the remark is equally true to all ranks of society. The maidservant in Victoria has the pertness, the independence, the mode of asserting by her manner that though she brings you up your hot water, she is just as good as you, – and a good deal better if she be younger, – which is common to the American 'helps'. But in Victoria, as in the States, the offensiveness of this, – for to us who are old-fashioned it is in a certain degree offensive, – is compensated by a certain intelligence and instinctive good-sense which convinces the observer that however much he may suffer, however heavily the young woman may tread upon his toes, she herself has a good time in the world. She is not degraded in her own estimation by her own employment, and has no idea of being humble because she brings you hot water. And when we consider that the young woman serves us for her own purposes, and not for ours, we cannot rationally condemn her. The spirit which has made this bearing so common in the United States, – where indeed it is hardly so universal now as it used to be, – has grown in Victoria and has permeated all classes. One has to look very closely before one can track it out and trace it to be the same in the elegantly equipped daughter of the millionaire who leads the fashion in Melbourne and in the little housemaid; but it is the same. The self-dependence, the early intelligence, the absence of reverence, the contempt for all weakness, – even feminine weakness, – the indifference to the claims of age, the bold self-assertion, have sprung both in the one class and in the other from the rapidity with which success in life has been gained. The class of which I am now specially speaking is an aristocrat class; but it is an aristocracy of yesterday; and the creation of such an aristocracy does away with reverence and puts audacity in its place. The young housemaid does not shake in her shoes before you because you have £10,000 a year, and the young lady has no special respect for you because you are her father's old friend. Her father and her father's friends have had their time. It is her time now. It is for her to stand in

the middle and for them to range themselves on one side. She
will do her duty by her father and mother, – but she does it as
a superior person attending on those who are inferior. To her
grandfather and her grandmother she alludes as poor things of
the past, to whom much tenderness is due. But the attention is
paid after a fashion which seems to imply that old folk, in the
arrangements of life, should not interfere with their betters
who are young. Luckily for fathers and grandfathers in
Victoria the power of the purse remains with them, otherwise
they would I fear be ciphers in the houses that were once their
own. The Australian girls and young married women are not
cruel, false, or avaricious, and I will not call them Gonerils and
Regans; but I have seen old men who have put me in mind of
Lear.

There is a manifest difference between women who have
come out from England and those who are 'colonial-born',
which is not at all points favourable to the former. If we are to
take personal appearance as the good thing most in request by
the female sex, I think that the girls born in the colony have
the pre-eminence. As a rule they are very pretty, having
delicate sweet complexions and fine forms. They grow
quickly, and are women two years earlier in life than are our
girls, – and consequently are old women some five years
sooner. They are bright and quick, hardly as yet thoroughly
educated, as the means of thorough education for women do
not grow up in a new country very readily; but they have all
achieved a certain amount of information which they have at
their fingers' ends. They never appear to be stupid or ignorant, – because they are never bashful or diffident. We do not
criticise very accurately the law as laid down to us by a pretty
woman, – being thankful for any law from bright eyes and
ruby lips. Sometimes at home we can get no law, no opinion,
no rapid outflow of sweet-sounding words, – because some
modest sense of the weakness of feminine youth restrains the
speech. It must be admitted, however, that even at home this
failing is less general than it used to be.

Women, all the world over, are entitled to everything that
chivalry can give them. They should sit while men stand.
They should be served while men wait. Men should be silent
while they speak. They should be praised, – even without

desert. They should be courted, – even when having neither wit nor beauty. They should be worshipped, – even without love. They should be kept harmless while men suffer. They should be kept warm while men are cold. They should be kept safe while men are in danger. They should be enabled to live while men die in their defence. All this chivalry should do for women, and should do as a matter of course. But there is a reason for this deference. One human being does not render all these services to another, – who cannot be more than his equal before God, – without a cause. A man will serve a woman, will suffer for her, – if it come to that will die for her, – because she is weaker than he and needs protection. Let her show herself to be as strong, let her prove by her prowess and hardihood that the old idea of her comparative weakness has been an error from the beginning, and the very idea of chivalry, though it may live for awhile by the strength of custom, must perish and die out of men's hearts. I have often felt this in listening to the bold self-assertion of American women, – not without a doubt whether chivalry was needed for the protection of beings so excellent in their own gifts, so superabundant in their own strength. And the same thought has crept over me when I have been among the ladies of Victoria. No doubt they demand all that chivalry can give them. No ladies with whom I am acquainted are more determined to enforce their rights in that direction. But they make their claim with arms in their hands, – at the very point of the bodkin. Stand aside that I may pass on. Be silent that I may speak. Lay your coat down upon the mud and perish in the cold, lest my silken slippers be soiled in the mire. Be wounded that I may be whole. Die, that I may live. And for the nonce they are obeyed. That strength of custom still prevails, and women in Victoria enjoy for a while all that weakness gives, and all that strength gives also. But this, I think, can only be for a day. They must choose between the two, not only in Victoria but elsewhere. As long as they will put up with that which is theirs on the score of feminine weakness, they are safe. There is no tendency on the part of men to lessen their privileges. Whether they can make good their position in the other direction may be doubtful. I feel sure that they cannot long have both, and I think it unfair that they should make such demand. For the sake of those who are to come after me, – both men and women, – I hope that there may be no change in the old-established fashion.

I write these words in fear and trembling, lest the ladies of Victoria should condemn my book, and set me down as one who had accepted and betrayed hospitality. Let them remember all that I have conceded to them. They are lovely, bright, quick-witted, and successful. If, having said so much on their behalf, I venture to add a few words of counsel, they should remember that unqualified praise is always egregious flattery.

In speaking of men I can venture to use my pen with greater courage, and to say what I have to say without bating my breath. To their censure I can be deaf, and callous to their displeasure. The Victorian old man hardly as yet exists. Among those who are near the top of the tree it is rare to find even those who have been born in the other colonies. The men who have hitherto prospered best in Australia are they who came young from the old country, without much money, with great energy, and with a strong conviction that fortune was to be made by industry, sobriety and patience. These men succeeded, and they or their descendants are now the landed gentry of the country. Some are dead, and their places are filled by their sons. Some are tottering in old age, and their work is carried on by their sons. But there are enough of them still left in hale strength to give a tone to the entire colony. They smack of England, – or of Scotland or Ireland, as the case may be, – and are very different in their manners from those younger than themselves, who have been born in Australia. There are of course many, still young, who have come out from England, – so many that they suffice to give a tone to the whole social life of the colony. But every year this becomes less so than it was the year before, and the time will soon come in which the colonial will be stronger than the home flavour. It is of interest to inquire whether the race will deteriorate or become stronger by the change.

Dividing the population into two classes, – which, in order that I may be understood, I will call the upper and the lower class, – I speak now of that which is by far the less important as being the less numerous. As regards the masses of the men who earn their bread by their manual labour I have no doubt whatever that the born colonist is superior to the emigrant colonist, – any more than I have that the emigrant is superior to his weaker brother whom he leaves behind him. The best of our workmen go from us, and produce a race superior to themselves. The labourer born in the colonies is better educated than the man who has come from the old country, and is very much more sober. He is better fed than the labourer at home, better housed, better clothed, and is therefore more of a man. I think that any observer seeing the artisans in an Australian town, the miners on an Australian gold-field, or the shearers in an Australian wool-shed, would come to this conclusion, – and would feel that no workman should remain at home who can make himself master of a passage to the colonies. I cannot speak with the same confidence of those who are born to positions which we regard as higher than those of a daily workman. The young Australian-born 'gentleman' has certain points in his favour. He who goes out from England belonging to that class has not uncommonly been sent there because he has not hitherto done very well at home. I have said that the best of our labourers emigrate; but we certainly do not send to the colonies the best of our youth from Oxford and Cambridge, our most learned young lawyers, our cleverest engineers, or the most promising sons of our merchants and tradespeople. The young colonial scion is not called on to compete with the élite of the youth of the mother country. But in the competition to which he is called, he hardly as yet holds his own. He rarely runs into bad vices. He does not drink, or gamble, or go utterly to the dogs. But he is too often listless, unenergetic, vain, and boastful. Up to a certain age, that of advanced boyhood, he is generally clever, quick at learning what he does learn, and very often superior in general information to a boy from Harrow or from Winchester. He has more to say for himself, is less addicted to mere boyish amusements, and comes out as a man at an earlier age. But he has that fault which belongs to all produce of field and garden which grows ripe too quickly. When Clara in 'Philip van Artevelde' boasted that she, being of the softer sex, was privileged to grow ripe on the sunny side of the wall, she had probably not yet learned that the fruit which hangs through the autumn has the finer flavour, and can be kept till the end of winter. The colonial young man, – a young man while he still should be a boy, – hardly keeps the promise of his early years, and seems to lack something of that energy which grows up among us during the protracted years of our juvenility.

It is common to hear this discussed in the colonies themselves, – where the old swans are by no means disposed to look upon their cygnets as goslings. It is acknowledged, at any rate, that the boy grows out of boyhood earlier than he does in the old country. It is common to attribute the change to the climate; and there certainly is apparent ground for doing so, as we know that puberty is attained earlier in warm than in cold countries. I do not, however, believe that the climate is accountable for the great difference which exists, – especially as there is another cause in operation which must, I think, have produced it without other cause. Hitherto the education of youths in the Australian colonies has been quick, perfunctory, and perhaps superficial. That it should have been of this kind, is so natural, – that it should gradually cease to be open to such censure as the modes of education are improved, is again so natural, – that we may be justified in looking for the decrease and gradual cessation of an evil so caused, whereas, were it attributable to the climate, any remedy for it would be beyond the reach of our energy and wisdom. We are apt, in the old country, to complain bitterly of the years which are devoted to the pursuit of limited knowledge very imperfectly mastered. At eighteen or nineteen our boys, though they have been at school for the last ten years, do not speak Latin, do not read Greek fluently, bungle in their French, and are novices at mathematics. But during the whole time they have been learning much which cannot be put into any examination paper, and which they cannot reckon up in the list of their acquirements. They may be idle, but they are rarely listless. They may dislike study, but they do not love to sit still and whistle.

Gradually there is growing up in the colonies a desire for protracted education on the part of fathers who can afford to bestow such advantage on their sons. There are universities at Sydney and Melbourne, which indeed are as yet only in their infancy in regard to numbers, but which have the means of giving, and which are intended to give, the protracted education of which I speak. Gradually they will grow into favour, and the example which they set will be followed by schools throughout the colonies. What is chiefly required on behalf of the colonial-born youth is that he should be kept a little longer from the appurtenances of manhood. He should be taught to cease to think that the prime of life has been reached at nineteen.

CHAPTER IX

NEWSPAPERS, BOOKS, RAILWAYS, ROADS, TOWNS, AND WINES

I dislike the use of superlatives, especially when they are applied in eulogy; nevertheless, I feel myself bound to say that I doubt whether any country in the world has made quicker strides towards material comforts and well-being than have been effected by Victoria. She is not forty years old, all told, – going back even to the date at which Mr. Henty landed at Portland, – and she has already at her command most of the enjoyments of civilized life. Of her great city, Melbourne, I have spoken, – and of her gold-fields and that wonderful gold-town, Ballaarat; also of the country life of her country gentlemen. But there are other matters in which she has advanced as quickly: – and I must say a word of her newspapers, her general produce, her railways, her roads and coaches, her country towns, and her native wines.

With all the prejudice of a genuine Briton, I think that no country has ever yet produced newspapers equal to those of England. This fact, – if it be a fact, – I attribute partly to her wealth, partly to her general energy, partly to her love of fair play, but chiefly to her determination that the press shall be free. In France many of the writers of newspapers are at any rate equal in talent to their brethren among us, and, as a rule, they stand higher in public estimation. They are known by name, and they have a wider reputation. But they do not produce the same sort of article. The French newspaper is more confined than the English, and either more vapid in its obedience to authority, or more violent in its opposition. There is no catering for information at all approaching in extensiveness to that practised by our great metropolitan and provincial daily papers; and the means expended on the production of a newspaper are infinitely less. The article when

produced is readable in regard to language and type, and has
opinions of its own, perhaps very strongly developed, as to
the central political subject of the day in France itself; but
beyond that it is generally barren of information, and is often
half filled with extraneous matter, which might be more
conveniently used in the form of a volume. But if the French
newspapers dissatisfy us, what are we to say of those of the
United States? With a fair experience of their journals, with a
conviction favourable in general to American habits and
American institutions, with strongest feelings of social friendship for Americans whom I know and of political friendship
for Americans generally, I am bound to declare that I never
had a newspaper of the United States in my hand without
suffering during the whole time I was reading it. The sensational headings, spread over an amount of column often
greater than that afterwards devoted to the subject itself,
disgust and irritate. There will be a dozen such headings in
every paper, and not a scrap of news to create sensation
afterwards. The language is bombastic, vulgar, and very
frequently so faulty as to leave on the mind an impression that
the persons employed cannot generally belong to the same
class as do our writers for the daily press. Their type is bad.
Their paper is bad, – and when you have read a journal
through with the greatest diligence, you declare, as you throw
it aside, that there is nothing in it whatever. An American can
give a good lecture, – much better generally than any Englishman, – can make a good speech, can build a good house,
can cook a good dinner, can bake good bread, can tell a good
story, can write a good book, can do, as I think, anything on
earth requiring intellect, energy, industry, and construction, –
with this one exception. He cannot, – at any rate as yet he has
not turned out a good newspaper.

But Victoria, with her 750,000 souls, has a good daily
newspaper, – as has also New South Wales, with her 500,000
souls. Indeed, in this respect I intend to give no priority to the
one over the other, having failed to form an opinion as to
which was the best. But I think that the Melbourne 'Argus'
and the Sydney 'Morning Herald' are the best daily newspapers I have seen out of England. Sydney is nearly a hundred
years old, and is perhaps entitled to a good newspaper; but it is

remarkable that there should be such a paper as the 'Argus' in a town which was a wilderness forty years since. Melbourne also has a weekly paper, the 'Australasian', which is as good in its way as the 'Argus.' Common report says that as pecuniary speculations these periodicals have been highly successful, – but then so also is the New York 'Morning Herald'!

General literature is perhaps the product which comes last from the energies of an established country. Men must eat before they can write, and all think of eating before they think of writing. Leisure, which is compatible only with fixed means of living, is necessary for the production of books. Books in these halcyon days do no doubt provide bread for the writers of them; but the man who with empty pocket attempts to begin the opening of his oyster by the production of a book, will too often have to endure almost starvation before his oyster is reached.

The production of books must follow the production of other things, and the growth of literature will be slow. Victoria, however, and the Australian colonies generally have produced many books. I cannot say that as yet their volumes are to be found crowding the shelves of European libraries. It would be odd indeed if it were so, as the country has not yet been open to European enterprise, or even to European footsteps, for a full century. I have been surprised to find not only how many books have been written in Australia, and sent home for publication, – books generally of colonial history, colonial experience, and colonial exploration, – which have made their mark, but also how vast a number of small volumes have issued in the colonies, from the presses of Melbourne and Sydney, which, alas! have as yet done but little either for the pockets or the fame of the writers. Very many of these little books, – the majority of the great number which reached my hands, – contained verse, verse that was heroic, verse that was burlesque, verse that was amatory, and very often verse that was plaintive. I never had one of these unpretending products of ambitious souls in my hand without thinking of the hopes which were once high, so soon to be dashed to the ground, – of the grand thoughts which heralded perhaps but a poor production, of the labour given without return, of the bitter disappointment, and, alas! too, of the money spent on the paper and printing which probably could be but ill spared. Taking each individual author, and regarding the agony which disappointed authorship entails, I could not but deplore the production of many a little book. Now and again the author would tell of all his trouble, and would complain of the hardness of the world which would not give him a hearing. But, looking at the thing as a whole, I know it to be good for the colonies that such efforts should be made. Success will always at last attend such struggles; not, I fear, success for each individual struggler, but success for the people collectively, whose total of energy is thus exhibited. The desire, and the ambition, and the purpose are there, and that which a people really desires it will achieve. I cannot thus allude to the literature of the colony at large without mentioning the name of Mr. Marcus Clarke, of Melbourne, whose Australian tales are not only known famili- arly by all colonists, but are almost as familiar to English readers.

Victoria has made her railways after a system, – as we are sometimes told that France did, as England certainly did not do, nor, as far as I could judge, the other Australian colonies. In the first place she has a line perfected, as far as her territory is concerned, in the direct route to Sydney. The Melbourne and Sydney road crosses the Murray at Albury, and the Victorian railway was, when I was there, nearly finished up to the Victorian side of the river, and has since been completed. I do not think that New South Wales is making any effort to fill up the gap. She has a line as far as Goulbourn, – 130 miles from Sydney; but the intervening space is so long, – about 300 miles, – that the general transit from one town to the other is still by water. The distance, and the poorness of the country to be traversed, will afford an excuse for New South Wales, the validity of which it is impossible altogether to deny; but it is, I think, notorious that Sydney is not desirous of the close intercourse which a continuous railway would create, and that she would dread the effect of the unrestricted rivalry which it would produce. The wool-growers of the intervening districts would buy in Melbourne as easily as Sydney, – and then there would be renewed difficulty as to border duties. If all the southern part of the colony, and much of the south-eastern part, as well as the Riverina, bought their groceries in Melbourne, how would New South Wales collect sufficient taxes?

The Victorian line, striking the Murray at Albury, is a branch from a main line, previously perfected, striking the same river at Echuca, lower down. By this main route the intercourse between the Riverina and Melbourne is carried on, and from this point the people of the Riverina are anxious that a line should be made into the heart of their country, or at any rate to Deniliquin, which they call their capital. But of this they have but faint hopes while the Riverina remains a portion of New South Wales. The line from Melbourne to Echuca passes directly through the great Victorian gold-fields of which Bendigo, or Sandhurst as they now call it, is the centre. There is a station at Castlemaine, and another at Sandhurst. The line to Ballaarat, the capital of the other great Victorian gold-field, – I am afraid to call it either the first or the second in regard to its gold, but in regard to its qualities as a town there can be no doubt that it is the first, – starts from the same station at Melbourne, but branches off a mile or two from the town. This line takes an indirect course, running down the north-western side of Port Phillip Bay to Geelong, and then turning north to Ballaarat. It is intended to continue this line into the rich farming districts of the west, towards Hexham, Hamilton, and Coleraine, but when I was in the colony there was a diversity of opinion as to the route which should be taken. There is apt to be a diversity of opinion as to the route to be taken by railways, when the money required for making them is to come from the colony at large.

Victoria, as she makes her railways, borrows the money on the credit of the entire colony, and pays the interest out of the general revenue, applying the earnings of the railways to the revenue also. In 1869 the total interest on the amount up to that date borrowed for the construction of railways, is stated to have been £505,676 and the expenses of working the railways to have been £250,657 making a total of £756,333 expended, – whereas the proceeds earned amounted to £544,414, leaving a deficit of £211,919 to be paid out of the general taxes of the country. I regard the result as highly satisfactory to the colony. The railways are still in course of construction, and in that condition must be less remunerative than they will be when perfected. I believe that comparatively a few years will make the Victorian railways self-supporting, and that an excellent discretion has been exercised in the manner in which the money has been borrowed and expended. But it may easily be imagined that money borrowed and expended on this system should give rise to conflicting claims. Why should one district be favoured above another, when all pay? It will be urged that this district will support a railway, while that other cannot do so. But such an argument will find no favour with the rejected district, which may perhaps be able to assert itself loudly by political support or political opposition.

Another short branch striking off from the Geelong line down to Melbourne, goes to Williamstown, which is the port of the capital, and completes the set of government railways belonging to the colony. There is a suburban line, belonging to a private company, which runs to the south and south-east, and enables the citizens of Melbourne of all degrees to live out of the city. It was a matter of wonder to me that a town of such a population as Melbourne should afford so very large a local traffic, – but I soon found how large a proportion of the population lived in the suburbs which it accommodated.

There are still large districts of Victoria not touched by railway, especially the entire eastern part of the colony, which is called Gippsland. and the Wimmera district which lies to the north-west. The Gippslanders talk eagerly of a railway, but as their pleasant little capital of Sale holds only 2,000 people, and is the centre of a thinly populated country, I cannot think that their hopes will be soon gratified. The Wimmera district I did not visit. It is more remote and more sparsely populated even than Gippsland, but had I gone there, I should probably have heard of the great projected Wimmera line.

I cannot speak as highly of the coach roads as of the railways of Victoria. One effect of railways in a new country is to anticipate and supersede the creation of ordinary roads. A perfectly new country, hitherto known only to a few shepherds, is opened up by a railway, – which is not carried hither and thither for the service of towns and villages, but creates them as it goes along. Then, the one great need of a central road having been achieved, neither the government nor the inhabitants are for a time willing to go to the expense of macadamization. The badness of the roads is, however, remarkable throughout Australia, – and it is equally remarkable that though the roads are very bad, and in some places cannot be said to exist, nevertheless coaches run and goods are carried about the country. A Victorian coach, with six or perhaps seven or eight horses, in the darkness of the night, making its way through a thickly timbered forest at the rate of nine miles an hour, with the horses frequently up to their bellies in mud, with the wheels running in and out of holes four or five feet deep, is a phenomenon which I should like to have shown to some of those very neat mailcoach drivers whom I used to know at home in the old days. I am sure that no description would make any one of them believe that such feats of driving were possible. I feel that nothing short of seeing it would have made me believe it. The coaches, which are very heavy, and carry nine passengers inside, are built on an American system, and hang on immense leathern springs. The passengers inside are shaken ruthlessly, and are horribly soiled by mud and dirt. Two sit upon the box outside, and undergo lesser evils. By the courtesy shown to strangers in the colonies I always got the box, and found myself fairly comfortable as soon as I overcame the idea that I must infallibly be dashed against the next gum-tree. I made many such journeys, and never suffered any serious misfortune. I feel myself bound, however, to say that Victoria has not advanced in road-making as she has in other matters.

There are three good towns in Victoria, towns which would receive such praise on the score of architecture and general arrangements in any country, whether new or old. These are Melbourne, Ballaarat, and Geelong. In some respects, a growing town with a look of growing prosperity about it, but with still something of the roughness of the bush in its unfinished streets, is more interesting than a full-fledged city. There are many such in Victoria, in which the churches, the banks, the schools, and the hotels seem to bear a very undue proportion to the shops and private residences. And in every such a town that has had any success there is a newspaper, – or perhaps two. For a mile or two on each side of such a town there will be made roads, and then, by gradual but quick decrease of road-making enterprise, the bush track will be reached. The population is very small, 3,000 being enough to justify corporate pride and a high position among boroughs, and even 500 sufficing for a mayor. In all these towns rough plenty prevails. In many of them I found that the rates of an artisan's wages were quite as high as in Melbourne, and in some higher. Large amounts of capital are occasionally expended on the erection of a store, or a huge inn, – which not unfrequently is lost to the speculator. But in a new country such losses do not even frighten other speculators, – do not frighten him who for the nonce has been ruined. The man who has lost his money 'clears out', and some other speculator comes in. I visited various such towns as these, Beechworth, Hamilton, Sale, Woods Point, Wangaratta, and others, and was invariably struck by their uncouth prosperity. You see them expanding and growing, as you do the young colonial girl of ten years old, who buds forth so quickly that the increase of her physical power becomes almost visible to you. Too often these towns are altogether ugly to the eye. How should an unfinished congregation of houses be otherwise than ugly when it is constructed with rectangular streets on a level plain? The pretentious dimensions of some two or three buildings, – of a church, a bank, or an inn, – adds to the ugliness of the houses generally, and gives to the stranger a feeling of mixed melancholy and of thankfulness that his lot has not been cast in so unsightly a place. When, however, he has learned on inquiry that every man there earns 4s., 5s., or 6s. a day, and that meat is 2d. a pound, and when he remembers that in his own pretty villages at home men are earning 2s. a day and that meat is 1s. a pound, the melancholy by which he is pervaded takes another direction.

From this general charge of ugliness I must except the pretty town of Beechworth, which is the capital of a large district, and which is graced by a lunatic asylum. But its charm does not depend on the greatness of its corporate condition, or even on its asylum. It is backed by the Australian Alps, and has had bestowed upon it the gift of fine scenery. I doubt whether there be a man alive who would prefer 2s. a day and grand mountains, to 5s. and a flat country, – but when the matter does not come home so closely to the spectators, a pretty landscape has a great effect.

Australia makes a great deal of wine, – so much and so cheaply that the traveller is surprised how very little of it is used by the labouring classes. Among them some do not drink at all, some few drink daily, – and many never drink when at work, but indulge in horrible orgies during the few weeks, or perhaps days, of idleness which they allow themselves. But the liquor which they swallow is almost always spirits, – and always spirits of the most abominable kind. They pay sixpence a glass for their poison, which is served to them in a cheating false-bottomed tumbler so contrived as to look half-full when it contains but little. The drain is swallowed without water, and the dose is repeated till the man may be drunk. The falseness of the glass seems to excuse itself, as the less the man has the better for him, – but the fraud serves no one but the publican, for though the 'nobbler' be small, – a dram in Australia is always a nobbler, – there is no limit to the number of nobblers. The concoction which is prepared for these poor fellows is, I think, even worse than that produced by the London publican. At home, however, beer is the wine of the country and is the popular beverage at any rate with the workmen of this country. In all the Australian colonies, except Tasmania, wine is made plentifully, – and if it were the popular drink of the country, would be made so plentifully that it could suffice for the purpose. All fruits thrive there, but none with such fecundity as the grape. One Victorian wine-grower, who had gone into the business on a great scale, told me that if he could get 2s. a gallon for all that he made, the business would pay him well. The wine of which he spoke was certainly superior both in flavour and body to the ordinary wine drunk by Parisians. It is wholesome and nutritious, and is the pure juice of the grape.

Accustomed to French and Spanish wines, – or perhaps to wines passed off upon me as such, – I did not like the Australian 'fine' wines. The best that I drank was in South Australia, but I did not much relish them. I thought them to be heady, having a taste of earth, and an after-flavour which was disagreeable. This may have been prejudice on my part. It may be that the requisite skill for wine-making has not yet been attained in the colonies. Undoubtedly age is still wanting to the wines, which are consumed too quickly after vinting. It may possibly be the case that though Australia can grow an unlimited quantity of wine, she cannot produce wines capable

of rivalling those of Europe. On these points I do not pretend
to have an opinion. But I regard a wholesome drink for the
country as being of more importance than fine wines, even
though they should equal the produce of the vineyards of the
South of Spain or the South of France. France and Italy are
temperate because they produce a wine suitable to their
climate. Australia, with a similar climate, produces wine with
equal ease, and certainly, – I speak in reference to the common
wines, – as good a quality. There is now on sale in Melbourne,
at the price of, I think, threepence a glass, – the glass
containing about half a pint, – the best vin-ordinaire that I ever
drank. It is a white wine, made at Yering, a vineyard on the
Upper Yarra, and is both wholesome and nutritive. Nevertheless, the workmen of Melbourne, when they drink, prefer to
swallow the most horrible poison which the skill of man ever
concocted.

CHAPTER X

LEGISLATION, GOVERNMENT, AND COMMERCE

The scheme of legislation and government is the same in Victoria as in the other colonies, but it has been carried out after a more entirely democratic fashion, and with a more settled intention of throwing the political power of the colony into the hands of the people. There are, of course, the three estates, – King, Lords, and Commons, represented here by the Governor, with his appointment from Downing Street, the Legislative Council, and the Legislative Assembly. The Governor has, of course, the royal veto; and he has also, which is much more commonly used, the power of reserving bills which have passed the two colonial houses for the approval or disapproval of the home government. The Upper House, or Legislative Council, is elective, as it is also in South Australia. In Queensland and New South Wales it is nominated. The nominations in the latter colonies are, indeed, practically made by the premier for the time, who is the minister of the people; but a House is thus constituted much less democratic and at the same time more influential than when elected by popular constituencies. Political power necessarily belongs chiefly to the Lower House, as the people devote all their energies and all their thoughts to the members whom they are to elect for the popular chamber.

The Legislative Council in Victoria is returned by six provinces into which the colony is divided, – each province returning five members. Of these five one goes out every second year, so that each member of the Council is returned for ten years. A property qualification is required both for the candidate and for the electors. The former must own property to the value of £2,500, and the latter must pay a rental of £50, or rates on property to that amount. The interest taken by Victorians in the election of the Council is not great. At those which were made in 1870 there was no contest in four out of the six provinces, and in the other two less than 50 per cent. of the electors polled. The Upper House seldom initiates laws, and is looked upon rather for protection than action. This is certainly the case in the other colonies also, but in none of them to the same extent as in Victoria. In Tasmania and South Australia I found the prime minister in the Upper House. In Queensland and New South Wales I found one of the cabinet there; and, in the latter, many of the leading men of the colony held seats in the Council. In Victoria the cabinet is no doubt represented in the Council; but the representation is generally feeble, and the gentlemen selected have of late held no office and, I believe, received no emolument.

The Lower House is elected for three years, by manhood suffrage, and no property qualification is required either for the candidates or for the electors. The votes for both Houses are of course taken by ballot. In regard to the ballot in Victoria, it is as well to point out that its value consists not in any security afforded by secrecy, – as to which the voters are happily quite indifferent, – but in the tranquillity at elections which it ensures. In Victoria, and in Victoria alone among the Australian colonies, members of parliament are paid. They receive £300 a year for their services, and are entitled to travel free by railways and mail-coaches. The system of payment has not, however, as yet been permanently adopted. Unless renewed by another bill, it will lapse after the first year of the parliament next to be elected, and would thus cease in 1875. Whether it will be renewed not a few of the colonies profess to doubt; but I observe that the doubters are those who think such payment to be objectionable. I have but little faith myself in the moderation of a dog that has once tasted blood, and do not therefore believe that the members of the next Victoria parliament will be endowed by so strong a spirit of patriotic martyrdom as to abandon by their own act the salaries which they will be then enjoying. I will not trouble my reader here by attempting to prove that this making a profession of parliament, this power of living poorly on the small means which parliament will produce, must be injurious to the legislature of the country, as the system has but few advocates at home. It has now been practised for many years in the

United States, and certainly has not served there to raise the House of Representatives. It has not been long tried in Victoria, but it certainly has not as yet had that tendency.

The mode of carrying on the government in Victoria subject to the approval of parliament is almost identical with that which is familiar to us at home. The governor nominally appoints his minister, – selecting one chief who selects his own cabinet; but the choice is in fact made by the Lower House, whose chosen leader remains in power as long as he is the chosen one, and gives way by resignation as soon as some other favourite has usurped the votes of the majority. The mode of changing ministers is nearly the same as with us at home, – but the power of the minister is in one respect confined within narrower limits. The outgoing minister in his last and generally futile attempt to regain that which he has lost, recommends the Crown to dissolve Parliament, so that the country at large may have an opportunity of reversing the last decision of its representatives. We at home now think that the Crown is bound to follow the advice so tendered, thereby obeying the great constitutional rule that the sovereign can do no political act except by the advice of his ministers. The practice is not as yet recognised, – is at any rate not as yet established as constitutional usage, – in the colonies. During my sojourn in Australia I saw a ministry outvoted in New South Wales and another in Victoria. In each case the outgoing minister appealed to the governor for a dissolution. In New South Wales the governor acceded, – and was then blamed by every one for doing so. In Victoria the governor refused, – giving his reasons in a paper which was read to the House, and every one praised him for refusing. In the one case as in the other there was a general feeling that nothing could be gained by a dissolution, – as in New South Wales nothing was gained by the outgoing minister. Nevertheless it will come to be accepted in the colonies before long as good constitutional doctrine that in this matter, as in all other matters of political practice, the governor should be guided by his responsible advisers.

A member of a colonial cabinet is not so great a man as a cabinet minister at home. He is not even relatively so great a man, and does not hold a position among his fellow citizens proportionate to that enjoyed by our own statesmen at home; but he holds very much more than proportionate powers, and exercises very much more than proportionate patronage. Everything is centralized. The roads, the bridges, and the railways of the colony are constructed by government. Asylums and gaols are erected and managed by the government. The lands of the colony, not as yet alienated, are the property of the government at large, and are sold or leased by the government. The local magistrates are appointed by the government. Municipal institutions are growing, and as they grow this centralization of power will be lessened; but, in the meantime, the ministers of the day, who may be men but very little qualified to bear the weight of such responsibility, are called upon to arrange details affecting the interests of individuals which it would be impossible for any minister, however great, to adjust with true impartiality. Things are, in truth, adjusted with an eye to electioneering majorities. When a member for some remote district becomes a cabinet minister, that district at once expects all the good things which patronage can give. Should a Roman Catholic be prime minister the Roman Catholics throughout the colony expect government places, – and every porter at a railway holds a government place. But the minister for lands is he upon whom the greatest pressure is brought to bear. A supporter of the ministry considers himself entitled to buy good land cheap, – and considers also that every impediment should be thrown in the way of those who oppose the ministry but still wish to buy land. Tenders of contracts for the conveyance of mails are sent out in the name of the postmaster-general, who happened also to be prime minister when I was in Melbourne. Tenders for government clothing are sent out in the name of the treasurer. The same practice prevails throughout the cabinet, and produces a feeling that staunch support of the government may be quite as influential in procuring the desired job as favourable terms. The injustice done to individuals is not in itself so great an evil as the growing conviction throughout the colony that all this is a matter of course, and that it forms a recognised part of that concrete institution which we welcome under the name of Constitutional Government.

I do not wish to say hard things of Victorian ministers of
state, – nor do I condemn any individuals when I assert that
the whole colony is permeated by a conviction that the power
of government is used for jobbing. While matters are centralized as they are now, – while members of the cabinet are
compelled to exercise their own judgement in the appointment of gaolers, railway porters, and letter-carriers over the
entire colony, – while tenders are sent in, not to the politically
powerless head of a department, but to the political minister
himself by name, – it would require more than human energy
and impartiality to avoid jobbery. In the present circumstances
of the colonial executive departments is it not probable that
the energies of ministers will be prompted to take quite the
other direction? Indeed no man could sit for a month on the
Victorian ministerial bench who determined to manage his
office without any reference to his parliamentary position. It is
taken as a matter of course that he will use his patronage for
the promotion of his party.

In this matter I do not know that even yet we have our
hands at home quite clean. I think I do know that they have
not at any rate been long clean. But the sin has been all but
abolished among us, chiefly by the intense desire of statesmen
to be quit of a business that had been thrown upon them
gradually by the increasing propensity to raise bulwarks for
political powers, but which they at last found to be not only
onerous and disreputable, but also unserviceable. In the
United States the system is still rampant, – though there it has
been somewhat lessened by the general feeling which prevails
as to its iniquity. In all the Australian colonies it exists. In each
of them ministers are driven to seek parliamentary support by
manipulating patronage. Fortunes already made are not
common among legislators in a new country, – so that it may
often happen that the brothers, sons, and kinsmen of a
minister may themselves be in need of places. A ministry that
was beaten in the parliament of Victoria in June, 1872, was
turned out solely on the ground that it had misused its
patronage. There may, perhaps, be room to hope that such an
example may be of service, and that it may tend to teach the
people generally that parliamentary government does not
mean the partial advancement of a certain class who may

support this or that set of politicians. There can be but little doubt that a decentralization of local management would greatly tend to save colonists themselves from falling into a miserably false view of politics, which at present it is almost impossible that they should avoid.

The revenue of the colony for the year ending 30th June, 1872, was £3,721,648. This included about three-quarters of a million raised by the sale of public lands and by pastoral leases. It included also the amount collected on the railways, for water-supply to the city of Melbourne, for telegraphs, pilot-dues, and postage, and various other items, all of which are brought to the account of the public purse, though they have no connection with the taxation of the country. The absolute burden on the country, raised in the shape of taxes, does not exceed a million and a half, and is therefore not above £2 a head on the population. The public debt amounts to twelve millions, – but it has been borrowed exclusively for the construction of public works, and almost exclusively for the construction of railways. It must be admitted that the burden of taxation on the public is light in the colony, and is so although the government has undertaken enterprises on the public behalf, which no private companies could have achieved.

The two great staple articles of commerce in Victoria are wool and gold. Of the gold-fields of the colony I have said enough, but it may be well to add a comparative statement of the value of those two sources of wealth. In 1870 the gold exported from the colony was sold for £6,119,782, and the wool for £3,205,106. Gold maintains its nominal value, whereas wool vacillates so much that within twelve months the price may be nearly doubled or halved. Between March, 1871, and March, 1872, the price of wool did rise fully 80 per cent. But since 1852, the first year of extended gold production in Victoria, the Victorian wool has never come near to the Victorian gold, and during the whole of that period has amounted to little more than a quarter of it. Nevertheless the established wealth of the wealthy man in Victoria has been made by pastoral pursuits rather than by mining. The aristocracy is essentially an aristocracy of squatters, – that is of gentlemen who have made or are making their money by grazing cattle and shearing sheep. The gold may cost as much to raise it as it is worth, – may indeed, and often does, cost much more. But the sheep increase in numbers and are shorn with comparatively little outlay. Here, as in most other countries, land is more coveted, and seems to convey a higher influence, than any other property. The squatter, even though he do not own his own land, but runs his sheep on waste lands, as a crown tenant with a short lease, and no certainty of tenure even as to that, is still regarded as a territorial magnate. Though the gold produced in the colony be annually worth double the wool, and though the raids of the free-selecter on the squatter have been more cruel in Victoria than even in the other colonies, still the production of wool is the most popular and certainly at the present moment the most remunerative occupation in Victoria.

In 1870 the total imports into the colony amounted to £12,455,758, and the exports to £12,470,014, thus very nearly balancing themselves. Each amount is about a million lower than it was ten years before, – in 1861. But I doubt whether this can be taken as showing any decrease in the substantial prosperity of the colony. The decrease in the exports has been chiefly on gold and live-stock, with a wholesome rise on most other articles of Victorian produce. The export of wool increased during that period by more than a third, showing that it was better worth the while of stock-owners to keep their sheep than to send them into the other colonies for sale. The produce of gold is necessarily fluctuating, and cannot be taken in any one year as an indication of the trade of the country. The decrease in the imports was chiefly on grain and flour, thus showing that the country had progressed in the important work of feeding itself. No doubt, whenever new gold-fields are opened, creating new 'rushes', or gold-fields show themselves for a time specially productive, there will be a sudden influx of migratory population, and successful miners will spend money freely. They will thus raise the imports by their consumption, and the exports by the gold which they send away. A gold-producing country must be subject to these fluctuations, but they can hardly be taken as a proof either of the decay or the rise of substantial prosperity. As to the substantial prosperity of Victoria, no one, I think, who has visited that country can entertain a doubt. It is to be seen in the daily lives of the colonists, in the clothes which they wear, in the food which they eat, in the wages which they receive, in the education of their children, and in the general comfort of the people.

NEW SOUTH WALES

CHAPTER I

EARLY HISTORY OF THE COLONY

On reaching Sydney the traveller should remember that he is visiting the spot on which our Australian empire was commenced, amidst difficulties of which we in England in these days think very little. We know something of Australian explorers of a later date. We do hear of Oxley, of Hume and Hovell, of Cunningham, Mitchell, Eyre, Sturt, Kennedy, Leichardt, Gregory, Stuart, Burke and Wills, and others who have succeeded in opening up new regions in Australia or have lost their lives in the attempt, – but we hear nothing of the perils endured and the efforts made by those who first brought convicts out to Botany Bay, and who were called upon to perform the almost impossible task of feeding and of governing them there.

Captain Cook landed at Botany Bay, a few miles south of Sydney Harbour, – or Port Jackson, as it is properly called, – in 1770, and took possession of the land on behalf of the English Crown. But Captain Cook was by no means the first to find Australia. Manoel Godenho, a Portuguese, is supposed to be the right claimant of that honour, and is said to have landed on the north-west corner of the continent in 1601. A Dutchman was the next, by name John William Verschoor, who is said to have touched at Cape York, the northern point of the great Queensland promontory, in 1606. Dirk Hartog in 1616, another Dutchman, was the third; and then, for many years, the Dutch continued to discover parts of the coast and various islands of what was then called Terra Australis. They have left their names behind them in many places, – in Nuytsland, a most dreary region on the southern coast, at present utterly useless, so called from Peter Nuyts; in the great Gulf of Carpentaria in the north, so called from Peter Carpenter; in Tasmania, – Van Diemen's Land, as it used to

be, – discovered by Abel Jan Tasman, who called it Van
Diemen's land after the governor of the Dutch East India
Company, who had sent him on his voyage, and since
re-christened Tasmania because a flavour of convicts had
attached itself to the former name. Indeed the Dutch did so
much and were so energetic in their voyages, that they were
justified in calling the new continent New Holland; and it
seems now to be marvellous that a people so enterprising, and
at that time so prone to get and to keep territory, should have
lost their hold of the great 'Terra Australis'. It appears that
they defeated their own object by their own secrecy and
mystification. They published no records of the voyages
made, and no charts of the newly discovered seas, fearing that
the great future possession would become too well known to
other explorers. Consequently, even among themselves, the
doings of their sailors were unknown and unappreciated, and
no natural desire was created for possession of the land.

It seems that a Frenchman was on the coast before any
Englishman, one M. de St. Alouran having anchored off Cape
Leuwin, – the great south-eastern corner of the continent, – in
1670. After him came William Dampier, an English buccan-
eer, who in 1688 landed on the western coast, and was, as far
as we know, the first Englishman to put his foot on the soil of
our great dependency. For eighty years after that English,
Dutch, and French, with intermittent energies, endeavoured
to become masters of New Holland. In 1770 Captain Cook,
not only landed at Botany Bay, but actually surveyed a large
portion of the eastern coast, and formally took possession of
the country in the name of the King of England. This he did,
having first touched at New Zealand, which had been discovered by Tasman in 1642. In 1777 Captain Cook made
another voyage into the Pacific, – in the course of which
enterprise he was murdered at the Sandwich Islands. It was at
this time that he recommended the English government to
send out to Botany Bay the convicts from England which
could no longer be sent to the revolted colonies of America. In
1787 Commodore Phillip, the first Australian governor, was
despatched in accordance with Cook's advice to form a penal
settlement at Botany Bay. Finding Botany Bay and the
territory immediately around it to be altogether unfitted for

the purpose he had in hand, with no fertile land around it, and no sufficient supply of water, Commodore Phillip sailed northward, entered Port Jackson, – as Cook had already called it, – and founded the settlement for British convicts.

In the same year a French captain, La Perouse, also landed at Botany Bay, anchoring there as it happened on the very day on which Commodore Phillip hoisted the English colours at the head of Port Jackson. La Perouse perished on his road home, but Commodore Phillip created the colony of New South Wales, – from whence have sprung all our Australian colonies.

Mr. Rusden, who knows Australian history probably as well as any man living, commences his account of the discovery, survey, and settlement of Port Phillip, or of the colony of Victoria as it is now called, with the following words: – 'American colonization sprang mainly from private adventure. The foundation of colonies in Australia was not the result of private enterprise, but of the policy of the ministry of which Pitt was the real as well as the nominal head'. There can be no doubt that Mr. Rusden is right in his statement that our possession of Australia is due to the government of the day, and not to any gallant adventurer such as was Raleigh, or to any band of Puritan brothers going forth in search of freedom, as did they who landed from the *Mayflower* on the shores of Massachusetts. The expedition to Botany Bay was planned by government, – whether actually by Pitt or not I do not know that we can now say, – with the view of finding a shore on which we might rid ourselves of our ruffians. It was to be governed by martial law, and was based on the footing of a penal settlement. After that the French still made renewed attempts, and endeavoured to call the whole southern district of Australia 'Terre Napoléon'. This was intended to include, with much other territory, all that country which is, perhaps, now better known as Victoria, than by the imperial name then given to it.

Governor Phillip, with his convicts and few attendants, had by no means a pleasant time of it. He had indeed about as bad a time as any government servant of whom we now read. There were two establishments for convicts in his hands, one at Sydney, and the other at Norfolk Island, – where the descendants of the mutineers of the Bounty are now dwindling back to the insipidity of savage life amidst the charms of Utopian

freedom. In Governor Phillip's time the life on Norfolk Island
was by no means idle or Utopian. There was a great deal of
rebellion and running away, a great deal of punishment of a
kind which now seems to us to have been very barbarous, but
without which the convict element would probably have got
altogether the better of the governing element. And there was
terrible want, not only at Norfolk Island, but also on the
mainland, – want so dire as almost to have become starvation.
Nearly all the food consumed for the first years had to be
brought either from England, or from some other distant
land, such as Batavia or Bengal. The land round Sydney, on
which attempts were made to create farms, was found to be
poor and barren. The few cattle which the settlers or, rather,
which the governor possessed, strayed away or were killed by
the blacks. And then these black men, the aboriginals, were a
source of difficulties for which no satisfactory solution could
be found. If only they would be friendly all might be well, –
but how could friendship be expected from a race whose all
was being taken from them by a handful of strangers who
spoke a strange language, – and who had fire-arms? If the
blacks would be friendly it would be well; but if not – then
they must be repressed, as were the convicts. The settlement
was not to be abandoned because savage tribes could not be
made to understand quickly the benefits of civilisation, and the
blacks were repressed, and driven away, and sometimes
starved, to the great affliction of the first governors.

For five years Governor Phillip fought his battle against
convicts, black men, recusant settlers, famine, floods, and
drought, and he fought it like a hero. In every emergency, –
and every day created a new emergency, – he was forced to
think for himself. He had no ministers, and no council. He
was commander-in-chief, and the life of every man was in his
hands. But he was responsible to the King's government at
home, and to public opinion in the colony. From day to day
there was pressed upon him the fear that, one after another,
they might all perish from want. If this vessel or that did not
come at the expected time, there would not be even half a
day's rations per day either for convicts, freemen, or for the
governor. That modicum of half a day's rations was, more
than once, the allowance for them all. I do not know where to

look for a better story of great, continued, unpicturesque heroism than in the records of Governor Philip's career. In these days it is very pleasant to be a governor of a colony. A charming house is provided, there are aides-de-camp and private secretaries, there is a liberal salary, there is probably much hospitality, and just enough of work to enable the governor of an Australian colony to feel that he earns what is bestowed upon him. But in truth he governs nobody, and is simply a medium of communication between the ministry of the colony and the Secretary of State at home. In Governor Phillip's time it was very different. He had indeed to govern, – to rule all and everything, and to do so with an iron hand that could not dare to relax its severity. His hand was of iron, but his heart was very soft. He had no rest from providing for the wants of those around him, and when they were put on half rations, and on less than half, his own were always as scanty as the scantiest.

At the end of five years Governor Phillip went home, and after a lapse of two years, – which two years were very injurious to the young settlement, – was succeeded by Captain Hunter, who had come out with Phillip. Hunter again, after five or six years, was succeeded by another officer who had come to Botany Bay with Phillip's first band of convicts, – namely Governor King. And these men also were heroes in their way, facing terrible difficulties, – difficulties in regard to the black men, difficulties in regard to the convicts, difficulties in regard to food, and, perhaps worst of all, difficulties in regard to a certain New South Wales Corps, which had been sent out from England with an idea that perhaps by such military body the convicts might be controlled, – and perhaps also, in some degree, the governor also. The officers of this corps soon became dominant in the colony, and used their dominion after a strange fashion. They obtained the right, or at any rate the power, of an almost exclusive monopoly, at first in spirits, and afterwards in all imported goods. When Governor Hunter and Governor King had resigned, the battle was carried on by Governor Bligh, – the famous Captain Bligh of the Bounty, – who thus became king and lord over the very island on which are now settled the descendants of those who took his ship away from him and sent him adrift upon the waters. Governor Bligh was a very rough man, but seems to have been a manly fellow, with a strong idea of his duty. In the third year of his government he was arrested by the commanding officer of the very troop which was supposed at home to be at his hand for his support. His government was then brought to an end, and the New South Wales Corps was sent home.

Thus were passed the first twenty years of the new colony, amidst struggles of which the history has not yet been fairly written. Great efforts in the meantime had been made to extend the settled district. Farms were established up the Paramatta River, on grounds now rich with orange groves, but which were gradually found to be utterly unfit for cereal crops. The first attempts at growing corn in the neighbourhood of Sydney were failures, sad enough to break the hearts of all but heroes. The Hawkesbury was discovered, – a magnificent river which makes its way into the ocean about fifteen miles north of Sydney Harbour, – and on the Upper Hawkesbury, where now stands the town of Windsor, the land was found to be a rich alluvial deposit, capable of growing anything. But no sooner had settlers made their young home on this seemingly happy soil, than floods came and washed everything away, and there is Windsor now, with its rich lands, and its constant floods, – and some 2,000 inhabitants, who must surely be web-footed. Various also were the attempts made under these first governors to find a way out from the narrow strip of territory occupied along the shore across the mountains into the interior. These are the Blue Mountains, which are blue indeed, and very lovely, – now crossed by the Bathurst railway, but over which in those days the settlers long found it impossible to make their way. Wool had become an article of export during these early years, and did at last give rise to the energies which in time forced a passage through the Blue Mountains. Captain Macarthur, who had been one of the officers belonging to that wretched New South Wales Corps, introduced merino sheep into the colony, and obtained a grant of 10,000 acres of land. Then others took to massing flocks. In 1813 there came a great drought, and Messrs. Wentworth, Blaxland, and Lawson got through the mountains in search of grass for their sheep.

In 1805 a second dependency on New South Wales was established on the northern shore of Van Diemen's Land, for the purpose of removing thither convicts from Norfolk Island, – which place was abandoned, as the governor found it impossible to supply food to a settlement at such a distance. The abandonment of the station was, however, only temporary. Thus was commenced the second in date of our Australian colonies. In 1825 Van Diemen's Land was, at its own request, separated from New South Wales, and established as a penal colony on its own bottom, with its own governor, and its own expenses. Its name soon became as familiar with us as that of the parent colony, – but we viewed them both only as the homes of our exported rascaldom. In 1836 Port Phillip, – which is now the colony of Victoria, – became a dependency under New South Wales. In 1851 she was allowed to go alone, and is now, at any rate in her own opinion, the first in importance of all the colonial children of Great Britain. In 1839 New Zealand became a dependency under New South Wales, – but the child did not remain long in leading-strings. In 1840 New Zealand received a governor of her own from England. In 1859 the Moreton Bay district, constituting at that time the northern half, – or something more than half, – of what was left of the colony of New South Wales, was cut off, and the separate colony of Queensland was established. In this way New South Wales was the parent of all our present Australian colonies, except South Australia and Western Australia, both of which originated in efforts made from home.

In 1856, five years after the separation of Victoria, responsible government was established in New South Wales, and governors of the happy, hospitable, sleek, and unburdened kind came into vogue. This happened during the reign of Sir William Denison, who came out in 1853 with the task of inaugurating the change. He, however, still kept the title of Governor-General of Australasia, which was not borne by his successor, Sir John Young. Perhaps of all her governors, Sir Richard Bourke is the one best remembered and the most esteemed in New South Wales. He came to the colony in 1832, and remained there for the normal period of six years. A large statue to his memory, standing at the gate of the Sydney domain, helps to keep alive his honours. He was no doubt a firm, considerate man, excellently well qualified for his duties. He was preceded by Governor Darling, and succeeded by Governor Gipps, as to both of whom it is now recorded in the colony that, if diamonds, they were rough diamonds.

CHAPTER II

SYDNEY

I despair of being able to convey to any reader my own idea of the beauty of Sydney Harbour. I have seen nothing equal to it in the way of land-locked sea scenery, – nothing second to it. Dublin Bay, the Bay of Spezzia, New York, and the Cove of Cork are all picturesquely fine. Bantry Bay, with the nooks of sea running up to Glengarrif, is very lovely. But they are not equal to Sydney either in shape, in colour, or in variety. I have never seen Naples, or Rio Janeiro, or Lisbon, – but from description and pictures I am led to think that none of them can possess such a world of loveliness of water as lies within Sydney Heads. The proper thing to assert is that the fleets of all nations might rest securely within the protection of the harbour. How much acreage of sea the fleets of all nations might require I cannot even surmise, – but if they could be anchored together anywhere, they could surely be so anchored at Sydney.

In none of the books which I have seen respecting the early settlement of the colony, or of its subsequent difficulties in progress, is much stress laid on the scenery of Sydney Harbour, or of the Hawkesbury River which is near it. Nor is much said of the glorious defiles of the Blue Mountains. Such books have been generally circumstantial and statistical, – either despondent or hopeful, according to the opinions of the writers. They have always insisted much, – and have done so with well deserved zeal, – on the great efforts made by Australian discoverers. They have told us of the drawbacks of the land, – which are very great, as the soil is often poor, is encumbered with forests, deficient in water, and subject to a climate which is not propitious to cereals. On the other hand, we have from them much of Australian wool, and for the last twenty years of Australian gold. We gather from these books many facts as to the past events of Australia, and many opinions as to its future. But we hear very little of Australian scenery. Consequently we, at home in England, are inclined to believe that Australia, as a country, is displeasing to the eye. The eternal gum-tree has become to us an Australian crest, giving evidence of Australian ugliness. The gum-tree is ubiquitous, and is not the loveliest, though neither is it by any means the ugliest, of trees. But there are scenes of nature in Australia as lovely as are to be found in any part of the world, – not so closely congregated as in Western Europe, but quite as much so as in North America. They are often difficult of access, – and must remain so, till the population is large enough to stretch itself about the country, and to make railways, and to run river steamers.

The people of Sydney are by no means indifferent to the beauty of their harbour, and claim for it the admiration of strangers with something of the language, but not with the audacity, of Americans, when they demand the opinions of their visitors as to their remarkable institutions. There is something of shamefacedness, a confession of provincial weakness, almost an acknowledgement that they ought not to be proud of a thing so insignificant, in the tone in which you are asked whether, upon the whole, you do not think Sydney Harbour rather pretty. Every Sydney man and every Sydney woman does ask you the question, – as does every American ask that other question; but it is asked in Sydney with bated breath, and with something of an apology, 'Of course you have been bothered out of your life about our harbour, – but it is pretty, – don't you think so?' It is so inexpressibly lovely that it makes a man ask himself whether it would not be worth his while to move his household gods to the eastern coast of Australia, in order that he might look at it as long as he can look at anything. There are certain spots, two or three miles out of the town, now occupied generally by villas, or included in the grounds of some happy resident, which leave nothing for the imagination to add. Greenoaks and Mount Adelaide, belonging to two brothers, Mr. Thomas and Mr. Henry Mort, are perfect. Sir James Martin, who was the prime minister when I was first there, and who, I hope, may soon be so again, has a garden falling down to the sea, which is like

fairyland. There is a rock outside, – or probably inside, – the
grounds of Woolhara, belonging to Mr. Cooper, on which the
blacks in the old days, when they were happy and undisturbed, used to collect themselves for festive, political and
warlike purposes. I wonder whether they enjoyed it as I did!
How they must have hated the original Cooper when he came
and took it, – bought it for 20s. an acre, out of which they got
no dividend, or had a grant of it from the English Crown!
Woolhara is a magnificent property, covered with villas and
gardens, all looking down upon the glorious sea. In England it
would be worth half a million of money, and, as things go on,
it will soon be worth as much in New South Wales; and
perhaps some future Cooper will be Duke Cooper or Marquis
Cooper, and Woolhara will be as famous as Lowther or
Chatsworth. It is infinitely more lovely than either. I envied
the young man, and almost hated him for having it, –
although he had just given me an excellent dinner.

I doubt whether I ever read any description of scenery
which gave me an idea of the place described, and I am not
sure that such effect can be obtained by words. Scott in prose,
and Byron in verse, are both eloquent in declaring that this or
that place is romantic, picturesque, or charming; and their
words have been powerful enough to send thousands to see
the spots which they have praised. But the charm conveyed
has been in the words of the writer, not in the beauty of the
place. I know that the task would be hopeless were I to
attempt to make others understand the nature of the beauty of
Sydney Harbour. I can say that it is lovely, but I cannot paint
its loveliness. The sea runs up in various bays or coves,
indenting the land all around the city, so as to give a thousand
different aspects of the water, – and not of water, broad,
unbroken, and unrelieved, but of water always with jutting
corners of land beyond it, and then again of water and then
again of land. And you, – the resident, – even though you be a
lady not over strong, though you be a lady, if possible not
over young, – will find, unless you choose your residence
most unfortunately, that you have walks within your reach as
deliciously beautiful as though you had packed up all your
things and travelled days and spent pounds to find them. One
Mrs. Macquarie, the wife, I believe, of Governor Macquarie,

made a road, or planned a road, or at any rate gave her name
to a road, which abuts on the public domain, and is all but in
the town. A mile and a half from the top of Hunter Street
carries the pedestrian all round it. Two shillings does as much
for him or her who prefers a hansom cab, – and the Sydney
hansoms are the very best cabs in the world. At the end of it is
Mrs. Macquarie's chair, – with a most ill-written inscription,
but with a view that affords compensation even for that. The
public gardens, not half a mile from the top of Hunter Street,
beat all the public gardens I ever saw, – because they possess
one little nook of sea of their own. I do not love public gardens
generally, because I am called upon to listen to the names of
shrubs conveyed in three Latin words, and am supposed to
interest myself in the locality from which they have been
brought. I envy those who have the knowledge which I want;
but I put my back up against attempts made to convey it to
me, knowing that it is too late. But it was impossible not to
love the public gardens at Sydney, – because one could sit
under the trees and look out upon the sea. There is a walk
from the bottom of Macquarie Street, – not Mrs. Macquarie's
Road, but the old governor's own street, – leading round by
the fort, under the governor's house, to the public gardens.
The whole distance round may be a mile and a half from the
top of Hunter Street, which opens on to Macquarie Street. It
runs close along the sea, with grassy slopes on which you may
lie and see the moon glimmer on the water as it only glimmers
on land-locked coves of the ocean. You may lie there prostrate
on the grass, with the ripple close at your feet within a
quarter-of-an-hour of your club. Your after-dinner cigar will
last you there and back if you will walk fairly and smoke
slowly. Nobody ever is there at that hour, the young men of
Sydney preferring to smoke their cigars in their arm-chairs.
Then there is the little trip by steam ferry over to the north
shore, where lives that prince of professors and greatest of
Grecians, Doctor Badham, of the university. I should like to
be the ferryman over that ferry to Lavendar Bay on condition
that the Doctor met me with some refreshment on each
journey. Sydney is one of those places which, when a man
leaves it knowing that he will never return, he cannot leave
without a pang and a tear. Such is its loveliness.

The town itself, as a town, independently of its sea and its suburbs, was, to me, pleasant and interesting. In the first place, though it is the capital of an Australian colony, and therefore not yet a hundred years old, it has none of those worst signs of novelty which make the cities of the New World unpicturesque and distasteful. It is not parallelogrammic and rectangular. One may walk about it and lose the direction in which one is going. Streets running side by side occasionally converge – and they bend and go in and out, and wind themselves about, and are intricate. Philadelphia, which has not a want in the world, and is supplied with every luxury which institutions can confer upon human nature, is of all towns the most unattractive because it is so managed that every house in it has its proper place, which can be found out at once, so long as the mind of the seeker be given to ordinary arithmetic. No arithmetic will set the wanderer right in Sydney, – and this, I think, is a great advantage. I lived at 213 ½ in a certain street, and the interesting number chosen seemed to have no reference to any smaller numbers. There was no 1, or 5, or 20 in that street. If you live at 213 in Philadelphia, you know that you are three doors from Two Hundred and Ten Street on one side, and seven from Two Hundred and Twenty Street on the other. Information conveyed in that manner is always to me useless. I forget the numbers which I should remember, and have no aid to memory in the peculiarity either of the position or of the name.

The public gardens at Sydney deserve more than the passing mention just made of them. The people of Australia personally are laudably addicted to public gardens, – as they are to other public institutions with which they are enabled to inaugurate the foundation of their towns, by the experience taught to them by our deficiencies. Parks for the people were not among the requirements of humanity when our cities were first built; and the grounds necessary for such purposes had become so valuable when the necessity was recognised, that it has been only with great difficulty, and occasionally by the munificence of individuals, that we have been able to create these artificial lungs for our artisans. In many of our large towns we have not created them at all. The Australian cities have had the advantage of our deficiencies. The land has been public property, and space for recreation has been taken without the payment of any cost price. In this way a taste for gardens, and, indeed, to some extent, a knowledge of flowers and shrubs, has been generated, and a humanizing influence in that direction has been produced. There are, in all the large towns, – either in the very centre of them or adjacent to them, – gardens rather than parks, which are used and apparently never abused. Those at Melbourne in Victoria are the most pretentious, and, in a scientific point of view, no doubt the most valuable. I am told that, in the rarity and multiplicity of the plants collected there, they are hardly surpassed by any in Europe. But for loveliness, and that beauty which can be appreciated by the ignorant as well as by the learned, the Sydney Gardens are unrivalled by any that I have seen. The nature of the land, with its green slopes down to its own bright little sea bay, has done much for them, and art and taste combined have made them perfect. It may be said that of all drawbacks to public parks distance is the greatest. We know that, in London, Hyde Park is but of little service to those who live at Mile End. The great park at New York, though it is connected by omnibuses with the whole city, requires an expedition to reach it. The gardens of the Crystal Palace at Sydenham are so far off from the multitude that the distance rather than the cost of entrance deters the crowd which might take delight in them. Even the Bois de Boulogne are too remote for daily purposes. But the gardens of Sydney are within easy reach of every street of the combined towns of Sydney and Wooloomooloo. A little beyond the gardens, almost equally near to the town, are the sea baths, – not small, dark, sequestered spots in which, for want of a better place, men and women may wash themselves, but open sea spaces, guarded by palisades from the sharks which make bathing in the harbour impracticable, large enough for swimming, and fitted up with all requisites. It is a great thing for a city to be so provided; and it is a luxury which, as far as I am aware, no other city possesses to the same degree. There is no place for bathing in England like it, or at all equal to it. That at Kingstown in Ireland is perhaps as good; but Kingstown is six or seven miles from Dublin, and has to be reached by railroad. A man or a woman may walk to the bathing-place at Sydney in a quarter of an hour.

I was much surprised at the fortifications of Sydney harbour. Fortifications, unless specially inspected, escape even a vigilant seer of sights, but I, luckily for myself, was enabled specially to inspect them. I had previously no idea that the people of New South Wales were either so suspicious of enemies, or so pugnacious in their nature. I found five separate fortresses, armed, or to be armed, to the teeth with numerous guns, – four, five, or six at each point; Armstrong guns, rifled guns, guns of eighteen tons weight, with loopholed walls and pits for riflemen, as though Sydney were to become another Sebastopol. I was shown how the whole harbour and city were commanded by these guns. There were open batteries and casemated batteries, shell rooms and gunpowder magazines, barracks rising here and trenches dug there. There was a boom to be placed across the harbour, and a whole world of torpedoes ready to be sunk beneath the water, all of which were prepared and ready for use in an hour or two. It was explained to me that 'they' could not possibly get across the trenches, or break the boom, or escape the torpedoes, or live for an hour beneath the blaze of the guns. 'They' would not have a chance to get at Sydney. There was much martial ardour, and a very general opinion that 'they' would have the worst of it. For a time I could not gather who 'they' were to be. But 'indirect damages' were on men's tongues, and so I knew who were the 'they' at that moment uppermost in the thoughts of my companions. It would be the same in regard to any other enemies of England, either in esse or in posse. I hope that New South Wales may never have to fight for England, and certainly that she may not have to fight America. But the feeling of loyalty in the colony is so strong that, were there a fight on hand, she would be unhappy not to be allowed to take some share in it. But, in viewing these fortifications, I was most specially struck by the loveliness of the sites chosen. One would almost wish to be a gunner for the sake of being at one of these forts.

Three different localities are combined to make Sydney. There is the old city, – old as the age of cities is as yet counted in Australia, – in which are George Street and Pitt Street, so called from George III, and his minister, running parallel to each other, from the centre. The other chief streets are all

named after the old governors, – Macquarie Street, King
Street, Bligh Street, Hunter Street, and Phillip Street. Among
these, Macquarie Street takes a proud pre-eminence,
containing the Houses of Parliament, the Treasury buildings,
the entrance to Government House, and the old hospital.
During a portion of its length it is built up but on one side, and
looks on to the public domain, – for there is a public domain
or park, as well as public gardens. Indeed, according to the
maps of the city, there are an inner domain and an outer
domain, and a Hyde Park. To the south of these rises the
important town of Wooloomooloo, – as to the remarkable
spelling of which name the reader may take my assurance that
I am right. Wooloomooloo has become almost as big as
Sydney, and much more fashionable; and beyond
Wooloomooloo, on and over various little coves of the sea, –
Elizabeth Bay, and Rose Bay, and Double Bay, and Rushcut-
ter's Bay, – cluster the various villa residences of the wealthy
families. It is here that the rising generation of Sydney desires
to dwell, and there is much to justify its choice. Then there is
the 'North Shore,' less fashionable, but almost as beautiful as
the hills round the southern coves. The North Shore has to be
reached by steam ferry from Sydney Cove, which is now
better known as the Circular Quay, where is congregated the
shipping of the port. When the wool ships from England are
here, lying in a circle all round the margin, no port has a
pleasanter appearance. This is during the summer months,
from October perhaps up to March. I was at Sydney both in
summer and winter; but during the winter the port seemed to
be deserted. Crossing the main harbour from the Circular
Quay, the inhabitants of the North Shore reach their side of
the town in ten minutes. Here are St. Leonard's, which is
fairly fashionable; Balmuir, which is less so; and up higher, the
township of Pyrmont, which will perhaps hardly excuse me if
I say that it is not fashionable at all. But then, on the other
hand, Pyrmont is reached by a bridge, while the inhabitants of
St. Leonard's are driven to use the ferry. I can hardly complete
this attempted description of the city, without explaining that
the Government House stands between the Circular Quay and
the public gardens, with grounds sloping down to the sea. The
position is one of great beauty, and the house has an air of

magnificence about it, such as should belong to the residence
of a viceroy. I have been told, however, that as a house it is not
as good as it should be. Looking at it with the eyes of a humble
private individual, I thought that it was all that a house need
be.

The antiquity of Sydney, – perhaps I should say the
comparative antiquity, – strikes an Englishman as being
almost absurd, as he remembers that in his father's lifetime the
place was covered by gum-trees and peopled by savages.
There are houses so old that they are in almost ruinous
condition, – seeming to be as low, as comfortless, and almost
as picturesque, as do some dilapidated tenements in the old
streets of our old towns. These are chiefly of wood; but the
eyes become so used to wooden houses that this speciality is
not observed. Two or three were pointed out to me, each as
being the oldest in the town, and which certainly were built
when the hearts of the young colonists were heavy with many
troubles. Little was thought then of the beauty of position, of
gardens down to the water's edge, and of views over the
land-locked sea. How were the inhabitants to make themselves safe against black savages, against convicts who were
still more savage, and against fire? It seems that the first
comers into any land have rarely thought much about scenery.
Trouble as to food and security is too heavy on the minds of
pioneers to allow them to indulge in the luxury of landscapes,
and the taste for scenery is one of latter-day growth. In the last
century Englishmen travelled to see cities, and to see men, and
to study the world, – but in those days mountains were
troublesome, and dark valleys were savage and glaciers were
horrible. Much is said by those who first landed at Botany Bay
and Port Jackson on the trees and plants and herbs·of the new
country, – what I believe is now called 'the Flora'; but I do not
remember a word in praise of its loveliness.

Among other old buildings at Sydney there is an old church
and a very old hospital. The hospital, I was assured, is quite
antiquated. It seemed to be airy, easy, and as pleasant as is
compatible with the nature of such an institution. St. James's
Church is pewed round with high dark panels, and is as much
like an English comfortless church of the last century, as
though it stood in a second-rate town in an Eastern county. I

went there once, and found it impossible to hear a word, either from the gentleman who read the lessons, or from him who preached. But it is a fashionable church, and is supposed to be that at which the governor and his family should say their prayers. The cathedral, on the other hand, is new, and very well arranged. I heard an excellent sermon there, in which I was told that it was the practice of St. Paul to teach his own religion rather than to abuse that of others, – a lesson which is much needed at home, and by no means unnecessary in the Australian colonies.

CHAPTER III

RELIGION AND EDUCATION

It is natural that a visitor to any country should think most, and therefore speak with greatest fulness, of that sect in religion to which he himself belongs. He will be most prone to meet the pastors of that Church; and, unless he keeps his mind alert on the subject, he will, – if he be an Englishman of the Church of England, – fall into the error of thinking that the Church of England is the only important Church. The feeling is very common at home, – but even there it is a mistake. In the colonies the blunder would be much more egregious. As long as the colonies were Crown colonies, governed directly from home, a certain amount of Church of England ascendency was established. Bishops were appointed by the Crown, who still have, by virtue of their patents, some social precedence. They are recognised as titular lords, – having some stronger claim to the appellation than their Roman Catholic brother prelates. But in all these colonies every branch of the Christian religion is now supposed to stand on an equal footing, – and to have an equal title to whatever support the State may be able and willing to give. In each of the colonies the energy of the various pastors and of their flocks, and the munificence of individuals, have added something to the clerical incomes, which are for the most part provided by the voluntary payments of the people. I should only trouble my readers with unnecessary particulars were I to attempt to explain in detail the sources from which such funds have arisen, and the manner in which they have been expended; but it may perhaps interest some to know that there are five bishops of the Church of England in New South Wales, the Bishop of Sydney being the metropolitan for the Australian colonies, with a salary of £2,000 per annum. The total income of the clergy of the Church of England in New South

Wales is £13,963 per annum, – of which £12,386 is the amount paid voluntarily be the people, and £1,576 that coming from the General Church Fund. The usual stipend of an incumbent is £200 per annum. There are 229,243 members of the Church of England in the colony.

One Roman Catholic Archbishop has the Romish Church under his government, with a salary of £800 per annum. The total income of the Roman Catholic Church is £7,607 per annum, of which £6,583 is the sum derived from the subscriptions of the faithful, and £1,024 that from the Church Fund. The incomes of the parish priests are £200 or £150 per annum. There are 145,932 Roman Catholics in the colony.

The Presbyterians and Wesleyans have of course no bishops, but they also pay their ministers at the rate of about £150 each, the Presbyterians drawing altogether £326, and the Wesleyans £180, from the General Church Fund. The large remainder of the necessary sum is made up by the voluntary subscriptions of the flocks, – the Presbyterians paying £2,179 per annum, and the Wesleyans £1,572. The number of Presbyterians in the colony is 49,122, and that of Wesleyans 36,275. There are nine other Christian sects who have parish ministers and places of worship of their own, and who together number 26,447 souls. There were also two Jewish synagogues, – and there is a congregation of Christian Israelites, as to whose religious doctrines I must own myself to be altogether ignorant.

Very much praiseworthy energy has been used throughout the colonies to bring religious teaching within the reach of the people under very disadvantageous circumstances. No doubt the fact of an endowed Church at home, and the theory of endowments which was brought from home to the colonies, has given rise there as well as here to an idea that religion and religious teaching and rites should be administered to a people without any demand upon them for direct payment. People in Australia will commonly make it a matter of complaint that no clergyman has ever been near them, that no religious aid has ever been sent to them, – although they themselves have taken no measures and paid no money towards bringing a clergyman into their districts. For the doctor and the lawyer they know they must pay, – as the Roman Catholic knows also that he must for his priest. But the normal English Protestant, – even when dissenting from the Church of England, – thinks that his spiritual pastor should be sent to him by some unknown authority which is supposed to have such matters in keeping. If the spiritual pastor be not sent, the Protestant goes on without clerical assistance, perhaps complaining, – more probably troubling himself very little on the matter. He would go to church if there were a church near him; but if there be none within reach the fault does not rest with him, and thus his conscience is at rest. And again the sparseness of the population and the great distances which lie between the small towns, add greatly to the difficulty. Clergymen of all denominations are, when employed in the pastoral districts, obliged to take charge of wide areas of country rather than of parishes, – of areas so wide that services can be held by each perhaps only once a fortnight, and perhaps only once a month. The travelling also is expensive, laborious, and very disagreeable. It necessarily follows that in many places there is no religious worship set on foot with clerical aid, and that squatters with their families, and their attendant shepherds, stockriders, shearers, and the like, recognise Sunday only as a day of rest.

I should, however, be wrong not to add that in New South Wales, and in the other colonies, a system has grown up under the direct sanction of the bishops of the Church of England for the performance of the Church Service by laymen. The morning prayers, with the lessons and litany, are read, – and often also a sermon. I believe that Episcopal injunctions against original sermons by laymen are very strong; but I imagine they are sometimes disobeyed. Whether the Presbyterians and Wesleyans employ lay readers I am unable to say. As a matter of course the Roman Catholics do not do so, – and on this account I think that the Roman Catholics as a sect are more neglected than their Protestant brethren, although they are doubtless under stricter coercion in regard to the payment of clerical dues.

I feel myself bound to record my opinion that religious teaching and the exercise of religious worship are held as being essential to civilisation and general well-being by the people of Australia. Taking the inhabitants of the colonies all through, I

think the feeling is stronger there than it is at home, first and
chiefly because the mass of the population is better educated, –
secondly, because they who are foremost in education, rank, and
society are less highly educated.

That the first should be the case will surprise no one, and will
generally be admitted as a consequence, if it be allowed that the
colonial education is superior to that which we have as yet
achieved at home. The tendencies and influences which send
children to school, send them and their parents to church also, –
even though the schools be in all respects secular. Teaching
produces prosperity; prosperity achieves decent garments, – and
decent garments are highly conducive to church-going. Among
us in England that portion of our rural population which never
goes to church, and which is utterly ignorant of all religious
observances, consists of the unfortunates upon whom the kindly
dew of instruction has never fallen, and who have been left in
almost brute-like ignorance. Among all communities in the
colonies the children are taught. Wherever there is any
community, however small it may be, there is a school; and
where there is a school the children attend it. And almost as
universally, wherever there is a community there arises a church,
or more commonly churches. Though there be only two or
three hundred persons within a twelve-mile circle, affording
perhaps an average church attendance of less than a hundred,
there will be a Presbyterian and a Roman Catholic church
alongside of each other, or a Church of England and a Wesleyan
church. Sometimes in a small township, containing ostensibly
little in the way of buildings beyond the four public-houses, the
blacksmith's shop, and the bank, there will be three places of
worship. The people are fond of building churches, and are
proud of having them in their villages, – though they are
unfortunately less addicted to pay annually for their clergyman
than to defray the cost of their churches. You can, too, go in
debt for a church, – but hardly for a clergyman. There is, I think,
undoubtedly a general desire that the comfort and decency of
religious teaching should be recognised in the colony, and this I
attribute mainly to the healthy state of education.

It would be more difficult to show that a lower condition of
education among the better educated classes in the colony than
that which has been reached at home, should have a similar

tendency, but I think that such is the case. There can be but little doubt that education among the most favoured classes at home does range higher than in the colonies. It would indeed be most disgraceful to England, with her wealth and her endowed colleges and schools, if it were not so. And it has come about as one result of such advanced teaching, – not in England only but in every country in which erudition has been valued, – that the erudite have learned to disregard and in part to dispense with the services of the priesthood. I do not say that infidelity has been thus produced, – but rather a tendency in the man's mind to think that he can best suffice to himself as his own priest. This feeling, operating from men to their wives, from fathers to sons, and from mothers to daughters, – but ever more strongly among men than women, – has in all highly intellectual communities had a certain tendency to weaken confidence in the administrations of church services. In the colonies this condition of society has hardly been yet reached. That it will come, – whether it be for good or evil, – is certain. In the meantime the absence of the condition has the tendency which I have alleged, of making the feeling in favour of religious teaching stronger among the higher classes in the colonies than it is among our higher classes at home.

I find by the statistical register of New South Wales that the average Sunday attendance at various places of worship amounts to something over one-third of the whole population. On 31st December, 1870, the population was 502,861, and during that year the average Sunday attendance had been 172,320.

It must be admitted on behalf of the colony, that New South Wales has supplied itself with schools on the most liberal footing; but it must be admitted also by the colony that too large a proportion of the expense of these schools has been thrust on the general taxation of the country. There are 796 public or common schools, – open to all classes, though not open without payment except under special circumstances, – of which 267 are denominational and 529 are secular. The total cost of these is £150,866 per annum, of which only £39,583 is paid by the subscriptions of the scholars, leaving the large sum of £111,283 as a burden on the revenue of the country. And it must be remembered that this is the case in a country in which

the wages of artisans average 7s.6d. and those of rural labourers
4s. a day. These schools are all subject to the Council of
Education, and in 1870 they taught 59,814 scholars. Including
those at private schools, the cost of which cannot of course be
given, there were, in 1870, 74,503 scholars under tuition in the
colony – a number which I think will be regarded as high for a
population of half a million, which is continually being increased
by the immigration of adults.

The glory of Sydney in the way of education is its University,
and certainly a great deal of spirit has been shown by the colony
in the creation of the institution and in the erection of the
building. As regards the building, I think no one will dispute the
assertion when I say that the college-hall, – or public room, for it
is put to none of the comfortable festive uses for which
college-halls have been built at our universities, – is the finest
chamber in the colonies. If I were to say that no college either at
Oxford or Cambridge possesses so fine a one, I might probably
be contradicted. I certainly remember none of which the proportions are so good. In regard to the Sydney University itself, it
must be remembered that it has been instituted simply for
education, and not as a place of residence either for fellows,
scholars, or commoners. It consists, therefore, of the hall,
library, lecture-rooms, museum, and a residence for one of the
professors. It knows nothing of gaudy days, of high tables, of
sweet Latin graces, or of audit ale. It lacks the social charms to
which the frequenters of Oxford and Cambridge have been
accustomed; but perhaps the education on that account is not the
worse, and certainly it is very much less expensive.

In a fiscal point of view, I cannot say that the university has
been as yet a success. In 1870, – and I can give the figures for no
later year, the total cost of the university, consisting chiefly of
the salaries of the professors, was £5,938, of which no less than
£5,000 was paid from the taxes of the colony. There were but 41
scholars, whose friends contributed a trifle over £22 per annum
for their education, amounting in all to £938. But there are three
professors attached to the college, each of whom enjoys an
income in excess of the sum so subscribed, besides other
professors less liberally remunerated.

There are also affiliated colleges, in which it is proposed that
students from a distance shall live, – as they do at our English

colleges, – under the charge of a Warden or Rector. Two of these have been already built, and are inhabited, by the Warden of St. Paul's, which is a Protestant establishment, and by the Rector of St. John's, which is intended for the Roman Catholics. These gentlemen's salaries, of £500 each, are paid out of the taxes; but the affiliated students have not yet come in large numbers. When I visited the university, the happy Rector of St. John's was troubled with, I think, but one inmate, whereas the Warder of St. Paul's had three or four.

I am very far, however, from intending to sneer at the Sydney University. Amidst a population so sparse, it was of course necessary that the beginning, if made at all, should be made by the government, and be paid for with government money. It has not yet had time for success. Every effort has been made to lead to success, especially in procuring first-class teachers for its service. The reputation for scholarship of Dr. Badham, the classical professor, is as high in England as it is in Sydney, – or nearly so; for in Sydney he is now regarded as the one living incontrovertible authority in all questions of Greek literature. Mr. Pell, the professor of mathematics, stands equally high in his own line. There is no institution in the colonies which excites and deserves the sympathies of an English traveller more completely than does the Sydney University.

CHAPTER IV

LEGISLATURE AND GOVERNMENT

The first parliament under which responsible government was inaugurated in New South Wales commenced its action on the 22nd of May, 1856, and the first responsible ministry came into office on the 6th of June, 1856. Sit William Denison was then governor. When he was sent to the colony, the governor really governed, having a policy of his own, in the execution of which there was not much to disturb him as long as he carried the English Secretary of State with him in his measures. But from May, 1856, all this was changed; and from that date parliamentary rule has prevailed in New South Wales. The sixth parliament is now sitting, and the fourteenth ministry was formed in 1872. Australian ministries are not long lived, and it may well be that before these pages are published Mr. Parkes, who was premier and colonial secretary when they were written, will have given way, and a fifteenth ministry, – possibly under the presidency of Sir James Martin,– will be sitting on the treasury benches. Sir James Martin and Mr. John Robertson seem to be two statesmen whose services are most generally in request by the colony. Sir James Martin has been five times attorney-general, and has three times, while holding that office, been also premier. Mr. Robertson has been in six cabinets, and has twice been premier. There can be but little doubt that a turn in the political wheel of fortune will restore them to the seats on that bench to which they are so well accustomed. The only question is as to the duration of their exclusion.

There are many other gentlemen who are well known in the colony as parliamentary politicians, – men who come into office for a time and go out, perhaps, for eternity. But as to the two whom I have mentioned, there is a feeling that they are normal ministers – gentlemen who have almost a right to be in parliament, and, being in parliament, almost a right to be in the cabinet. It is very hard to define parties in the colonial parliamentary contests, as they are defined with us. Of these two colonial statesmen, I should say that Mr. Robertson was a strong Liberal, and Sir James Martin a very strong Conservative. Mr. Robertson's name and fame are connected especially with the administration of the crown lands, in regard to which he has been regarded as the friend of the free-selecters, and therefore as the enemy of the squatters. Sir James is, I fear, a protectionist at heart. He is a proclaimed foe to separation, strong in loyalty to the Crown, very English, very confident in his own colony, perhaps a little jealous of others, very pugnacious, a consistent and thorough-going politician, and almost a Tory. He is, I think, certainly the best Australian speaker that I heard. Mr. Robertson, who was lately Sir James's colleague, but for many years his opponent, is entitled to the singular merit of having won for himself high parliamentary reputation in spite of organic impediments to speech which would have made a less energetic man dumb for life as regards all public assemblies.

When I was first in Sydney, the parliamentary question which was then exciting the minds of men in New South Wales, – and the minds of men also in Victoria, – was that of the border duties. I do not feel quite sure that these border duties would interest my readers as keenly as they interested me, or that I could in any way make the subject palatable to them. In the colonies they are of vital interest, not only from the effect they have had and must have on the intercourse between the two leading colonies, Victoria and New South Wales, but because the discussion which they are producing may probably assist in bringing about that one great measure, which is of all measures most essential to the future welfare of the colonies, a customs union which shall bind them together as one country in regard to duties on imported goods.

These border duties were so much in the ascendant, both when I first visited Sydney and when I returned thither, that I hardly heard other matters of much importance discussed in the New South Wales parliament. There was a divorce bill brought forward, and I then was surprised to learn that the people of New South Wales, alone among English-speaking races, are without any legalised means of separating a wife from her husband, or a husband from his wife. On this occasion the divorce bill was thrown out, and the peculiarity still remains. The practice of the British parliament as to counting out and observing the presence of strangers has been adopted, and is of course much more frequently used than it is at home. I was surprised to find how very large a proportion of the time of the House was occupied in personal discussions and appeals to the Speaker, – as to some of which I could not but feel that the gentleman had by no means a bed of roses. A Speaker in an Australian House of Assembly should be a stout man, not thin-skinned, prone rather to content himself with a low level of conduct in his House than to attempt the maintenance of high dignified decorum, – but capable of speaking a very strong word if a member should occasionally fall into a bathos lower than that low level. With some trains a driver feels that it is much to get along at all. The House at Sydney does certainly succeed in making its journeys. When there, I often felt that an exercise of some great act of authority would be useful, – that an order to the sergeant-at-arms to carry away an offending member and lock him up in some parliamentary black-hole would be beneficial. I longed for the moment to be the Speaker, that I might be authoritative. But I perceived gradually that the work did get itself done, and that the gentleman in the chair knew what he was about. I was not so sure that he was right, when on an occasion, – a new bill respecting the border duties being then in committee, – he spoke from the benches as a member of the House, not simply on the clause under discussion, but with considerable party violence on the subject of the bill at large. I could not but think that his authority as Speaker would be injured by his descending into the political arena.

That a very commonplace man may make a fair debater was a lesson I had learned before I ever entered an Australian legislature. Such a one will not become a great orator. He will not overcome his hearers by reasons, or carry them away by passionate eloquence. But he may be very serviceable, – as flour is serviceable in the fabrication of a pudding. Indeed, a pudding with much flour and but few plums will answer its purpose better than one in which the plums have nothing to

hold them together. In the House of Assembly at Sydney there
was a sufficiency of farinaceous matter to prevent the plums
from cloying the appetite and injuring the digestion.

The Lower House, or House of Assembly, at Sydney
consists of seventy-two members. They are elected members
for four years, the house being, of course, subject to dissolution by the governor, – as is our House of Commons at
home. Manhood suffrage prevails, and votes are given by
ballot. There is no power of scrutiny after the ballot, and I was
told by many that personation of votes is common. I am
inclined to think that the ballot has acted well in the colony, –
serving, as it certainly has done, to preserve tranquillity at
elections. I do not think that any conclusion should be drawn
from this as to the expedience of the ballot in England. In New
South Wales no voter is desirous of concealing his vote. It is
not for secrecy, – to protect the voter from intimidation, or
from bribery, – that the ballot is needed, but as a measure of
police precaution for the day.

The Upper House, or Legislative Council, in Sydney is
dignified and conservative. As in Queensland, the members
are elected by the Crown, and are elected for life. Practically
the nomination is made by the premier of the day. The great
majority of the present members have sat in the Lower House,
and have thus learned the use of a debating chamber before
entering the Council.

The Executive Council consists of the Governor and seven
ministers, – one of whom must be in the Legislative Council.
The following are the officers who generally compose the
Cabinet, – the Colonial Secretary, the Attorney-General, the
Solicitor-General, the Colonial Treasurer, the Secretary for
Lands, the Secretary for Public Works, and the Postmaster-
General. Any one of these officers may be premier, though the
premier generally chooses to be Colonial Secretary. Sir James
Martin, when premier, has always been Attorney-General.
Mr. Robertson was at one time premier and Secretary for
Lands. The conduct of public business is almost the same as
with us in England, the one exception being that the Gover-
nors have the power of reserving bills passed by the two
Houses for the sanction of the home government; and that the
home government, even when bills have not been so reserved,

may put its veto on a bill, even when it has been passed by the two Houses and the Governor, at any time within two years of the date of its receipt by the Secretary of State.

By the last census, taken in 1871, the population of New South Wales was 503,981. At the beginning of 1872, the revenue was £2,218,699. Of this sum, £1,729,722 was made up by taxation, and £497,977 was revenue derived from the sale and lease of crown lands. The public debt was £10,614,330, and the interest of the debt was £530,514 per annum; thus requiring every individual in the colony to bear a burden of about £1 per annum on its account. It must, however, be explained that nearly all the money so borrowed has been expended on public works, – such as roads and railways, and that the sum expended on railways, amounting to £6,500,000, returns an interest of nearly 2 ½ per cent, in the shape of profit. It can hardly be boasted on behalf of the colony that this outlay of money has been directly remunerative, as we know that 7 ½ per cent. is nearer to the mark of normal interest in New South Wales; but when we consider the general good that is done by an easy means of transit to a community in which the ordinary means are difficult, slow, and expensive, we can hardly look upon the debt in the light of a national incubus, as we should do had the money been laid out on the current expenses of the year, or in defraying the charges of past extravagance.

The total payment demanded from every inhabitant is higher than it is at home. With us it is less than £2 10s. a head. In New South Wales it is very nearly £3 10s. a head, – after giving the colony the advantage of the sum derived from the lease and sale of crown lands; but £3 10s. a head is not nearly so heavy a burden in the colonies as is £2 10s. in England. The rate of rural wages throughout Great Britain is not above 14s. a week, whereas in New South Wales it averages about 24s.

CHAPTER V

COUNTRY TOWNS, RAILWAYS, AND ROADS

The country towns of Australia, generally, are not attractive, and it is hardly to be expected that they should as yet be so. There are, of course, exceptional instances, – Ballaarat, Geelong, and Beechworth in Victoria are exceptions, as are also Launceston in Tasmania, and Strathalbyn and Mount Gambier in South Australia, which, from peculiarity of situation or the energy of individuals, have become either well-built cities or pleasant little towns. No doubt there are others which I was not able to visit. But, generally, there is a raw newness about these congregations of houses, an initiation of streets which as yet are no more than initiated, a deficiency in pavement and macadamisation which leads either to dust or mud, an apparent mixture of pretension and failure which is indeed indispensable to towns founded with hopes of future greatness, but which creates a feeling of melancholy sadness in the mind of a stranger. It could hardly have been otherwise, and yet it grieves us to see that they who have diligently made their plans, intending to produce comfort, social neatness, and sometimes even urban magnificence, should as yet have succeeded in producing only discomfort, untidinesss, and insignificance. In old countries, such as our own, towns have grown up almost without an intention on the part of any founder. Cities have formed themselves out of villages, because it has first suited this man and then that to earn his bread in this or that locality. Consequently our streets have been narrow and crooked, our spaces confined and often ill arranged, and our supplies of water and air insufficient for an increasing population. We are daily compelled to pull down that we may rebuild, – and are almost angry with ourselves or with those who went before us, in that there has been so little foresight among us as to the wants of mankind. But it has resulted from all this that we are not, as a rule, incomplete, pretentious, or unpicturesque. The new countries, however, have taken a lesson from the deficiencies of the old countries, and have commenced their towns on a certain plan, with wide streets, and large spaces, and straight long lines, so that coming generations of thronging men may be able to build their houses in spots properly prepared, and to move about without knotting themselves into inconvenient crowds as men have to do in the old cities. When the generations shall have come, this will be very well, and the wisdom of the founders will be acknowledged, – but in the meantime the new towns are ugly, and generally dirty.

They who have travelled in the United States beyond the big cities, – who have seen something besides New York, Boston, and Chicago, – must have felt this ugliness very strongly. It was the appreciation of this deformity, excited to its greatest intensity by the unfortunate youthfulness of the place then under inspection, and by the imagination of the artist, which produced that picture of a town in the wilderness which Dickens painted and called Eden. The founders of his Eden had sought the confluence of two great navigable rivers, and had planned long quays and broad streets, – but, up to Dickens's day, had produced nothing but mud and ague. I have seen no Australian town so bad as Eden, which certainly when I visited it still deserved all the evil things which have been said of it. Such a picture of any Australian town, even if I could draw it, would be untrue. But I cannot say that as yet these communities possess many beauties to recommend them to the eye, or have much to please a stranger.

And yet in these towns there is ample evidence of energy. The population of such places may be said to vary from 7,000 to 500, the great majority having less than 2,000 inhabitants. Exclusive of Sydney there are but six towns in the whole colony of New South Wales which have a population over 2,000 and of these four, Newcastle, Maitland, Paramatta, and Bathurst, have a population varying from 5,000 to 7,500. In all these towns, – even in places with less than 500 souls, – there is a bank. In most of them there are two or three banks. In all these there is a church, – in most of them there are churches. The hotels are more numerous even than the banks and churches, and, – though I heard them abused as inns are always abused in all countries, – I found them fairly comfortable, and very much better than I had expected from the sparseness of the population over so wide a district. Almost all inns in Australia, however small, have a bath-room, though it may be of rude construction. I wish I could convey this information to hotel-keepers in England. I found, too, that the shops were better than they looked, and that the means of comfortable life were to be found in towns which were not attractive in their appearance.

In New South Wales many of the towns have been absolutely created by the gold-fields, and are still being created. Some of the gold-field towns are already in a state of decay, and are almost passing away. Still something of life remains, but of all the sad places I ever saw they are the most melancholy. They are 'bush' towns. Readers who desire to understand anything of Australian life should become acquainted with the technical meaning of the word 'bush.' The bush is the gum-tree forest, with which so great a part of Australia is covered, that folk who follow a country life are invariably said to live in the bush. Squatters who look after their own runs always live in the bush, even though their sheep are pastured on plains. Instead of a town mouse and a country mouse in Australia, there would be a town mouse and a bush mouse, – but mice living in the small country towns would still be bush mice. A young lady when she becomes engaged to a gentleman whose avocations call upon him to live far inland always declares she prefers 'bush life'.

The mining towns are composed of the sudden erections which sprang from the finding of gold in the neighbourhood, and are generally surrounded by thick forest. But in their immediate vicinity the trees have been cut down either for firewood or for use under ground, – but have not been altogether cleared away, so that the hideous stumps remain above the surface. Around on all sides the ground has been stirred in the search for gold, and ugly bare heaps of clay are left. The road to and from such a place will meander causelessly between yawning holes, in each of which some desponding miner has probably buried his high hopes, – and which he has then abandoned. One wonders that every child in the neighbourhood does not perish by falling into them. At different points around the centre, which have once been supposed to be auriferous, there are the skeleton remains of wooden habitations, with here and there the tawdry sign-boards of deserted shops from which high profits were once expected. In some few of these skeleton habitations there are still inhabitants, – men and women who having a house have been unwilling to leave it, even when the dreadful fact that gold is not to be found in paying quantities has been acknowledged. In the centre there is still the town, though day by day its right to the name is passing from it. There are still the publicans, and still the churches, – though the services become rare and still more rare, – and there is the bank holding its position as long as an ounce of gold is to be extracted from the unwilling soil. Here congregate Chinese in gangs, who are content to rewash the ground which has already been perhaps twice washed by European or Australian Christians, and who, with the patient industry which is peculiar to them, will earn perhaps each 1s.6d. a day by the process. I will name no such town, because by doing so I might offend the susceptibilities of some still-hopeful denizens of the place specified, but they are easy to find by those who travel in New South Wales. There are, however, other mining towns in the colony in full life. Men are still crowding to them; and at these habitations cannot be put up fast enough to cover the eager seekers after wealth, nor shops opened quick enough to supply their wants. Of them I will say a few words in another chapter.

Other towns, and they probably the best and most enduring of the country towns of New South Wales, have been built in the wheat districts, – in those parts of the colony which have been found most fitted for cereal produce. Among these are Maitland, Bathurst, Goulbourn, Armidale, Albury, – and Wagga Wagga, celebrated for ever in the annals of the colony as having been once the residence of the great Tichborne claimant. Maitland and Goulbourn I did not visit, – of Bathurst I cannot speak otherwise than kindly, because of the kindness I received there. It stands in a fertile plain, just across that range of Blue Mountains which in the early days of the colony were so cruelly inaccessible to the first settlers. When at last their energies prevailed they got down upon the happy wheat-bearing land through which the Macquarie runs, where the town of Bathurst now stands with its broad streets and

numerous churches. Bathurst has 5,030 inhabitants. There
must surely be room there for treble the number, – so spacious
is it, and so great are the distances. Truth compels me to state
that the mud in their streets can be very deep in wet weather.

Newcastle, in population and importance, is second to
Sydney. It is essentially a city of coal. As I must speak again of
the coal of the colony, I need do no more here than mention
the name. It remains that I should say a word in honour of
Paramatta, the city of oranges, and the scene of some of the
greatest efforts made by the early settlers to obtain subsistence
from the ungrateful soil of the districts adjacent to Sydney.
The Paramatta River, – called by the natives by that or by
some similar name, – runs down into Sydney Harbour, and on
this river, about fifteen miles above the city, now stands the
pleasant and almost old-fashioned little town. It is quite unlike
any other colonial place of the same size, having been established before the new order of things had commenced, – when
men were struggling for existence rather than thinking of
sanitary arrangements and future grandeur. The early colonists tried to grow wheat here and failed. Those who have come
since have planted oranges and have made money. Now
Paramatta is known far and wide for its fruit, – so that no man
or woman is supposed to have seen Sydney aright who has not
visited Mr. Pye's orange groves, and shaken hands with Mrs.
Pye, who in the matter of conserved oranges stands far above
all competitors in any country. Either the soil or the climate,
or both together, contain the requisites, whatever they may
be, for this peculiar growth, so that neither Jamaica nor the
South of Spain, not Malta or the Havanna, can beat Paramatta
in this especial article of produce. And as a consequence the
consumption of oranges is very great throughout all the
colonies. December and January are the months in which they
culminate, but they are picked ripe throughout the entire year.
On the 1st of July, in the very middle of winter, I ate
fresh-picked oranges in Sydney which were ripe and perfectly
sweet, and at the same period of the year they are exported in
great numbers. At Paramatta I found an hotel so like an old
English country inn, – that when there I could hardly believe
that I was in the colony. But Paramatta, like Sydney, is not a
mushroom, as are other colonial towns, but has an old history

and savours of the last century. Steamers ply to it up the Paramatta River, and it lies also on the Sydney and Bathurst Railway, – so that it may almost be regarded as a suburb of the city.

In New South Wales there are three lines of railway nearly equal in length, comprising altogether 394 miles. The amount does not seem much for so great a country, – but it must be remembered that the very great distances create the difficulty. The population is scattered so far and wide that the towns to be connected are too small to pay for railway traffic. The Great Northern starts from Newcastle, and runs up through the coal district to Maitland, Singleton, and Musclebrook. The average cost per mile of this line was £13,000, and it is carried over 124 miles. The Great Western and the Great Southern, – it is of course necessary that the English pattern should be followed, and that all railways shall be Great, – are one and the same from Sydney as far as Paramatta. This morsel of railway, 14 miles in length, the first opened in the colony, cost no less than £50,000 a mile to construct it, the total sum expended on it being six times the amount originally subscribed by a private company to make the entire railway to Goulbourn, a distance of 135 miles! At Paramatta the lines diverge, the Southern branch going to Goulbourn, and the Western across the Blue Mountains to Bathurst. The latter crosses the Nepean River at Penrith, and immediately ascends the hills. It is taken up by a zigzag ascent, and after running 60 miles through the mountains, by the only passable track which they afford even for foot travellers, it is brought down again by another zigzag. On the ascent from the Nepean the steepest gradient is 1 in 30, – on the descent towards Bathurst it is 1 in 42. The whole work is said to be, and appears to be, a wonderful feat of engineering enterprise, – and is not the less so certainly because it cost £25,000 a mile; whereas the portion of the line between Sydney and Paramatta, which cost double the money, runs through a perfectly flat country. The scenery through the Blue Mountain ranges is so grand, that the traveller should not content himself with looking at it from a railway carriage. There are three or four points on the line at which he should stay a few hours, and explore the defiles around him. The ranges which are so passed run all the length of the eastern side of Australia, dividing a narrow strip of land along the sea-shore from the huge plains of the interior. From Paramatta the Southern line branches to Goulbourn, also passing the ranges, – but doing so at a spot in which the ascent is comparatively insignificant. But in this work also the gradients for three consecutive miles are 1 in 30. The line to Goulbourn from Paramatta cost £13,000 a mile.

The total cost of the railways in New South Wales up to the end of 1871 had been £6,532,184, and in that year the receipts taken on the 394 miles open were £365,322. The working expenses were £197,065, and the net profit on the sum expended £158,257, giving an interest on the capital invested of 2.42 per cent. These railways are exclusively in the hands of the government, are made with public money, and are managed by a minister of state, – as are the post office and electric telegraph with us. The greater portion of the debt of the colony has been borrowed for the purpose, and has been so expended. As 7 ½ per cent. may perhaps be named as the present normal rate of interest in the colony, it cannot be said that the business is directly remunerative as a speculation. The railways are still being extended, and it may probably be long before any material increase in the rate of direct profit will be realised, – but that adequate profit of an indirect nature is realised, amply sufficient to justify the outlay, no one I think can doubt.

Nevertheless, these railways are open to an objection which strikes an Englishman very forcibly. With a few exceptions as to short lines for local traffic, all the Australian railways have been made by the Australian government, and have necessarily been made under the authority of centralized officials. When it is determined to spend a million on railways, some individual has to determine whether the money shall be expended for the advantage of this or that district. No doubt the proposition must be sanctioned by parliament, but we all know what is the power of a man 'in power;' and we know also how prone such men are to use their power, perhaps unconsciously, towards the promotion of their own parliamentary interest. They who do not know it would soon be taught the lesson by a visit to the Australian colonies. When a change of government is effected, and a new set of men obtains possession of the treasury bench, the happy localities by whom the new ministers are sent to parliament immediately become assured that roads and bridges will be showered upon them, and they become loudly expectant of railways. But these benefits are to be procured by money subscribed by the colony at large, which should therefore be expended on behalf of the colony at large. When the member for Wonga-jonga becomes the honourable Secretary for Public Works, it is a matter of course that the inhabitants of the Wonga-jonga district should expect great things; and it is almost equally a matter of course that the Secretary for Public Works should do, if not great things, at least little things. He will do probably as little as may suffice to secure his popularity; but he will hardly be able to forget altogether his own interests in his public duty, and he certainly will not be encouraged to forget his own interests by the general feeling which prevails around him.

Nor would it be possible for any minister, let his sense of duty be ever so strong, to adjust the expenditure of public money on local objects so as to deal fairly with all by whom the money is subscribed. Consequently there is a continued outcry that money is unfairly spent. None of the railways of New South Wales confer any appreciable benefit on the inhabitants of the great Riverinan district, or on the district of Illawarra, which lies south from Sydney along the coast; but Riverina and Illawarra pay as much towards the Bathurst and Goulbourn railways as do the localities benefited. Consequently a certain amount of suspicion and distrust is the necessary consequence of the system adopted.

The ordinary roads of New South Wales would probably more thoroughly astonish an Englishman hitherto altogether ignorant of the condition of the colonies than any other phenomenon that he would meet. The extreme length of the colony along the seaboard is 900 miles, and its mean breadth about 500 miles. It is about three times the size of Great Britain and Ireland, and larger than any state in Europe except Russia. Throughout the whole of this enormous country there are but 604 miles of metalled roads, by far the majority of which are closely adjacent to the towns. In the island of Ceylon, which has not been in our possession longer than New South Wales, and which is smaller than Ireland, there are 2,606 miles of principal roads, all of which are metalled and completed. Ceylon is a Crown colony, in which everything is done by almost despotic rule, whereas New South Wales enjoys the privilege of representative government.

I trust it may not be thought that I make this comparison as tending to show that a Crown colony is in a more blessed state than one under representative government, or that the native races of Ceylon are in a happier condition generally than the people of New South Wales. In Ceylon the labourers on the roads receive, I am told, about 1s. 2d. a day, and they live upon rice. Roads may therefore be made cheaply. In New South Wales the road-makers eat meat three times a day, and are paid certainly not less than 4s. a day. Roads, therefore, are costly. The contrast, however, will serve to show how very small a portion of the free colony has received an accommodation which we at home regard as one of the primary requisites of civilised life.

In addition to the 604 miles of completed road, there are 1,255 other miles in different states of incompletion, of which the majority, in the summer of 1872 had been simply cleared. The lines had been surveyed, and the forest-trees had been cut down. As a consequence of this condition of things, journeys are made over forest-tracks, and are made so constantly, and with such a fair amount of average punctuality, that the traveller is at last driven to ask himself whether, after all that has been said on the subject, roads are a necessity.

This travelling through the endless forest of gum-trees is very peculiar, and at first attractive. After awhile it becomes monotonous in the extreme. There is a great absence of animal life. One may go all day through a pastoral country without seeing even a sheep. Now and again one hears the melancholy note of the magpie, or the unmelodious but cheerful gobble of the laughing jackass, and sometimes the scream of a cockatoo; but even birds are not common. Travellers one meets occasionally, – a man on horseback, with his swag before him on his saddle, or a line of drays drawn by bullocks, or perhaps a squatter in his buggy, – but they are few and far between. The road, such as it is, consists of various tracks, running hither and thither, and very puzzling at first to a 'new chum', – till he learns that all these tracks in the bush are only deviations of one road. When the bullock-drays have so cut up a certain passage that the ruts are big enough and deep enough to swallow up a buggy or to overset the stage-coach, the buggies and the stage-coach make another passage, from which they move again when the inevitable bullock-drays have followed them. The government shows its first care on these roads in making bridges over the streams, but even bridges are not absolutely essential. With some rough contrivance, when any contrivance is absolutely necessary, the vehicles descend and ascend the banks, though the wheels be down to the nave in mud. Over many of these bush roads, Cobb's coaches travel day and night, passing in and out through the trees, up and down across the creeks, sticking here and there in the mud, in a rough, uneasy, but apparently not very insecure fashion. Now and then one hears that a coach has been upset, and that the passengers have been out in the bush all night; but one very rarely hears that any one has been hurt, unless it be the coachman. The average pace of the travelling in New South Wales is about six miles an hour.

But more go in their own buggies than by coach, and perhaps more on horseback than in buggies. In Australia every one keeps horses, – every squatter keeps horses by the dozen; and a buggy is as necessary a part of his establishment as a dinner-table. These vehicles are either American or are built on the American plan, and are admirably adapted for bush work. They are very light, and go over huge logs and across unfathomable ruts almost without feeling them. To upset them seems to be an impossibility. They are constantly being broken, – hopelessly broken to the mind of an ignorant stranger; but they go on apparently as well without a pole as with one, and are indifferent to bent axles and injured wheels. There are always yards of rope at hand, and supplementary timber can be cut from the next tree. Many scores of miles through the bush I have travelled in these buggies, – and have sometimes felt the hours to pass by very slowly; but though there have been no roads, – nothing that in England would be called a road, – I have encountered no injury, not have I been aware of any danger.

But the pleasantest mode of bush travelling is on horseback. It is open to this objection, – that you can carry nothing with you but what can be strapped on to your saddle before you. Two changes of linen, a night-shirt, a pair of trousers, with hair-brush, tooth-brush, and a pair of slippers, is about as much as can be taken. But, on the other hand, bush-life requires but little in the way of dress, and a man travelling on horseback is held to be exempt from rules which he should observe if he travelled in a buggy. The squatter travelling alone through the country generally takes two horses, leading one and riding the other, and in this way makes very long journeys. The work which Australian horses will do when immediately taken off the grass is very surprising. I have ridden forty, fifty, and even as much as sixty-four miles a day, – the whole weight on the animal's back being over seventeen stone, and have come to the end of the day's work without tiring the horse. According to the distance to be done, and the number of consecutive days during which you require your steed to travel, will be your pace. The fastest which I ever did from morning to evening was eight miles an hour throughout, resting two hours and journeying eight; but six miles an hour will perhaps be the average rate. The stories, however, that we hear are very wonderful, – for, in matters of horseflesh, gentlemen in Australia do not hide their lights under bushels. I have heard men boast of doing ten miles an hour for ten hours running; and one very enterprising horseman assured me that he had ridden seventy-five miles in four hours. The bush horses are, generally, not shod, – though I would always recommend shoeing for a long journey, – and are very rarely stabled. They are expected, – to use a bush phrase, – to cut their own bread and butter, or, in other words, to feed themselves by foraging. The two paces which are commonly adopted by horsemen in the bush are walking and cantering. Men seldom trot, and consequently many horses altogether lose, or never acquire, the habit of trotting. I have been assured that Australian horses will get over the ground at a fast pace with greater ease to themselves by a continual canter than by changing that pace for a trot. That such a theory is altogether wrong, I have not the slightest doubt. I have found in Australia, as all horsemen know in England, that horses carrying heavy weights will make much longer journeys if made to trot than they can do if required to canter hour after hour. The canter is the easier pace to the man, and therefore it has been adopted. Not uncommonly a horse will knock up with his rider on the road. On such occasions the rider turns into the nearest squatter's station, and borrows another. The fact that everybody's horses, and everybody's saddles and bridles, are always at somebody else's house and never at the owner's, is one of the most remarkable and perhaps not least pleasing phases of Australian life. Nevertheless it tends to some confusion.

CHAPTER VI

LAND

It must be remembered that, at the commencement of colonization in Australia, all land was the property of the Crown, – and that on the transfer in each colony of the power of government from the Crown to representative institutions, the land became the property of that colony, except in regard to such comparatively small tracts as had been already alienated to individuals. In other words, the land from the beginning has been held in trust, to be administered for the benefit of those who have ventured to go to it and look to it for their future means of subsistence. Great difference of opinion has existed among men as to the way in which this trust should be administered, and undoubtedly many mistakes have been made. Equally without doubt, I fear, the trust has been occasionally betrayed by grants of land which there has been nothing to justify. Sales, too, have been made with partiality, – so that land has been transferred to the favoured for sums much less than it is worth in the open market. And political influences have been brought to bear upon the disposition of land, concessions having been made to the supporters of one interest at the expense of those who have been regarded as opponents. These differences of opinion have been so wide, the mistakes made have been so serious, the breaches of trust have been felt to be so obvious by men who have not themselves been favoured, and the political jobbing has been a thorn so sharp in the side of those who have considered themselves to be injured, that the matter in the colonies is discussed on all sides as though the only principle on which it was possible to act, – that of the land being in truth the property of colonists who would go and use it, – had been forgotten, thrown over, and abandoned. But the principle has never been forgotten and has never been abandoned. The adherence to it has perhaps been as close as has been compatible with the customary infirmities of human administrators. Under the old despotic governors, and under the government as since carried on by parliamentary ministers, there has ever been an attempt at a system founded on this principle. Mr. Wakefield's idea that the land should be sold for a price, and not given away, has been fully adopted. The idea of those who generally agreed with him, that the money so obtained should be expended on emigration, has been partially tried, but has fallen to the ground. The price paid for the land has become a part of the revenue of the colony, and has in this way been used for the benefit of those who paid it. It is now a fixed rule in all the Australian colonies that the public lands shall be sold to those who desire to buy them, in accordance with certain laws, – and that these laws shall settle the price, the area that may be bought, the way in which it shall be selected, the amount of credit that shall be given, and the terms as to residence and cultivation, by a compliance with which the purchase may at last be completed. These laws have been made with the expressed object of dealing fairly not only with the would-be purchasers of the land, but also with the interests of a set of men who, by their capital and energy, have gradually become the ascendant class or aristocracy of Australia. It must be remembered always that the would-be purchasers have rarely, if ever, proposed to settle themselves on lands altogether unoccupied. There have been settlers before them who have used the land, but who, while using it, were under no necessity to possess it. These were patriarch squatters, – owners of sheep who drove their flocks on the public pastures, and 'squatted' on the land, conscious that it was not their own, but conscious also that by taking such temporary occupation they were making themselves the pioneers of civilisation, and were legitimately carrying on the true purposes of colonisation. It is not too much to say, that all the early success of Australia was due to the squatters of New South Wales, who followed the steps of Captain Macarthur, the man who introduced merino sheep into Australia. At first the sheep of the squatters ran free, – but it was soon recognised as a fact that as the foraging of sheep was profitable, the graziers should pay some rent for the land, – the land so used

being still the property of the colony and not the property of
the graziers. Then it became necessary not only that a rental
should be fixed, but also terms arranged as to the continuance
of the lease. I have not heard that in New South Wales there
has been much heart-burning as to the price demanded, – but
there has been much as to the continuance of the squatter's
holding. The squatter's pastoral run has been made fairly his
own, as against other squatters, but it has been opened by law
to the choice of the free-selecter. Any would-be farmer may
take a bit more here or there, may choose the choice water-
holes of the run without which the sheep cannot be pastured,
may make his own of any portion of the squatter's holding.
And ten, twenty, forty free-selecters may make their own of
as many portions of it till they absolutely take his pastures
from him. And perhaps this is not the worst aspect of the
squatter's case. The man who comes and calls himself a
free-selecter may at heart, and in very deed, be no farmer at
all, – but a professional thief intent on living on his neighbour's goods. Or he may be joint farmer and thief, – growing
perhaps a little maize and a few pumpkins, but still having an
eye to the squatter's sheep or the squatter's oxen. That there is
very much of such theft in New South Wales is certain, and
also that it is very difficult to punish the offender. The flocks
are so numerous and the spaces so vast, that it is often long
before the stolen animals are missed, and often impossible to
bring evidence against the thief, although the squatter knows
well where his beef and mutton have gone. And there is
another evil-minded free-selecter who is very odious to the
squatter. This man purchases his tract of land, something
between 40 and 320 acres, simply in order that he may be
bought out. He knows that he can be so disagreeable as a
neighbour, that his neighbour will be fain to buy him out. He
also succeeds, too often, to the great grief of the squatter. The
squatters urge that they had leases or promises of leases which
should have preserved them for a term of years, and that their
rights were ignored by new laws. I found the question to be
very intricate in New South Wales, and I do not know that I
can do any service by expressing an opinion one way or the
other. Land ministers in New South Wales have been
confident in proving to me that no existing rights were ever

infringed by the operation of a new land law. Squatters have been equally confident in proving to me that their rights were altogether ignored, and that the terms made with them were infringed. I have endeavoured to believe both when listening to them, and do not doubt that they were all proclaiming truths undoubted to themselves. In speaking of Victoria I shall be obliged to return to this subject, – for in Victoria I think that the squatter's rights, as confirmed by one law, were taken from them by a subsequent law. I mention the matter in regard to New South Wales in order that the reader may understand some of the difficulties with which the distribution of the public lands has been surrounded. The professed object of the land laws has been so to adjust the disposal of the public lands as to attract small purchasers without injustice to the great squatters, and I believe that this object has been truly sought by those who have framed these laws in New South Wales.

When I was first at Sydney, a new land law was in the hands of the government, – which had then come hot from the brain of the indefatigable Mr. Robertson. It contained eighty-four clauses, and each clause required study for its comprehension, – so complicated is the subject. I was told that I could not hope to understand the bill unless I mastered all the details of the existing land law. I did my best, believing that the new bill would become a good law. But when I returned to Sydney, Mr. Robertson and Sir James Martin had fallen, and the new land bill with its eighty-four clauses had been shoved aside into pigeon-holes.

Under the existing law any would-be purchaser may select in New South Wales not less than 40, or more than 320 acres, – the price being 20s. an acre. Of this sum he pays down one-fourth, – £25 we will say for 100 acres. He then enters in upon possession, and no further claim for payment is made upon him for three years. At the end of that time he may pay the other three-fourths, as to which no interest is charged against him for those three years. If he does so, and can satisfy the officials of the land office by certain declarations that he has complied with expressed stipulations as to residence and expenditure of money on improvements, the fee-simple of the land is made over to him. But this the free-selecter need not do, – and very rarely does. He may pay the outstanding 75 per cent. of his purchase-money and get his title-deeds, but he need not do so. Instead of that he may pay 5 per cent. interest on the debt for an indefinite term of years, having the while the undisturbed use of his land; and as his money is worth to him more than 5 per cent., this is what he does do. The farmer, therefore, in New South Wales with 100 acres of land will have paid £25 down, will have had the use of his land without further payment for three years, and will then pay a rental of £3 15s. a year, – which obligation he can terminate at any time by paying down a further sum of £75.

The terms seem to be very easy, but yet, as far as I could learn, the free-selecters in New South Wales are not so prosperous a class as one would wish to find them. It must be remembered in the first place that they enter in upon their land in its rough state, unfenced, and probably with heavy timber on it. They then become almost invariably subject to, I will not say ill-usage, but hostility from their richer neighbours. No doubt they can retaliate. – and can injure the squatter much more materially than the squatter can injure them. They can steal, and if provoked can set fire to fences. They can sell grog, either with or without a licence; and a grog-shop in the vicinity of his station is regarded by the squatter as one of the most grievous injuries which can be inflicted on him. But the state of hostility which is thus engendered cannot tend to the man's comfort or to his material advantage. The climate, however, is the most severe enemy which the free-selecter has to encounter in New South Wales. Land capable of producing cereals he can obtain, but through the uncertainty of the climate he cannot be secure of his crop. Once in three years his crop is good, – but twice in three years it will hardly pay the price of production. In the year ending 31st March, 1870, there were in New South Wales 189,452 acres under wheat, and the crop amounted to nearly 17 bushels an acre. That was a good year. Nevertheless the area under wheat sank in the next year to 147,997 acres, and the produce did not amount to 7 bushels an acre. That was a very bad year. Wages are so high, – averaging never less than 24s. a week, including the cost of board, when labour is hired only for a short time, – that unless a farmer can do his work with his own family, he will be worse off than his own labourer. And then his markets are probably far from home, and the roads to them are very bad. The condition in which the free-selecter of New South Wales seemed to thrive the best was that in which the farmer, who is his own master and perhaps the employer of labour during a part of the year, condescends to be the paid servant of a master during another portion, and to take the squatter's wages for work done in the wool-shed or at the washpool. I should have added, when stating the terms on which the free-selecter obtains his land, that he is entitled by his initiated purchase to certain grazing rights. He has such privilege under the existing law; but this arrangement has been found to work so prejudicially both to the selecter and to the squatter, – adding a fresh ground of contention between the two, – that by the new bill to which I have alluded, that privilege would have been abandoned, under the conviction that it had done more harm than good.

I am far, however, from expressing an opinion that the cause of the free-selecters should be given up in New South Wales, or that efforts made to attract such a class should not be continued. It is by the influx of such men that the labour market of the colony must be maintained, and the body and life of the colony be supported. The condition of the free-selecter, – that of ownership of a piece of land to be tilled by the owner, – is the one which the best class of immigrants desire. It is the hope of attaining this condition which tempts men to come, such as all colonies are desirous of possessing. It is impossible not to sympathize with the efforts of colonial law-makers to assist the growth of such bone and blood in the body of the colony with which they have to deal. As time goes on the sheep-stealing and the cattle-stealing, which are less rife than they were ten years since, will become exceptional as they are with us. And as time goes on the gradual improvement of the climate which follows occupation, and the creation of roads, and increased skill in farming, will all tell in favour of the free-selecter. In describing the present condition of this most interesting of all colonists I have endeavoured to paint the picture as I saw it.

When describing the manner in which the public lands are alienated by the colonist on behalf of the colony, I should also state the terms under which the runs of the squatters are let to them. Leases are now granted for terms of five years, which are renewable. The tenure under these leases is in fact so good that a squatter buys or sells the right to pasture on a run without fear of interference or loss of his grazing ground at the expiration of the term. But the lease affords no protection to the squatter against free-selecters. The rent demanded from him is calculated after a complicated and no doubt most sagacious fashion which I cannot explain, as I have failed to understand it. Practically he pays about 2*d*. a sheep. In the assessment of his rent 200 head of cattle are supposed to be equal to 1,000 sheep. The payment demanded by the government from the squatter in New South Wales is not above a fourth of that exacted in Victoria.

The squatter himself is almost invariably a free-selecter, as he buys the ground on which his homestead stands, and his water frontage, and horse paddock, and wool-shed, to save them from other free-selecters. Not unfrequently he goes much further than this, and by calling in the aid of friends and dependants, makes large purchases, which are entirely opposed to the spirit of the act. For the land laws here, as in all these colonies, have been framed with the view of preventing, – though they have never succeeded in preventing, – the accumulation of large domains in the hands of territorial magnates. I must add here that there are large landowners in the colony whose title-deeds are more ancient than any of the laws which now regulate the sale of lands. In the early days of New South Wales vast grants of land were made to early colonists who undertook the charge of convicts, – were made, too, sometimes under other circumstances not always with strict impartiality. These grantees, or more frequently their descendants, still own the estates thus conferred, and are exempt from rent, and exempt also from selecters. There are others, too, who have purchased large properties. But the bulk of the land of the colony is still the property of the colony. At the close of 1870, 8,437,638 acres had been alienated in the colony, – but there were still left 104,618,436 acres unsold.

In 1872 there were no fewer than 3,495 pastoral holdings, or runs held under the Crown in New South Wales. It should, however, be explained that one squatter generally holds two or three of these runs, and not unfrequently one squatter or one firm of squatters will hold eight or ten. In Queensland there were in the same year 2,310. In Victoria only 973, – the comparative smallness of the number being due to the fact that the greater part of the pastoral land in that colony has been already purchased. In South Australia there are 778 runs. The small number is there due, as far as I could learn, to the fact that the land has been taken up in larger tracts than in the other colonies.

CHAPTER VII

MEAT

By the latest returns which I could get before leaving the colonies, I found that there were in Australia 4,340,638 horned cattle and 41,366,263 sheep. In these numbers the cattle and sheep of New Zealand are not included. In Great Britain and Ireland, at the beginning of 1872, there were 9,346,216 horned cattle and 31,403,500 sheep. The population of Australia then amounted, in round numbers, to 1,700,000. That of Great Britain and Ireland to 32,000,000. There was therefore for every 100 of the population in Australia over 250 cattle and over 2,400 sheep; and for every 100 at home less than 30 head of cattle, and less than 100 sheep. In other words, every Australian has 2½ head of horned cattle and 24 sheep to his or her own share, whereas every Briton staying at home has but a third of a bullock and one sheep. The price of meat ranges from 2*d*. to 4*d*. a pound in Australia, ranging perhaps from 8*d*. to 1*s*. in England. At the same time the wages of a labouring man in Australia are about double the wages of his brother at home. Consequently the labouring man, let his labour be what it may, eats meat three times a day in the colonies, and very generally goes without it altogether at home. That is a plain and, I think, a true statement of the case. In regard to almost all other necessaries of life such great inequality of price and consumption is prevented by the easy transport of the article produced. The price of wheat nearly equalises itself in all the great cities of the world. Tea, sugar, clothing, spirits, and tobacco are carried about so readily, that any difference in their prices is due rather to the fiscal necessities of the country importing them, than to the cost or difficulty of carrying them. But meat has hitherto been an exception to this rule, – from a cause that is manifest to every one. It becomes decomposed, and is destroyed by contact with the air. Hence has arisen the very important question, – important equally to the countries which have too much meat, and to those which have not enough, – whether the skill of man cannot devise some plan by which meat can be carried as securely, and at the same time as cheaply, as other commodities.

The glut of meat, or rather of meat-giving animals, in the colonies, has been so great, that for many years past flocks and herds have been boiled down to produce simply tallow, – because tallow can be easily exported. In 1870 there were, in the one colony of New South Wales, 48 boiling-down establishments, at which in the previous year 290,550 sheep and 246 bullocks were converted into 67,175 cwt. of tallow. The carcases of all these animals, for any other purpose than that of giving tallow, were absolutely wasted, while we at home were paying 11s. or 12s. for a leg of mutton, or going without the mutton because we could not afford to pay for it.

In circumstances such as these, the wit of man has, of course, been set to work to devise plans by which the meat might be taken to the market. Hence have arisen various meat-preserving companies, some of which I visited in Queensland, and have spoken of them in my account of that colony. The difficulty of sending meat home that shall be eatable has been easily overcome. The sheep and oxen are slaughtered. The meat is cut roughly from the bones, and is cooked in closed tins. During the cooking the tins have a vent, which is closed when the cooking is done, and the meat comes out of the tins in England in a condition fit for use. But it does not come out in a condition pleasant to the eye, – nor, as regard flavour and nutrition, can it be said to be equal to fresh meat. The prices in England have latterly ranged from 4½ to 6d. a pound, – and the pound of meat so bought is without bone. There can, I think, be no doubt that these preserved meats, even as they have hitherto reached the English markets, have been of great value to both countries. They have caused a marked rise in the price of sheep, for which, in regard to meat, there was almost no market at all in many parts of the colonies previous to the opening of these establishments; and they have added, at any rate, something to the very limited diet of the poorer classes at home. All the meat which could be exported from Australia, even were it as easy to export meat as flour, would not, at present, go far towards feeding the people of England. But the pastures of Australia are unlimited, and if the trade were fully established, the Australian flocks and herds would be multiplied for the supply of the markets across the water. Australia is not a corn-producing country. Her capabilities, at any rate, do not lie especially in that direction. But she is especially a grazing country. European animals have not only been acclimatized in the colonies with the greatest ease, but have proved themselves to be much more quickly procreative there than in the countries from which they or their ancestors lately come. Horses have bred so freely, that in many places they roam wild through the bush, and are a scourge to the squatters, whose grass they eat, and whose fences they destroy. Oxen also, whose sires and dams have escaped from the herds of the grazier, roam wild and unowned through the distant bush. Sheep are more valuable than horses and oxen, because wool is the staple produce of the country, but sheep have multiplied so quickly, that there are at present in the colonies about twenty-four sheep for every man, woman and child inhabiting them. In Great Britain and Ireland there is not much above a sheep apiece for each individual. If meat can be brought home in a condition to meet the requirements of the British purchasers, the Australian pastures will go as far towards supplying England with meat as do the prairies of the United States with corn, – and they will do so with the advantage of being a part of the empire which they supply.

The one great fault found with the meats hitherto sent to England is that they are over-cooked. Those which I saw and ate before I left England were almost tasteless on account of this fault. They come out, too, from these tins in a guise which creates a prejudice against them, which I have found to be very strong in the minds of poor people. I have heard them say that, if they can't have English meat, they will do without Australian meat. Servants are averse to it, thinking that they are ill-used if asked to eat it. I have found the managers of meat-preserving companies in the colonies quite aware of this, and have thought that they were disposed rather to think that these prejudices should be made to sink before the undoubted superiority of over-cooked meat to no meat at all, than to express a hope that they could remedy the evil by sending the meat to England at the same time secure and with the ordinary juices in it. If the evil be inseparable from the enterprise, of course they are right. The meats, ugly as they are, unappetising, and either dry or greasy, are wholesome, nutritious, and cheap. But if anything better can be done, of course that better will be very welcome.

When I was at Sydney, I was asked to lunch on preserved meats by a gentleman who was managing a Queensland meat-preserving company, of which that distinguished and well-known old colonist, Sir Charles Nicholson, is chairman. My attention was especially called to some roast beef which had been preserved by 'Jones' Patent'. What may be the specialities of Jones' patent I did not learn, but as to that special joint, I protest that I never ate better cold roast beef in my life. It was not over-cooked, and judging from its colour, appearance, and flavour, it might have been cooked and put into the larder on the previous day. Whether it can be made to travel to England, in the same condition, I cannot say. Our host assured me that it would do so, – but he told us at the same time that it could not be sold for less than 8d. a pound. Let the meat be as good as it may, any meat that finds its way ready cooked to England will encounter a certain amount of prejudice, and I fear that the price of 8d. a pound will be too high to stand against this dislike.

But the enterprise which promises most in regard to the exportation of meats from Australia is that at which Mr. Thomas Mort of Sydney has been at work now for many years. No man is better known in New South Wales, – perhaps no one is so highly regarded, – for commercial enterprise, joined to science and ingenuity, as the gentleman I have named. In Sydney Mr. Mort is as well known as are the most familiar objects of the streets, and all who know New South Wales well are ready to declare that no inhabitant of the colony deserves better from her than Mr. Mort. He has set on foot a scheme for sending meat home in ice, – or, to speak more correctly, a scheme for sending meat home in a chamber the temperature of which shall be always kept below the freezing point by the use of ice. As the quantity to be sent home must be very great, in order that the meat may be sold

cheap, and still at a remunerative price, the ice for the purpose
cannot be carried with the meat, but must be daily fabricated
on the journey by chemical appliances. The difficulty is not in
regard to the meat, but in regard to the ice. That ice can be
made in any quantity by a process which I will not attempt to
describe, but in which ammonia is the principal ingredient,
admits of no doubt; but unless it can be made at a low expense,
the speculation will not be remunerative. For years Mr. Mort
has been working at this matter, and has spent very large sums
of money on the work. We know that the first attempt made
at sending frozen Australian meat to England, – in 1873, – was
unsuccessful. But great commercial feats are always heralded
by failures.

   Should this be done, the meat will reach England, not
cooked, nor cut into junks, – but in the shape of joints, as we
at home are accustomed to buy them in the butchers' shops. I
ate at Mr. Mort's house a portion of a leg of mutton, – which
had been frozen I know not for how long, – as to which it
would have been impossible for any one to know that it had
been treated otherwise than in the ordinary way. Mr. Mort
imagines that meat thus prepared may be sold in England for
6d. per pound. The meat when received will simply want
thawing before it is cooked, – as is often necessary with
home-grown meat in winter. If this plan can be carried out,
there is no reason why all the carcases in Australia, not
required for the food of the people there, should not make
their way to the English market, and that in a form which will
not render them unfit even for the most fastidious.

CHAPTER VIII

METALS

I was in New South Wales in October, November, and December, 1871, and again in June and July, 1872. During my former visit very little was said in Sydney about gold or other metals. The tone of the public mind on the subject of mining was very different from that prevailing in Melbourne and Victoria generally. Indeed there seemed to be a feeling, in which I sympathized, that though gold-fields when found should of course be worked, the finding and working them could hardly be regarded as an unmixed good to a community. Such operations led to gambling, disturbed the ways of legitimate commerce, excited men's minds unduly, and were dangerous. Victoria was very keen about gold, believed in gold, was willing to trust to gold for her greatness and population. Victoria prided herself on being a gold colony. Let it be so. New South Wales was conscious of a pride in better things. That perhaps may be taken as an expression of the general mind as I read it. When I returned after an interval of six months all this was changed. No one in Sydney would talk about anything but mining shares. It was not only gold, nor, as I think, chiefly gold, that was in men's mouths. Copper had been found in the west, – in the district between Bathurst and Orange, – and tin in the north, – in New England. It seemed that all they who had been so sober before were now as mad after mining shares as the gentlemen who congregate under the verandah in Melbourne. Everybody had shares in copper, and almost everybody shares in tin. Gentlemen went about with specimens in their pockets, and seemed to think that any conversation diverging from the one important subject was frivolous and unneeded. 'You find us a little changed; don't you?' one old friend of the last year said to me. When I acknowledged that I had recognised an altered tone, he assured me that Sydney had now shaken herself and had ceased to be dull. Copper and tin were at the moment in the ascendant; but gold, too, was very 'lively'. The glories of Hill End, and of Hawkin's Hill in the Tambaroora district, had culminated since I had before been in the colony, and Tambaroora itself had come to be talked about as perhaps the future greatest gold-field of Australia. I was asked whether 'I had visited Tambaroora?' I replied that I had not, and now could not do so. Then I was told that I had then missed the one place in all that eastern world which more than any other would make Australia wealthy, happy, and great.

Though I did not visit Tambaroora or Hill End, I did go to other gold-fields in the colony. Gold, as I have said, was very 'quiet' when I was first in New South Wales, – but it is not therefore to be inferred that there were no gold-seekers in the colony, or that the business was not being carried on with individual enterprise at this or that happy, or less happy, 'rush.' The quiescence described was that of the colony at large, as evinced by the feeling in the metropolis, – as was also subsequently the reverse of quiescence. Since the days of Hargreaves, the reputed discoverer of gold in New South Wales, there has never been a time when the search for gold has been abandoned in New South Wales, or in which large quantities have not been extracted from the earth. Whether the gold-seekers have or have not prospered as a body, it is impossible for any one now to say with accuracy. A statement sufficiently true of the value which has been got from the soil can no doubt be made. Such statements are published from year to year with all the correctness usual to statistical records. We know that in 1862 New South Wales produced gold to the value of £2,212,534, which amount in 1870 had actually fallen down to £763,655. But we do not know, and never can know, all the money expended, and the value of the time expended, not only in extracting the gold when the site of it was found, but in seeking for the sites in which it might perchance be hidden. The search has even been going on, and there has usually been some new 'rush' to which miners could hurry themselves with renewed energy and hopes still green.

To the stranger personally uninterested in the search, it seems that the known presence of gold beneath the earth begets a fury in the minds of men compelling them to search for it, let the risk, the danger, the misery, the probable losses, be what they may. That a thing in itself so rich, so capable of immediately producing all that men most desire, should lie buried in the dirt beneath their feet, loose among the worthless pebbles of the rivers, mixed at haphazard with the deep clumsy lumbering rocks, overcomes the imagination of the unconscious thinker, and takes possession of his heart and brain. For a while he makes no estimate as to the cost of his labours as contrasted with the value of his chance of success. It is gold that is there, – gold that is customarily treasured, gold that is kept within bars and dealt out in tiny morsels as the recognised reward of the sweat of many hours, gold that is thought about, talked about, dreamed about, gold that is longed for, worked for, gambled for, and sinned for; and this gold may be got by the handful, if only the lucky sod of earth be turned. There is a feeling almost impersonal in the would-be miner's breast, as he feels it to be a shame that the dirty earth should hold, and hold without in any way using, the treasure of all treasures that is sweetest to the heart of man. 'Cogere humanos in usus', should certainly be the motto of the gold-seeker.

When I was leaving Sydney in October, 1871, with the intention of travelling westward into the colony, the rush to Gullgong was the rush of the day, and to Gullgong I went in company with the gold commissioners of the district. I have already given some description of Gympie, in Queensland, but Gympie when I was there was an old-established place, and the rush thither was a thing quite of the past. The rush to Gullgong was recent. The great attraction proposed to one visiting a rush seemed to consist in the sight of a congregating together of a great many men, without any of the ordinary comforts of life, and with but few of those appliances which are generally regarded as necessaries. I was told there were 12,000 people at Gullgong, all of whom had collected them-selves thither within a few months. The place had begun to be a place about a month since, – but the real rush had only lately commenced. I confess that I felt an interest in seeing a town without streets, and people collected together with houses made of canvas and rough boards, – an interest akin to that which induces others to see a criminal hung. Our journey thither was one of three days from Bathurst, and was performed in the commissioner's buggy. As we went we saw parties of men, generally ten or twelve in number, either leisurely tramping along the road with their swags on their back, or taking their mid-day siesta under the gum trees. The man who travels on foot in Australia, whether he be a miner, shepherd, shearer, or simply beggar, always carries his 'swag' with him, – which consists of his personal properties rolled up in a blanket. The blanket is an essential necessity, because the man sleeps out in the bush beside a fire. And he carries also a pannikin and a 'billy'. The latter is an open pot in which he boils his water and makes his tea, – for the bushman will always have a bag of tea within his swag. The billy is as essential as the blankets. A bushman of any refinement has the pannikin for drinking; but the rough old chum will dispense with it as a useless luxury, and will drink his tea out of his billy.

And these men were making a rush! They seemed to me to rush very leisurely. I hardly know what I had expected, – whether to see each miner galloping on his steed, or running continually towards his gold-field at the rate of eight miles an hour. Though the influx of men to such a place as Gullgong is a 'rush,' and when very numerous may be described as a stampede, the men themselves are orderly and slow. They have probably done it before, and know, if not the tale of the hare and the tortoise, at any rate the moral of the tale. But the men I saw were journeying some one way and some the other. Backs were turned upon Gullgong as well as faces towards it. Then I learned that such was the case with almost all rushes. Men would try their luck for a month, or perhaps for a fortnight, and if they failed, or did not meet success to satisfy them, would pack up their swags and would betake themselves elsewhere. In this way the population at a rush is very precarious, falling as quickly as it rises, receiving or losing a thousand in a few days, as the place gives or refuses to give its treasures. And, as a matter of course, the trade by which the place is supplied with meat and bread, with tea, sugar and sweet-meats, – the articles of food on which miners chiefly live, – must be equally precarious.

On our route we passed the little town of Sofala, which was in point of time the second established gold-field in New South Wales, Ophir having been the first. Sofala is now a poor little town, containing 644 inhabitants, of whom a considerable portion are Chinese. It is built on a river, the channel of which contained the gold which created the town. The hills rise abruptly on each side of the stream, and give to the place a quaint picturesque appearance, – as though it were altogether out of the world. Here we found about a dozen Chinamen 'fossicking' after gold amidst the dirt of the river, which had already been washed by the first gold-seekers. These men 'washed up' while we were looking on, and we saw them reduce the dirt collected during the day to a few dim specks of the precious metal. They then told us that they estimated their earnings for that day at 1s. each. They seemed to think that this was bad, but were not at all demonstrative in their disappointment.

Two days' travelling from Sofala took us to Gullgong; we stayed a night on the way at Mudgee, a clean little town, celebrated for the special breed of sheep produced in its neighbourhood. At Mudgee I was taken to visit the Mechanics' Institute, at which place I found a great number of well-thumbed novels. There were other books certainly; but the Mudgee shepherds certainly prefer novels. All these small towns have public libraries by one name or another. Mudgee boasts no more than 1,786 inhabitants, but seemed to be very much better off in the way of churches, hotels, institutes, and schools than towns of more than double the size in England.

Gullgong was certainly a rough place when I visited it, but not quite so rough as I had expected. There was an hotel there, at which I got a bedroom to myself, though but a small one, and made only of slabs. But a gorgeously grand edifice was being built over our heads at the time, the old inn being still kept on while the new inn was being built on the same site. The inhabited part of the town consisted of two streets at right angles to each other, in each of which every habitation and shop had probably required but a few days for its erection. The fronts of the shops were covered with large advertisements, – the names and praises of the traders, – as is customary now with all new-fangled marts; but the place

looked more like a fair than a town, – perhaps like one of those
fairs which used to be temporary towns and to be continued
for weeks, – such as some of us have seen at Amsterdam and at
Leipsic. But with this difference, – that in the cities named the
old houses are seen at the back of the new booths, whereas at a
gold-rush there is nothing behind. Everything needful,
however, seemed to be at hand. There were bakers, butchers,
grocers, and dealers in soft goods. There were public-houses
and banks in abundance. There was an auctioneer's establishment, at which I attended the sale of horses and carts. There
was a photographer, and there was a theatre, at which I saw
the 'Colleen Bawn' acted with a great deal of spirit, and a
considerable amount of histrionic talent. After the theatre a
munificent banker of the town gave us an oyster supper, at a
supper-room. It may be inferred, therefore, that the comforts
of life have not been altogether neglected at Gullgong. In the
middle of the day there had been a public dinner or lunch, at
which there was much speaking. I cannot say that the
Gullgong oratory was as good as the Gullgong acting or the
Gullgong oysters.

I think that the town of Gullgong, including its general
inhabitants and mode of life, was more interesting to me even
than the mines. I was charmed to hear that a few nights before
there had been a most successful public ball. But I was
distressed to find that there had been some heart-burning.
Where was the line to be drawn in reference to the ladies? The
postmistress would not attend the ball unless barmaids were
excluded. The barmaids, – I think very properly, – were
admitted, and the postmistress, who enjoyed the reputation of
being the beauty of Gullgong, remained at home.

Of course, having come to Gullgong, I had to see the mines.
I went down the shaft of one, 150 feet deep, with my foot in
the noose of a rope. Having offered to descend, I did not like
to go back from my word when the moment came; but as the
light of day faded from my descending eyes, and as I
remembered that I was being lowered by the operations of a
horse who might take it into his brutish head to lower me at
any rate he pleased, – or not to lower me at all, but to keep me
suspended in that dark abyss, – I own that my heart gave way,
and that I wished I had been less courageous. But I went

down, and I came up again, – and I found six or seven men working at the bottom of the hole. I afterwards saw the alluvial dirt brought up from some other hole, puddled and washed, and the gold extracted. When extracted it was carried away in a tin pannikin, – which I thought detracted much from the splendour of the result.

Of the men around me some were miners working for wages, and some were shareholders, each probably with a large stake in the concern. I could not in the least tell which was which. They were all dressed alike, and there was nothing of the master and the man in the tone of their conversation. Among those present at the washing up, there were two Italians, an American, a German, and a Scotchman, who I learned were partners in the property. The important task of conducting the last wash, of throwing away for ever the stones and dirt from which the gold had sunk, was on this occasion confided to the hands of the American. The gold was carried away in a pannikin by the German. Why should he not have put in his fingers and appropriated an ounce of the fragments to his own use? I know it is mean to suspect; but among us in England checks are necessary. No doubt the German to whom the pannikin was confided was respected far and wide for his honesty. Of the courtesy of all these men it is impossible to speak too highly, or of the civility of the miners generally; and in saying this I do not allude to the demeanour of the men to myself or to other chance visitors, but to their ordinary mode of conducting themselves. The Australian miner when he is in work never drinks, – and seems to feel a pride in his courtesy. It must be understood that his is not a submissive deportment, prone to the touching of hats and a silent reverence of his betters, – but a manly bearing, which enables him to express himself freely, but which never verges on distasteful familiarity.

I found that miners working for wages at Gullgong were earning from £2 10s. to £3 a week, – but I found also that many were there who could not get such work to do. No doubt a glut of labour would soon tend to lower the wages, – but the population did not seem to be fixed enough to have produced that result. Men came, and tried their fortune on little speculations of their own, and failed. Then, if they could

not at once get wages to their mind, they took up their swags
and departed to some other rush. I found also that many men
were employed on the most singular and easiest task that I
ever met in my travels. When a mining speculator had taken
out his claim to a piece of land, the law required him to occupy
it. If he did not at once work it, he must hold it by his own
bodily presence or by that of some deputy for at least two
hours a day. I think I was told that this minimum of
occupation for two hours must be before noon, either from
nine to eleven or from ten to twelve. This duty was called
'shepherding', – and the wages of a man to shepherd a claim
were 25s. a week. But these mining shepherds are not miners.
I asked a miner whether it would not suit him to earn 25s. a
week by shepherding, and then to take a day's work, or a part
of a day's work, at his own enterprise. But he gave me to
understand that shepherding a claim was dishonourable for a
miner.

It seemed to me, when I was at Gullgong, that the rush was
not regarded as a success. The population was decreasing; and
though much gold had been extracted, much useless labour
had been expended on 'duffers'. A shaft sunk without any
produce from it is a duffer. Looking around, an inexperienced
stranger would think that gold about Gullgong was ubiquitous. There were holes everywhere, and the ugly masses of
upturned clay which always mark the gold-seeker's presence.
But of these excavations the majority were duffers. It is the
duffering part of the business which makes it all so sad. So
much work is done from which there is positively no return!

I came away from Gullgong with a feeling that I had hardly
seen the rush in its most characteristic phase. The rush had
been rushed before I reached it. The place had become to a
degree settled, – and people were going out at any rate as fast
as they were coming in. But there was another rush to a place
about 150 miles from Gullgong, – a place called Currajong,
which was described to me as being quite new, and I went
there also. It was new, and a more wretched spot I never saw
in my life. I was told by one inhabitant that there were over
2,000 people, – by another that there were not above 500. Of
the number I could not at all judge myself, either by the
concourse of people or of habitations. There were a few

public-houses roughly constructed of timber, and a shop or two for the sale of general articles. The miners and their followers were living in tents scattered here and there among the holes they were digging. When gold was 'struck' at any of these holes, – when enough had been found to be regarded as a probable fore-runner of commercial success, – a red flag was hoisted. Here and there I saw the red flag, – but the holes and adjacent heaps at which there were no red flags were as legion to the distinguished few.

At Gullgong I had found satisfied miners, – men who said that they were doing well; at Currajong everybody seemed to be disappointed, unhappy and hopeless. The rush, it was found, was going to turn out a 'duffer' altogether. The street of the place, if it can be said to have had a street, consisted of a bush road, wider and more trodden than usual, with the trees standing close around, though the undergrowth and shrubs have been burned or otherwise used, and the trees themselves mutilated. Everywhere through the bush there were little tents, and holes and heaps. I visited one spot at which three men were working, one below filling a bucket, and two above drawing the bucket up. This they had been doing for a fortnight, and had found nothing. They did it for three weeks longer, and still finding no gold, had then gone away. One of them was the son of an English gentleman, who had thought that Australian gold-mining might probably be a road to easy wealth. He got his experience at Currajong, but he got nothing else. I can fancy no more heart-breaking occupation than the work of trundling up dirt out of a hole eight hours a day without results. There were drunken people about Currajong, – which I had not seen elsewhere, – and a rowdy aspect which made me think ill of the prospects of the place. I was told subsequently that for a while it was not a success, and that many left in disgust; but that afterwards gold-bearing quartz was found in large quantities, and that they who had stuck to the place through its early misfortunes did well there. Currajong, when I saw it, seemed to be the most hopelessly disappointing place I had visited in the colonies.

New South Wales contains coal as well as gold, and has coal-mines which are worked successfully. In this respect she is blessed above any other of these colonies. Coal is heard of and talked about in, I think, every province of Australia, – and specimens are shown in proof of its existence; but coal is worked successfully in New South Wales, and as yet in New South Wales only. Newcastle, as the head-quarters of Australian coal is properly called, has become the second city of the colony. Coal is the mineral product of New South Wales next in value to gold, but is so at a very great distance. The value of the gold raised in 1862 and 1870 was for the former year £2,212,534, and for the latter £763,655. That of the coal produced in the same years was, in 1862, £476,522, and for 1870 £316,385. As regards both there had been a falling off in value, – that of the gold being by about two-thirds. That in the coal is small, and does not at all indicate the amount produced, but only the price of the article. In 1862 thirty-three coal-mines in New South Wales produced 342,067 tons of coals, – and in 1870 thirty-two mines produced 868,564 tons. It seems that the increase in produce has gone on almost steadily, whereas the price has fluctuated considerably. In 1862 the coals at the pit's mouth were worth very nearly 13s. a ton, whereas in 1870, they were not worth 8s. At the end of 1871, when I visited Newcastle, they were still somewhat lower. The shareholders of coal-mines doubtless regard this falling-off in price as a great calamity, but the consumers of coal in Sydney and Melbourne and the owners of steam-ships plying to and from the colonies probably regard the matter in a different light.

In England we are accustomed to think that the possession of coal is the greatest blessing which Providence has bestowed upon us, and to believe that we owe to it our wealth, our population, and our greatness. I doubt whether there is a man of business in Great Britain who would wish to exchange our coal-mines for gold-fields. When the idea is presented to our minds we at once feel that the really productive powers of coal must be much more fertile in producing actual wealth than any amount of a metal, the value of which is in truth little more than nominal. No increase in the production of coal would at all diminish the real value of the article; but were the production to be increased suddenly, violently, and to a great extent, the value of the metal would fall away in a quickly increasing ratio in accordance with the increase of production.

Its value depends on its comparative rarity, – and, therefore, when we are told of some probable future development of Australian gold-fields at a hitherto unprecedented rate; when we are assured that Australian gold is as yet in its infancy, – as I have been assured very often, – we feel that even should it be so, the expected wealth will not follow the new discoveries. Should it come very quickly, the dislocation of prices, which is now being effected slowly by the gradual increase in the amount, and therefore gradual decline in the value of gold, would become rapid, and therefore ruinous to many. In such a case the wealth of the world would be increased only as far as gold is required, – not as wealth, – but as a symbol of wealth. Whereas every additional ton of coal that we get will contain as much power as every ton of coal that was got before it. Therefore, although the coal of Newcastle and Wollongong, in the present price paid for it, falls very far behind the gold of New South Wales, I regard coal as being the more important produce of the two. Had there been no coal found in New South Wales almost every source of wealth in Australia would have been stunted. Steamers could not have plied, nor rail-ways have been worked, unless at prices which would have made them inaccessible to the community. All machinery for mines and other works must have been procured from Europe. The copper must have been sent home unsmelted, and therefore at treble the freight now paid for it. It is useless to expatiate on this, – as who is there that does not know that a country with coal ought to be rich and blessed?

The most extensive coal region of Australia is that in the valley of the Hunter River, which empties itself into the sea at Newcastle, about 75 miles north of Sydney. The collieries are found for many miles up the river, – indeed along its whole length up to the base of the mountain ranges, – and are worked within three or four miles of Newcastle. They rejoice in the old well-known North of England colliers' names, – such as Wallsend, Lampton, Hexham, Alnwick, and the like. I should probably be thought guilty of exaggeration if I were to say that they are inexhaustible. After the disputes which have latterly taken place at home as to the growth, production, and consumption of coal, a plain man hardly dares to have an opinion on the matter. But there is a world of coal around

Newcastle, – which looks as though it would suffice for the wants of the South-eastern people to the end of time.

About 40 miles south of Sydney there is another coal-field, in the Illawarra district, for which Wollongong is the seaport. I did not visit Wollongong, but I learned that there were five different mines worked there, from which about 90,000 tons of coal were extracted in 1870. To the west of Sydney, there have also lately been opened coal-mines at Hartley, – which are as yet young, but which in 1870 produced 2,600 tons of coal. The Hartley coal is, I believe, used only for the production of gas; but shale is found there, and also at American creek, near Wollongong, from which kerosene is made. It is boasted on behalf of the shale oil of New South Wales that it is better than the American, – the advantage in favour of the Australian oil being that it will not ignite at a temperature ten degrees higher than that at which the purest American oil breaks into fire. I give this statement merely as I got it from the pages of the Report of the International Exhibition at Sydney, to which I have before referred, – and not as the result of any experiments made by myself into the qualities of kerosene.

I have said above that when I returned to Sydney I found all my formerly quiet-going friends in that city very much disturbed, and many of them considerably elated in regard to copper and tin. I can say nothing, from my own observation, on the resources of the colony as far as these metals were concerned. Copper-mines had previously been worked in the Orange district, and also near Lake George in the Goulbourn district, but not to such an extent as to have become a source of great public interest. Iron also has been found and worked at Nattai, in the south, but never as yet with any profit to the proprietors. That there is iron in New South Wales is a matter beyond doubt. Silver also has been found at Bronlee and Murrurundi, and cinnabar at Rylstone. There were also diamond-mines on the Cudgegong River, near to Rylstone, which some time since were worked by an Australian Diamond Mining Company; but the expenses exceeded the returns, and the work has been abandoned.

It was believed of Australia, when Great Britain first planted her colonies there, that she would prove to be a country

almost blank and barren in regard to minerals. It seems,
however, now, that few countries on the earth are richer in
ores than she is. If iron can be found on her hills, and worked,
she will probably become as populous and as rich as the
United States.

In the meantime the lately awakened but now energetic
speculators of New South Wales are all making fortunes out of
tin and copper.

CHAPTER IX

COUNTRY LIFE IN THE BUSH

When in New South Wales I spent a month at a small squatter's station in the distant bush, and as the difference between bush life in Australia and country life in England is more marked than I think any other difference between the two countries, I propose to describe the thing as I found it. I had already stayed at various sheep-stations in Queensland, but only for a few days at each; and these had been generally large places, where perhaps from one to two hundred thousand sheep were shorn, – and into which consequently the comforts and luxuries of civilised life had been imported. These were hardly typical bush residences. At that to which I now went, a young squatter beginning life owned not much more than ten thousand sheep, and was living quite 'in the rough.' The number of sheep at these stations will generally indicate with fair accuracy the mode of life at the head station. A hundred thousand sheep and upwards require a professed man-cook and a butler to look after them; forty thousand sheep cannot be shorn without a piano; twenty thousand is the lowest number that renders napkins at dinner imperative. Ten thousand require absolute plenty, meat in plenty, tea in plenty, brandy and water and colonial wine in plenty, but do not expect champagne, sherry, or made dishes, and are supposed to be content with continued mutton or continued beef, – as the squatter may at the time be in the way of killing sheep or oxen. During this month we killed mutton. After six months I returned to the same station, and beef was the provision of the day. Wool had gone up, and sheep had become valuable, and the squatter could not be persuaded to kill a sheep for love or money. He bought cattle as he wanted them, and found that his beef cost him 1½*d.* a pound.

The station I visited, and which I will call M—, was about 250 miles west of Sydney, and was decidedly in the bush. I have

already endeavoured to explain that nearly every place beyond
the influences of big towns is called 'bush,' – even though
there should not be a tree to be seen around; but in reaching
this place I journeyed for three days after leaving the railway
through continuous woodland, doing about forty miles a day
in a buggy. The house stood on a small creek, – hardly to be
called a rivulet, because the water does not continually run,
and in dry weather lies only in a succession of water-holes, –
and was surrounded by interminable forest. Close around it
was the home-paddock, railed in, and containing about 50
acres. Such an enclosure about a gentleman's house in England
is an appendage of great value, and constitutes with some who
are ambitious almost a little park. In the bush it is little more
thought of than as so much waste ground round the house.
Two or three cows may run in it, or a horse or two for
immediate use. It is generally found convenient to have a
horse near the house for the sake of 'running in' other horses.
One horse in the stable to catch two horses in the home-
paddock wherewith four horses when wanted may be run in
from the horse-paddock, make together a combination which
in the bush is considered to be economical and convenient. At
M— the home-paddock was partially cleared of timber, and
was pretty enough. Outside it, meeting the creek both before
and behind, was the horse-paddock, containing about 250
acres. This was supposed to be the domain appropriated to the
horses of the establishment needed for the working of it. At
that time there were about twenty, and I believe that there was
not one too many. My young friend also had his rams here
during a portion of the year, but hardly expected more from
so small an enclosure than food for the animals required for
use. A public road, such as bush roads are, ran through the
horse-paddock, – very inconvenient in that it caused the gates
to be left open, and brought travellers that way whose
presence was hardly desirable, but not without compensation,
as a postman with the mails passed each way twice a week.
The postman was a great blessing. If he wanted food for
himself or his horse, he got it; and in return he complied with
all requests made to him, conveying letters, telegrams, and
messages with wondrous accuracy. A mailman coming by, –
they are mailmen and not postmen in the bush, – is a great

addition to the comforts of bush life. At the back of the horse-paddock was the wool-shed paddock, containing about 1,200 acres, with the wool-shed at one corner of it, distant about a mile from the house. For many reasons the wool-shed should not be close. The squatter does not want to have his shearers always in the kitchen, nor to hear their voices close to his verandah. But as it is well for his superintendent to be there constantly during the shearing, and for himself to be there often, any great distance is inconvenient. As my young friend sorted his own wool himself, he was generally in the wool-shed before the shearers, and did not leave it till long after they had 'knocked off' work. The wool-shed was a wooden edifice, made of rough timber, roofed with bark, divided into pens, with room for eleven men to shear, and with outside pens for the shorn sheep as they leave the men's hands, – a pen for each shearer. It was constructed to hold about 300 sheep, – and that number would be put into it over-night, so that, even should rain come, there might be so many ready for the shearers in the morning, – for sheep cannot be shorn when wet. The form of the shed was that of the letter L, the base, however, being considerably larger than the upstroke. Along the base the shearers worked. At the corner were the sorting-table, and divided cribs for the different fleeces. In the upper part of the letter the wool was packed, and pressed, and stored, till the drays should come and take it away. My friend acknowledged that he did not think much of his own house, though he had built it himself, – but he was proud of his wool-shed, which was also the creation of his own ingenuity. About a quarter of a mile from the wool-shed was the shearers' hut, in which the men slept, and ate, and smoked their pipes. They had their own cook, who on this occasion was a Chinaman, – and, as is always the case with shearers, they gave their cook enough to do. He was generally to be seen outside the door of the hut chopping up onions. The cook had 25s. a week and his rations, – the shearers were earning on an average about 7s. 6d. a day, which was considered bad work. There was rain, and the weather was against the men. the shearers bought their own food from the head station, paying at the rate of 7s 6d. a week each for it.

There were three other paddocks on the run, – one containing 12,000 acres, and the others 7,000 acres each. The greater part of the fencing necessary for these domains had been put up by my friend since his occupation at an average cost of £25 a mile. There were over forty miles of fencing on the run, made either with logs laid at length on short round blocks, – called in the bush chock and log, – or of bushes laid lengthways and staked down with forked timber. This fencing suffices for sheep, but would be of no use at all on a run intended for cattle. When a run is not fenced, each flock of sheep requires a shepherd, and the sheep are brought up at night to an enclosure close to the shepherd's hut. When a run is 'paddocked', shepherds are not required, – but boundary-riders are employed, each of whom is supplied with two horses, and these men are responsible not only for the sheep but for the fences. They should see every portion of their fences at any rate three times a week, and repair the breaches. A bush fence is easily broken down, but is as easily put up again.

The natural grasses of the bush in the locality of which I am speaking would carry in ordinary weather a sheep to three acres. When the weather was damp and warm it would do much more; when there was either frost or drought, it would not do so much. At M— there was back ground outside the paddocks as extensive as the fenced area, and it was computed that the run might carry safely about 16,000 sheep.

The house was built at right angles to the creek, to the edge of which the little garden ran. It was of course only of one storey. A squatter rarely builds a two-storied house till he be a very large squatter indeed, and then his habitation loses most of the characteristics of the bush. It was of one storey, and contained but three rooms, – a sitting-room in the middle and a bedroom on each side, – but along the front there ran a verandah twelve feet wide, in which everybody lived, – using the sitting-room simply for meals. Life in the bush would be nothing without a verandah. The men of course spend their days mostly out of doors, – but in the evenings the verandahs are delightful. Here are congregated lounging chairs, generally very rough, but always comfortable, – with tables, sofas, and feminine nicknacks, if there be ladies, till the place has the appearance of a room open to the heavens. A verandah to be perfect should be curtained against the sun, and should be sheltered from the heat by creepers. Behind the house, about thirty yards distant from it, was the kitchen, with a servants' room attached to it, – and behind that again another edifice called the cottage, consisting of two rooms, in which slept the young men who were about the place, – for it must be remembered that there always are young men about a squatter's station. Then there were other buildings, – forming a quadrangle, which however was never as neat as such homestead quadrangle should be. There was a rough stable, and a rougher coach-house, – and that indispensable accessory the store-room. The place was altogether rough, and certainly not well kept; but it was comfortable and picturesque, and easily susceptible of improvement when increasing flocks and high prices for wool would justify the expenditure.

Almost all these pastoral homesteads are thus made up of various cottages, – till sometimes the place assumes the appearance of a village. When the station is large there will often be a church and a school, – and a separate house for strangers, and a shop for the stores, and an office. At M— no such grandeur had as yet displayed itself. But there was a garden, – in which the opossums would eat the vegetables, – and an orchard had been commenced.

There was one house at a distance of only three miles, which was a great drawback to my friend's happiness, – for it was inhabited by a free-selecter and a publican. I rather liked the publican, as he got up a kangaroo hunt for me, – but the vicinity of grog was looked upon as a serious evil by the squatter. And yet the men never drank when they were at work, – would work for weeks without anything stronger than tea. But if, on an occasion, any one of the station hands did take to drink, he would stay and drink till he was turned out of the house on the plea that he had consumed all his money. This public-house was a blistering thorn in the side of my friend. A gold-field town, whence the letters came, was twelve miles distant; but this was visited as rarely as possible, and was regarded as almost obtrusive in having caused itself to be built in a pastoral district. The nearest neighbours for any social purpose was another squatter, twenty-five miles off.

Of social gatherings, such as we know them, there are none in the bush. Squatters do not go out to dine, or ask each other to dinner. As a rule, I think, they rarely invite each other for country visiting. But they make the free-est use of each other's houses, – so that society of a certain kind is created. They do not make visits exclusively of pleasure, – but when business calls them from home they make no scruple of riding up to each other's doors, and demanding hospitality. A bush house is never considered to be full. If there be not rooms apiece for the guests, the men are put together and the women together. If there be not bedsteads, beds are made up on the floors. If room be still lacking, the young men wrap themselves in blankets and stretch themselves in the verandah. It is a point of honour that the house shall never be full, – unless some one very odious comes the way. But even for those who are odious shelter and food are provided in some outside hut or barrack.

I was at M— washing and shearing. I speak of course of the washing of sheep. It was the busiest time of the year, and the squatter himself was always out soon after five, and rarely back at the house in time for dinner at eight. He had two assistants, one of whom was his permanent first lieutenant on the run, and the other was borrowed for the occasion. The three, who were all young, certainly worked much harder than any other men about the place, and seemed to have more on hand than a British prime minister in June. I rode about at my ease, – from the washpool to the wool-shed, and from the wool-shed to the kangaroos, – giving now and then a fantastic opinion as to the doing of the work, criticising the roughness of the mode in which the poor brutes were hauled into the water, or the cruelty with which they were wounded by the shearers. But my friends were terribly in earnest. Now and again a man would misbehave, and squatters' law had to be exercised with prompt decision. If a man would not work, or worked amiss, he was sent away with a curt warning, – for the deed of agreement which is always drawn up, gives the squatter the power of judging as to the man's deficiency, and of punishing him for being deficient. The sheep were always being washed, and always being shorn, – but if the rain should come between the two operations, all would be spoilt. Rain did come, – but not thorough rain, and all was not spoilt. And then the 'yarding' of sheep by hundreds at a time, – getting them through one set of pens before washing, and through another set before shearing, – having them ready for the morning's work, and finished off before the dark night came, – weighing out tea and sugar and flour for the men, killing and preparing meat for them, sorting and packing the wool, pressing and labelling the bales, – all seemed to demand more than Herculean energy. At large stations this is done easily, because the greater number admit of divided labour. It seemed to me that the care of ten thousand sheep was the most difficult task that a man could have imposed upon him.

Those rides through the forest, either when I was alone or when I could get my host to go with me, – which was rarely, unless on a Sunday afternoon, – were very pleasant. The melancholy note of the magpie was almost the only sound that was heard. Occasionally kangaroos would be seen, – two or three staring about them after a half-tame fashion, as though they had not as yet made up their mind whether it would be necessary for them to run. When approached they would move, – always in a line, and with apparent leisure till pursued. Then they would bound away, one here and one there, at a pace which made it impossible for a single horseman to get near them in a thickly timbered country. It was all wood. There arose at last a feeling that go where one might through the forest, one was never going anywhere. It was all picturesque, – for there was rocky ground here and there and hills in the distance, and the trees were not too close for the making of pretty vistas through them, – but it was all the same. One might ride on, to the right or to the left, or might turn back, and there was ever the same view. And there were no objects to reach, unless it was the paddock fence. And when the paddock fence was jumped, then it was the same thing again. Looking around, one could tell by no outward sign whether one was inside or outside the boundary, – whether one was two miles or ten miles from the station.

Perhaps the most astonishing phenomenon on these runs is the apparent paucity of sheep. As a fact, there are thousands all round; but unless looked for they are never seen; and even when looked for by inexperienced eyes are often missed. If the reader will bear in mind that an enclosure of 12,000 acres contains more than eighteen square miles, he will understand how unlike to anything in England must be even the enclosed country in Australia. One seems to ride for ever and to come to nothing, and to relinquish at last the very idea of an object. Nevertheless, it was very pleasant. Of all places that I was ever in this place seemed to be the fittest for contemplation. There was no record of the hours but the light. When it was night work would be over. The men would cease as the sun was setting, – but the masters would continue till the darkness had come upon them.

There were four or five meals in the day. There was an early breakfast in the cottage for the young men, – there was another breakfast at nine for those who were idle, – for the ladies who were there and for myself. There was lunch at about two, to which one or two from the wool-shed might or might not rush in as things were going with them, – and there was dinner at about eight o'clock. My wife had brought a cook with her from England who was invaluable, – or would have been had she not found a husband for herself when she had been about a month in the bush. But in spite of her love, and her engagement to a man who was considerably above her in position, she was true to us while she remained at M—, and did her best to make us all comfortable. She was a good-looking, strong woman, of excellent temper, who could do anything she put her hand to, from hairdressing to confectionery up to making butter and brewing beer. I saw her six months afterwards, – 'quite the lady', but ready for any kind of work that might come in her way. When I think of her, I feel that no woman of that kind ought, as regards herself, to stay in England if she can take herself or get herself taken to the colonies. I mention our cook, because her assistance certainly tended very greatly to our increased comfort. The viands provided were mutton, bread, vegetables, and tea. Potatoes were purchased as an ordinary part of the station stores, and the opossums had left us lettuce, tomatoes, and a few cabbages. Dinner was always dignified with soup and salad, – which must not, however, be regarded as being within the ordinary bush dietary. In other respects the meals were all alike. There was mutton in every shape, and there was always tea. Tea at a squatter's table, – at the table of a squatter who has not yet advanced himself to a man-cook or butler, and a two-storied house, – is absolutely indispensable. At this squatter's table there was colonial wine and there was brandy, – produced chiefly to supply my wants; but there was always tea. The young men when they came in, hot and fagged with their day's work, would take a glass of brandy and water standing, as a working man with us takes his glass of beer at a bar. But when they sat down with their dinners before them, the tea-cup did for them what the wine-glass does for us. The practice is so invariable that any shepherd whose hut you may visit will show his courtesy by asking you to take a pannikin of tea. In supplying stores to men, tea and sugar, flour and meat, are the four things which are included as a matter of course. The tea is always bought by the chest, and was sold by the merchant at the rate of 1s.6d. a pound. There was but one class of tea at the station, which I found to be preferable to very much that I am called upon to drink in England.

The recreations of the evening consisted chiefly of tobacco in the verandah. I did endeavour to institute a whist table, but I found that my friends, who were wonderfully good in regard to the age and points of a sheep, and who could tell to the fraction of a penny what the wool of each was worth by the pound, never could be got to remember the highest card of the suit. I should not have minded that had they not so manifestly despised me for regarding such knowledge as important. They were right, no doubt, as the points of a sheep are of more importance than the pips of a card, and the human mind will hardly admit of the two together. Whist is a jealous mistress, – and so is a sheep-station.

I have been at very many bush houses, – at over thirty different stations in the different colonies, – but at not one, as I think, in which I have not found a fair provision of books. It is universally recognised among squatters that a man who settles down in the bush without books is preparing for himself a miserable future life. That the books are always used when they are there I will not say. That they are used less frequently than they should be used I do not doubt. When men come in from physical work, hungry, tired, – with the feeling that they have earned an hour or two of ease by many hours of labour, – they are apt to claim the right to allow their minds to rest as well as their limbs. Who does not know how very much this is the case at home, even among young men and women in our

towns, who cannot plead the same excuse of real bodily
fatigue? That it should be so is a pity of pities, – not on the
score chiefly of information lost or of ignorance perpetuated;
but because the power of doing that which should be the one
recreation and great solace of our declining years perishes
from desuetude, and cannot be renewed when age has come
upon us. But I think that this folly is hardly more general in
the Australian bush than in English cities. There are books to
be read, – and the young squatter, when the evening comes
upon him, has no other recreation to entice him. He has no
club, no billiard table, no public-house which he can frequent.
Balls and festivities are very rare. He probably marries early,
and lives the life of a young patriarch, lord of everything
around him, and master of every man he meets on his day's
ride. Of course there are many who have risen to this from
lower things, – who have become squatters, without any early
education, who have been butchers, drovers, or perhaps
shepherds themselves. That they should not be acquainted
with books is a matter of course. They have lacked the practice
in youth of which I have just spoken. But among those who
have had the advantage of early nurture, and have been taught
to handle books familiarly when young, I think that reading is
at least as customary as it is with young men in London. The
authors I found most popular were certainly Shakespeare,
Dickens and Macaulay. I would back the chance of finding
Macaulay's Essays at a station against that of any book in the
language except Shakespeare. To have a Shakespeare is a point
of honour with every man who owns a book at all, – whether
he reads it or leaves it unread.

I have said that squatters marry early. The reasons for doing
so are very strong; and those reasons for not doing so, which
are terribly familiar to us at home, hardly exist in the bush.
The man is alone, and can have at any rate no female
companionship unless he marry. In ordinary life, as we know
it, the unmarried man enjoys as many comforts, – unfortunately, perhaps, more luxuries, – than do they who take to
themselves wives. But in the bush the unmarried man is very
desolate, and will probably soon become forlorn and wretched
in his mode of life. He will hardly get a woman who will cook
for him decently, or will sew a button on his shirt when it is

wanted. And he will soon care nothing how his dinner is cooked, and whether his shirt be with or without a button. On the other hand, the cost of his household when he is married will hardly be more than when he is single. If his wife know how to keep a bush house, her presence will almost be a saving to him. At home, in England, the young man when he marries has to migrate from his lodgings to a house; he must make up an establishment, buy furniture, hire servants, and enter altogether upon a new phase of life. He must have ready money in his pocket to begin with, and a future income probably very much in advance of that he has hitherto been expected to expend. But on a station there is nothing of the kind. There is the house, in which it may be necessary to put a few additional comforts. There is the establishment, – already on so large a scale in consequence of the necessity of supplying men with rations that no recognised increase is created. When children come, and education is needed, expenses of course will grow; but at first the thing is so easy that the young squatter simply goes out in his buggy and brings home the daughter of some other squatter, – after a little ceremony performed in the nearest church.

As a consequence of this, life in the bush is decent and moral. The bulk of the labour is performed by a nomad tribe, who wander in quest of their work, and are hired only for a time. This is of course the case in regard to washing sheep and shearing them. It is equally so when fences are to be made, or ground to be cleared, or trees to be 'rung'. The ringing of trees consists of cutting the bark through all round, so that the tree cease to suck up the strength of the earth for its nutrition, and shall die. For all these operations temporary work is of course required, and the squatter seldom knows whether the men he employs be married or single. They come and go, and are known by queer nicknames or are known by no names at all. They probably have their wives elsewhere, and return to them for a season. They are rough to look at, dirty in appearance, shaggy, with long hair, men who, when they are in the bush, live in huts, and hardly know what a bed is. But they work hard, and are both honest and civil. Theft among them is almost unknown. Men are constantly hired without any character but that which they give themselves; and the squatters find from experience that the men are able to do that which they declare themselves capable of performing. There will be exceptions, but such is the rule. Their one great fault is drunkenness, – and yet they are sober to a marvel. As I have said before, they will work for months without touching spirits, – but their very abstinence creates a craving desire which, when it is satisfied, will satisfy itself with nothing short of brutal excess. Among the masters of these men, – among squatters with their superintendents and overseers, – drinking is not a common fault. I have seen a squatter drunk. I have seen a squatter very drunk. But he was a jovial exception.

Squatters, I think, do not as a rule go very frequently to church. Churches are not near to them, and as they are always either driving in buggies or riding on horseback in pursuance of their ordinary occupations, on Sundays they are not ready to add perhaps thirty miles, perhaps forty, to their week's work in quest of a sermon. I have spoken of stations which possessed churches of their own. When that is the case, the squatter is generally the parson for three Sundays, – being relieved by a real, but itinerant, clergyman on the fourth. I am, however, bound to acknowledge that Sabbath-day observances are laxly kept in the bush.

The resident squatter is generally a young man, – one at least not past the prime of life. For this state of things there are sundry causes. The squatter who succeeds in life, as he grows old does not cease to be a squatter. He sticks to his wool as closely as the lawyer does to his wig, or the banker to his ledger. He knows well every shilling that is spent and made. But he becomes an absentee squatter, – having a son, or a junior partner, or perhaps a manager, to manage the run and to send him the accounts. The money comes into his hand readily, as the produce of a sheep-station is never sold on the spot. London is almost always the rich squatter's market. then again the work to be done is hardly fitted for an old man. All that an old man can do, he can do away from the station. He has become tired of buggies and bucking horses, perhaps tired of tea and mutton; and he makes himself comfortable in a town.

And many no doubt are ruined before they grow to be old, – for to tell the truth of it, the growing of wool is at the best a precarious trade. Thousands have made their fortunes at it, –

but thousands also with small capitals have gone to the wall in
their struggles, and have been no more heard of among the
stations. What becomes of them I cannot say. Who knows the
fate of the ruined man? The business is always on a large scale,
– and being large and also precarious cannot but be dangerous.
With wool ranging from 1s. to 2s. a pound, a squatter with
20,000 sheep, and a small capital, may be made by high prices,
or marred by low prices, in one year. The year of favourable
circumstances in regard to weather and climate may put him at
his ease for life, – and a year's drought may beggar him. This
also tends to weed out the old men, and leave the young men
in possession. At fifty the squatter can afford either to live in
town or in England, – or else he can no longer afford to live on
his station.

CHAPTER X

THE RIVERINA

As in the old European countries so in the colonies, different districts have acquired different names, which have much significance in men's minds and are understood with sufficient clearness, though they have not recognised municipal or political standing. In New South Wales a northern part of the colony is called New England; a district lying on the seaboard south of Sydney is called Illawarra; and to the west, in the midst of the great rivers of the continent, is the Riverina, or Mesopotamia of New South Wales. The Riverina has characteristics of its own so marked and so important that they demand recognition from any one who desires to understand the position of the Australian colonies generally. It is bounded throughout on the south by the River Murray, – having in that direction a certain limit, as the Murray is the northern frontier of Victoria. But it has no other certain boundary, – unless it be the one hundred and forty-first line of east longitude on its western frontier, which line is the proclaimed division of South Australia and New South Wales. To the north it runs away into undefined space. To the east there is no recognised limitation by which it is divided from the remainder of the colony. The one hundred and forty-eighth line of longitude may perhaps be taken as the best demarcation that can be expressed; though this would be by no means correct throughout, as the squatters on the Boyne and the Macquarie rivers to the north, who are to the west of that line, certainly do not consider themselves as belonging to the Riverina. But in fact the Riverina consists of that part of the colony of New South Wales which finds that Melbourne or Adelaide are markets easier of approach than Sydney, the capital of their own colony. The geographical facts which have brought about this result, give to the people of the Riverina their distinctive interests, and force upon them a feeling opposed in politics to that which is general through the more thickly populated eastern half of the colony.

The Riverina, in area, comprises perhaps a full moiety of New South Wales, though in population it contains but little more than a twentieth part of the whole. The population of the colony in round numbers is half a million; that of the Riverina about 28,000. As the limits of the district cannot be defined with certainty, neither, of course, can the population be stated with accuracy. It lies, as the name implies, among the rivers, – among the only well-known great rivers of the continent. These rivers, with many tributaries, are the Murray, the Murrumbidgee running into the Murray, the Lachlan running into the Murrumbidgee, and the Darling running into the Murray below the Murrumbidgee. The Murray, carrying down the waters of an immense portion of the great Australian plains, finds its way into the sea at last by so poor an aperture as to forbid internal navigation on a scale greater than that which in other countries is achieved by canals. And the navigation afforded by these natural waters is only spasmodic. During a portion of the year it is interrupted by drought. At uncertain seasons in some years it is stopped by floods. Consequently large towns have not arisen on the river banks. And again nearly the whole of this country is unfit for agriculture. Though the soil in many parts of it is rich, the climate will not allow the soil to produce wheat. The average rainfall is not above fourteen inches in the year, – and the summer heats are very intense. Nevertheless, in the southern parts of the district, and on the frontages of the rivers, free-selecters are numerous, – to the great and, as I think, irrational displeasure of the squatters, for the free-selecter, if he cannot live on his land, must work for the squatter's wages. To the south-east, around Albury and Wagga Wagga, – if on behalf of the Riverina we may venture to say that those towns are within its limits, – wheat is grown. The rainfall here is greater and the heat less intense. But even in the localities named it seems to be a question whether cereals can be produced with sufficient constancy to repay the farmer. Nor is the Riverina a gold-producing district, – nor has it coal or copper. Gold has, I believe, been found within the limits above named, but not in sufficient quantities to attract a mining population. The Riverina is essentially a pastoral district, in which the squatters are patriarchs owning many flocks. But of all strictly pastoral districts of the world it is perhaps the best. As a wool-growing district I have no doubt as to its being the best in Australia. It consists of vast plains, a great part of which is completely without trees, and the whole of which is without hills or even rising ground. Where there is timber, the timber is light. And there is no stone, – not a particle of what the road-makers call metal, – in the country among the rivers. The houses are made of wood or brick. The roads are altogether unmade, and consist of tracks through the mud or dust. When anything is done towards the making of a road in or near the towns, clay is burned for the purpose into brickbats, or wooden blocks are used. The dust of Riverina I have never seen, but its mud is the most tenacious I ever encountered.

The secret of the wealth of the country for pastoral purposes lies in the salt which the soil possesses. A great proportion of the Riverina did, till lately, produce salt-bush, – a shrub about three feet high, pale in colour, and ugly to look at when it covers a whole plain, on which the sheep feed willingly, and which can stand great heat and great drought. I was told that the salt-bush was disappearing on runs which had carried sheep for many years, and that it certainly receded as the squatters advanced. But, though the salt-bush may go, the salt remains. Australian squatters who differ so widely among themselves on many pastoral questions, – who will dispute as to what breed of sheep is best, whether wool should be washed or shorn in the grease, whether, if washed, warm water should be used, whether sheep should be shorn early or late, whether wool should be sold in London or in the colonies, – are all agreed that a salt country is the best for sheep. In a salt country, though it seems to be as bare as a board, sheep will keep their condition, – and on a fat sheep wool will grow long and thick, while on a thin sheep the wool will also be thin. And on a plain country, sheep can be managed with very much less expense than among hills and valleys, and rock and thick timber. The knowledge that it is so comes upon the observer by degrees amidst infinite regrets.

The plains of the Riverina are not lovely to look at. The observing stranger, placing himself for a while, as every observing stranger will do, in the shoes of the observed, declares to himself at first that he will squat and lead his sheep afield amidst the rocks and gullies and widely spreading forest trees. He will know nothing at that time of the difficulty of mustering sheep in the midst of such picturesque impediments; he will not as yet understand how dingoes, or wild dogs, are harboured by them; he will hardly calculate how much farther afield sheep must travel for their food where trees are plentiful and grass is scarce, than on the open prairies where the whole strength of the soil is devoted to the production of the herbage; nor will he probably know that the unromantic animals find the food sweeter on which the sun shines openly, than that which they find beneath the forest foliage. But the squatter who has been at work for a year or two amidst timber and hills, sighs for the salt plains, and dismisses his aptitudes for the picturesque to the winds.

Such is the Riverina, – a wide, open, ugly pastoral district, on which squatters prosper and grow rich. Of its settled towns it cannot boast much. The two largest in the area which I have attempted to define as belonging to the Riverina are , Albury and Wagga-Wagga, nearly equal in size, and containing each something under 2,000 inhabitants. But Albury and Wagga-Wagga are all but outside the district, and do not especially partake of its idiosyncrasies. Deniliquin is the capital of the Riverina, and Deniliquin, according to the census of 1871, only boasts of 1,118 inhabitants. And I was told in its neighbourhood that the boast was hardly true of the town, – as, in the making up of that number, a large adjacent section of country had been included for municipal purposes. Nevertheless, were Riverina a separate colony, divided off from Victoria and Queensland, Deniliquin would probably be the chosen capital.

I should hardly have ventured to write a separate chapter on the Riverina district had not such a project of separation been entertained. I may as well say that as far as my own opinion goes, – which necessarily must be crude, – I think that the project will be renewed and consummated. I think also that this consummation, if effected, will be for the advantage of the

district itself, and for that of the adjacent colonies, – including
New South Wales, of which it at present forms a part. In order
to explain the question as well as I may be able to do, and in
giving a reason for my opinion, I must say a few words on the
terribly complicated and, I fear, rather tedious subject of the
border-duties, – for the Riverina district, and almost that
alone, is affected by them.

The government of Victoria have made a railway running
north from Melbourne across the colony to Echuca, a little
town on the Murray. They have, also, completed a second line
running north-east from Melbourne to Woodonga, another
small town higher up on the Murray, on the direct road to
Sydney, and just opposite to Albury, – ome of the towns I
have mentioned as belonging to the Riverina. By the former
of these railways, the wool and the sheep of the district, – in
which the wealth of the district altogether consists, – are sent
to Melbourne, and the stores required for the use of the
squatters are brought back from that city. The second railway
when completed will of course make the intercourse more
close, – though the line to Echuca must always be the one on
which the material prosperity of the Riverina must depend.
The communication between this district and Sydney is by a
succession of coaches till the New South Wales railway is
reached at Goulbourn. Deniliquin is nearly 500 miles distant
from Sydney, of which distance all but 130 miles must be
travelled by coach. The roads are not made, and the average
pace is about six miles an hour. But Deniliquin is reached by
coach in six hours from Echuca. The cost and labour of
passenger traffic are by no means the chief obstacles to close
connection between the western and eastern parts of the
colony; but they indicate the difficulty of other traffic. If a
four-horse coach cannot get from Deniliquin to Goulbourn in
less than eighty hours, a dray laden with wool, dragged
throughout by the one team of horses or bullocks, will be
nearly ten times as long. Hence has arisen the fact, that for all
commercial purposes the Riverina depends on Melbourne and
not on Sydney. In Melbourne it is often said that the money
which has populated the plains of the Riverina with sheep is
Victorian money, and that the squatting interests of the
district have all been created by Victorian energy. The boast

seems to me to be absurd. It might as well be said, on the other hand, that Victorian prosperity has arisen from Tasmanian energy, because many of the most prosperous graziers and wool-growers of Victoria found their way over to Port Phillip from Tasmania. The cluster of colonies is not only too small in population to admit of such divisions, but is too closely united by language, by nationality, by mutual dependence and loyalty to Great Britain, to allow of any real diversity of interests. Individual men may foster petty jealousies in their hearts, and politicians may fancy that they see an opening for their ambition in short-lived ascendancy of this or the other colony; but the interest of one of these colonies is in truth the interest of them all; and to all Australia Melbourne and Sydney are as Manchester and Liverpool, or as Nottingham and Norwich, are to England. It should matter nothing whether the Riverina send her wool to Port Jackson or to Port Phillip, – whether she buy her tea at Sydney or at Melbourne, – except to the individual tradesmen and merchants concerned. What does matter is this, – that the Riverina itself should be allowed to prosper if she have the means of prosperity within her borders; that she should at any rate be hindered by no quarrelling among outside parties.

But she is terribly hindered. At the present moment, as I write, every article carried across the Murray is subject to the interference of the custom-house, – as things used to be subject, and perhaps will again become subject, between Dover and Calais. The Riverina and Victoria, instead of being to each other as are Lancashire and Yorkshire, or as are New York and New Jersey, are in reference to their custom-house laws as are France and Germany. That a real cordon of custom-house officers should be maintained along a line over 500 miles in length, on each side, by two provinces whose joint population is a million and a quarter, is, of course, out of the question. But the hostile arrangement is carried on at the points which permit of the greatest amount of injury and inconvenience, at Albury and at Echuca. Elsewhere also along the line, – but especially at those places, – duties are collected. Passengers, as far as I am aware, are allowed to take their luggage over unexamined. No custom-house officer troubled himself with mine either at the one place or at the other. Nor do the custom-house officers do so at many of the European barriers. The trouble would find no results to pay for itself, and the nuisance would be intolerable. But articles brought down for purposes of commerce are treated as though they were going from one country into another.

This folly will probably be soon abandoned.* A bill having this object may probably be passed. But in that case one folly will have been abandoned by means of another folly, by no means so irritating as the first, but as irrational.

The one colony will again pay to the other a lump sum as the balance of exchange on behalf of these border duties. Victoria will pocket the duties collected on goods sent to the Riverina, and will pay £60,000 per annum to New South Wales. Goods will then be allowed to pass each way free, – in direct contravention of the terms of the constitution, which constitution in each colony gives to it its legal status, and is, in fact, so much British law equally binding on the colonies and on the mother country. By these terms Great Britain forbids her colonies to send their produce from one to another, except on payment of such duties as are levied on the same articles when imported from foreign countries. On the New South Wales side of the Murray wine is grown which finds its market in Melbourne. On the Hunter River also, in the northern portion of New South Wales, wine is grown which would find its market in Melbourne, – but that it is subjected to duty on entering Victoria by sea, as it must do if it enter Victoria at all. Under the arrangement, by which a lump sum is paid as balance by Victoria to New South Wales, the Murray wine will go free, in opposition to the British law; but the Hunter wine will be taxed, in obedience to the British law. The custom-house cordon will be maintained by sea, because it will not be absolutely unbearable, – but it will be abandoned by land, as constituting an infliction too irritating for men to endure.

I have endeavoured to make the matter plain, – not chiefly on account of these Murray border duties, which will probably

* Since this was written resort has been again had to the temporary expedient of a fixed sum settled between the colonies in lieu of border duties; but this is only an expedient, and the absurdity remains of custom duties chargeable between the colonies.

be made to vanish, and which can hardly be of much interest to ordinary readers, – but because I would endeavour to make clear the fatal injury which the colonies endure by the collection of any custom duties between themselves. The greatest present want of Australia generally is unity with itself. That the colonies should have been divided for purposes of local government was indispensable to their success. The different interests of the different parts were too divergent to allow of their being duly considered at one centre; and the distances were far too great for parliamentary legislation to embrace the whole from one capital. Further separation will probably take place, and will take place to the advantage of the colonies. But the divisions already made, and any new divisions which may be made, are not incompatible with national unity, and certainly need not be accompanied by the all but hostile feeling, by the unloving and unbrotherly condition, which is inseparable from custom-houses between the one and the other. The Australians are surely as closely knit together as are the Swiss in their several cantons, or as were the Germans of different kingdoms, who, in spite of various nationalities and dynastic jealousies, consented to trade with each other under the Zollverein. But the strongest example of their position, or that which is in every respect the most like to them, is to be found in the United States. They speak the one language, are subject, in regard to their foreign relations, to one central head, are the home of a spreading people determined to rule themselves, and have each their separate legislature for the purpose of doing so, – but they do not declare war against each other by border tariffs and internal custom duties.

Downing Street will answer to this, that the war is not perpetuated there. Downing Street is very fond of free trade, – as indeed are all English streets and English people, – and does not at all prohibit the colonies from the free interchange of commodities among themselves if only they will take them free from other countries. Downing Street also goes much farther than this, and will admit of a customs union between the colonies or between any two of them, – although such customs union would, in the opinion of Downing Street, inflict a grievous blow on free trade in the colonies by allowing them to import each other's goods while charging duties on foreign goods. And Downing Street now has gone still farther, and has said, under pressure, that if the colonies be imperious in their demands, she will permit them to import this or that article free, at their discretion, – adding, however, that any use of this permission in a direction hostile to free trade will have a tendency to loosen the bonds between the colonies and the mother country. Downing Street has all but given way in this matter, – and would give way altogether but that she fears to compromise herself by an apparent defalcation in regard to free trade. But there is no fairer ground for question of free trade in the matter than there would be between Middlesex and Surrey if the English parliament were to put a customs duty on some article of French produce, but which was produced also in one of those counties and carried thence into the other. The nationality between the Australian colonies is too close to admit of the doctrine of free trade having any bearing upon intercolonial commerce.

As the matter stands at present, Downing Street has simply notified her assent to a customs union between the colonies, should the colonies desire it. Two or three of them have agreed in principle to the arrangement, Tasmania having gallantly taken the lead. But the question has become so complicated among them by small diverse interests, – the jam-makers of Victoria, for instance, objecting to the free introduction of Tasmanian jam, – that no efforts made by some among themselves can, I fear, be successful. But if it were initiated from Downing Street, – if Downing Street would arrange the measure, and fashion the clauses, and give her earnest influence towards carrying it out, – it would be done. Victoria might not at first agree to it, – or Queensland, – or possibly New South Wales. But it would not require the agreement of all. Tasmania, South Australia, and New Zealand would agree. It is probable that the others would do so also, if the proposal were fairly made to them by the imperial government. But if three were combined, – if only two were combined, – not only with sanction from home, but also with British encouragement, – the union would soon grow till it included the whole.

In returning to the Riverina, I am bound to acknowledge that there has been proposed by many who are interested in her fate a remedy for the evil of border duties and for other evils, which is declared by them to be altogether effectual. But there must first be said a word as to those other evils. It has been explained that the Riverina is very far distant from Sydney; and it is thought by the people of the district that on this account she is greatly neglected by the Sydney parliament. She returns four members to a House of Assembly consisting of seventy-two members, having indeed her fair proportion according to her population. But what are four among so many? She cannot even 'log-roll'. If there be a proposition for spending public money in the north, or in the south, she is not strong enough to do aught by making her assent conditional on the spending of money also in the south-west. It must be remembered that very much is done in the colonies by public money which is with us accomplished either by private enterprise or by local contributions. Railways, bridges, and in a great measure roads also, are made out of taxes appropriated to that purpose by vote of the Assembly, – and are made under the superintendence, and are subject to the patronage, of a cabinet minister. How can any assembly be moved by four members; or what influence on a cabinet minister can be brought to bear by those forlorn ones? Consequently there are no roads, and no bridges, and not a mile of railway in the Riverina. But the Riverina pays taxes as do the other districts. When I was at Deniliquin an election was in progress for a member for the Murray district, and I heard the speeches. There were three candidates, and the man for the Murray, – which is the most centrically Riverinan of the constituencies of the Riverina, – was he who would give the loudest promise as to a certain bridge. The bridge ought to have been made years ago, connecting Victoria with New South Wales, – and the money had actually been borrowed for the Riverinan half of it. But not a pile had been driven, and now it was shrewdly guessed that an economical chancellor of the exchequer, – or treasurer as he is called in the colonies, – was going to swallow the money. I had not the slightest doubt in my own mind but that the money would be swallowed. But this or that gentle-man, if returned, would hurry up to Sydney, – probably to arrive too late because of the mud and the distance, – and would take that treasurer by the throat, if only he could get so far before the process of swallowing was completed. But it was manifest that not one man in the room expected the bridge, although the money had been voted, – and borrowed for the express purpose. What did Sydney want of a bridge over the Murray? Did not every one know that Sydney was more anxious to increase than to curtail the distance between herself and Melbourne? Candidates must say something, and it was as easy to promise a bridge as anything else. The feeling was general that nothing was to be expected from a Sydney parliament. Why should not the Riverina be annexed to Victoria?

The question was not asked at that meeting, as with the majority of those there assembled it would have been unpopular, but I heard it asked very often outside. In Victoria I have heard it put as though there could be but one answer to it. The genuine Victorian thinks that annexation to Victoria would be a road to fame and fortune for any colony or any nation. The inhabitants of Port Phillip, having separated themselves from New South Wales, would annex their parent to-morrow without compunction. But they will first annex Tasmania and Riverina. The Riverinans, however, – as also the Tasmanians, – do not seem to be in love with Victorian practices. Their deputies would be lost in the Victorian Assembly, – quite as much as those from the Riverina are now lost at Sydney; and, after a while, lawyers from Melbourne would represent them, receiving £300 per annum for their labour in doing so. And the Victorian land laws, – which have made themselves peculiarly odious to Victorian squatters, – are not at all to the liking of the Riverinan squatters. The Victorian Assembly might no doubt make promises as to pastoral leases, might declare that the sauce with which the goose to the south of the Murray had been cooked and eaten, should never be warmed up again on behalf of the gander in the Riverina, – but it is hard to bind a parliament by a promise, or to obtain obligations from a nation. There is a class of spiritual beings among whom, if you must be troubled by such an attendant, it is generally thought better to have an old friend than a stranger. The Riverinans do not much regard Sydney, – but they prefer Sydney to Melbourne.

It is well that it should be so, as it cannot be for the interests of Australia at large that the colony which is at present the most populous and the most important should be made greater and more important by annexing her sisters. It is for the advantage of England and of Englishmen, – for England will continue to feed Australia with Englishmen, – and of Australia and Australians, not that Victoria should be ascendant, but that Australia should be well governed and prosperous. That good government and prosperity would be promoted by a federation of the colonies, no one, I think, denies, – though there are various opinions as to the period at which such federation should, or can, be accomplished. Among the measures which will tend to produce federation, none will probably be so efficacious as the division of those colonies which are now too large in area for government from a central parliament in itself too weak in its elements to spread its arms afar; and among those which might retard federation none certainly would be so fatally strong as the increased preponderance of any one colony over the others. The preponderance of Victoria is at present the drawback most to be dreaded, – and to that a most injurious addition would be made, – not only as regards population, but in pride also, – were another colony or a section of one to add itself to the Victorian borders.

The only other remedy for the Riverina is Separation, – or, in other words, a setting up for herself among the colonies. That argument which I have attempted to use against customs duties would undoubtedly be a strong argument against further separation, if the continuance of such a barrier between cognate colonies were a necessity. Who would willingly multiply such barriers, and accumulate the sure means of intercolonial irritation? But if we look forward to a grouping of these Australian colonies under some form of government which may be combined in regard to external matters, but be separate as to local matters, – such as is the form of government adopted in the United States, – then the arguments against a small colony, or a poor colony, or a colony sparsely inhabited, fall to the ground. In saying this I trust that I may not be considered as specially advocating what we at home call 'American institutions.' Of those institutions this is not the place to speak. But the institutions necessary for the combined colonies would be no inch nearer to American institutions, and would be no inch farther removed from British institutions, than those which are at present used. Indeed I know not that any institution would be changed, – that any single 'Palladium of British Liberty' would be altered by the clipping of a hair. But I name the union of the American States as giving the best example which modern history affords us of a secure federation of self-governing communities.

There are, no doubt, objections which can be urged against such separation as that proposed, not only plausibly, but rationally, – objections which would perhaps be fatal, if the system of government in the Australian colonies, as at present administered, admitted of no change. The population of the Riverina is but 28,000, and it would seem to be absurd to saddle so small a body of people with all the expenses of a government house and a parliament, on the scale now adopted in the Australian colonies. It might be alleged, in answer to this, that when the separation of Queensland from New South Wales was sanctioned, the population of Queensland was under 18,000, and that in 1861, two years after its separation, it had only reached 30,000, – but it must be acknowledged, in behalf of Queensland, that her external circumstances gave better promise of a quickly increasing population than do those of the Riverina. The population of Queensland is now 125,000, and she supports what, for the sake of distinction, I will call a full-fledged parliamentary establishment. She is a bold, pushing colony, and will herself, probably, soon endure further separation. The progress of the Riverina will necessarily be slower, – but it may perhaps be well to accept such an opportunity as she would offer for ascertaining whether a separate colonial state may not be set on foot, with advantage to herself and to the group to which she belongs, on a more moderate footing. If it be allowed that a federation of the colonies would be for the advantage of the colonies, it will also, I think, be allowed that a federation of small states and of many states will be more easily constructed than one consisting of few and large states. That there should be equality of size between them is out of the question, – and with inequality of size there will of course be inequality of influence. Rhode Island and Delaware do not loom so large among the United States as New York and Pennsylvania. But Rhode Island and Delaware hold their own, govern themselves, and assist in forming a great nationality. Victoria and New South Wales may probably feel a mitigated jealousy in giving some co-ordinate power in a confederation to so small a people as that of the Riverina, when they remember that Virginia, New York, and Pennsylvania united themselves with Rhode Island and Delaware, on a basis which gave two senators each to small and to great states alike.

It is urged also, as a reason against such a measure, that the Riverina has no seaboard. Nor has Bohemia, as all readers of Shakespeare are taught to remember; nor have any of the Swiss cantons; nor had a dozen German nationalities; nor have half the states of the American Union. If a separate nationality, with custom duties and the like, be required for each political division of Australia, then seaboard may be essential. But if any unity be desired for Australia, – if the Australians of next century are to be one great people, instead of being denizens of a dozen little provinces, – then we may allow this question of seaboard to be passed as answered. It is not to be expected that another Melbourne will grow up in the Riverina, – nor that a Liverpool will establish itself in Oxfordshire. But Oxfordshire can hold its own among the counties by other influences than those to be derived from a great seaport.

In all these colonies the government is entirely centralized, and it is perhaps necessary that it should be so in new countries. When a small community is first established on some shore far distant from its parent country, the power of ruling must for a time rest in the hands of a few. Without such rule, there would be turmoil, anarchy, and destruction. But the effect of such centralized power is not, after awhile, beneficial to those who by their greater numbers are enabled to help themselves. It was the feeling of this unavoidable injustice which produced the various separations which have already taken place among the Australian colonies, and which will produce further separation. The Riverina would soon have roads and bridges, – would soon have a railway from Deniliquin to Echuca, if she stood so far alone as to have the management of her own internal finances for her own internal purposes.

TASMANIA

CHAPTER I

EARLY HISTORY

It seems hard to say of a colony, not yet seventy years old, that it has seen the best of its days, and that it is falling into decay, that its short period of importance in the world is already gone, and that for the future it must exist, – as many an old town and old country do exist, – not exactly on the memory of the past but on the relics which the past has left behind. England has towns of her own at home and colonies of her own abroad, – it would be invidious to name them, – of which this may truly be said. On visiting them the stranger feels assured that the salt of life has gone out of them. Trade dwells in them no longer, and prosperous men do not move about their streets. Their inhabitants are contented to be obscure, and generally have neither fears nor hopes. Society is mild and dull, and the remnant of the people who are left are for the most part satisfied to sit and wait. But a young colony should have young, sparkling, eager life. She should be hopeful, impetuous, and loud, with a belief in her destiny; and if she be given somewhat to boasting, she will not, indeed, thereby show herself to be possessed of an actual virtue, but will give evidence even by that vice of the strength of youth which makes a community at first buoyant and then prosperous. Such essentially are Queensland and Victoria, which force even upon unwilling ears a conviction of their strength by the loudness of their self-assertion and the vigour of their confidence. I by no means say that the dreamy, dusty quiescence of decay, the imbecility of old age which does not become actual death because so little of the energy of life is expended on the work of living from day to day, have become the lot of young Tasmania; but I do say that Tasmanians are almost united in declaring so of themselves, and that they have said so till the other colonies are quite united in repeating the story.

215

Tasmania as Tasmania is very young, – so young that many old-fashioned folk at home hardly recognise her under that name, and still know her as Van Diemen's Land. That name is now odious to the ears of Tasmanians, as being tainted with the sound of the gaol and harsh with the crack of the gaoler's whip; but it was under that name that the island was prosperous. England sent her convicts thither, and with her ruffians sent £350,000 a year for their custody and maintenance. The whole revenue of the island, including Customs, Inland Revenue, and Land Fund, does not now exceed £280,000. And the money sent from England was by no means all the wealth which the convicts brought with them. They had their thews and sinews, and the free squatters of Tasmania knew well how to turn such God-sends into money. And public works were done magnificently by them, – on the doing of which sufficiently, quickly, and without too close a regard to any immediate return of money, the welfare of a growing colony almost depends. Roads were made, and buildings were erected, and river-banks were cleared, and forests were cut down with a thoroughness which proved that convicts were at any rate useful. But though useful they were disgraceful. The Van Diemonians, – as colonists from other colonies are wont to call them with jeering mirth, – had a spirit of their own which could not be at ease within a prison, even though they themselves were the masters and wardens, and kept the keys of the prison. It began to be unendurable to them that their beautiful island, the sweetest in climate, the loveliest in scenery, the richest in rivers and harbours, the most accessible of all Great Britain's eastern colonies, should be known to the world only as Great Britain's gaol. So they spoke their mind, and of course had their way, – as has been the case with all Great Britain's children since the tea was thrown overboard at Boston. The convicts were made to cease, and Van Diemen's Land became Tasmania, – Tasmania with free institutions of its own, with representative government, with Lords and Commons, with a public debt, with its own taxes, and a right to govern itself by its own laws, – so long as it should enact no laws contrary to the spirit of the laws of England. It became, in fact, as were and are the other colonies, all but independent, and it threw off from itself also the £350,000 a year which in one shape or another the convicts used to bring with them from England, and it could make no more roads and put up no more public buildings except in the normal way of the world, by paying the market price for the works accomplished.

The feeling of disgrace, the aspiration for a different state of things, and the determination to be quit of the questionable well-being of a convict establishment, were very grand on the part of the free settlers of Van Diemen's Land. There was more in it than in the same resolution on the part of New South Wales, – for New South Wales was large, and was achieving property in another way when it resolved that convicts should be no longer received. New South Wales made no such sacrifice as did Van Diemen's Land. The government money, and the government works, and government employment were no longer at that time all in all to New South Wales, as they were to the small colony settled in the southern island, which had been created in the first place for the convicts, and then nourished by them. A great fight was made by the mother country to retain the right thus to dispose of her ruffians, and Sir William Denison, who was the governor of the day in Van Diemen's Land, was very eager in his attempt to perpetuate the arrangement, acting no doubt under instructions from the Colonial Office at home. But the feeling against the convicts was too general, and the people, though few in numbers, were too strong for Sir William Denison. In 1851 and 1852, when the agitation was going on, there were less than 75,000 free inhabitants in the colony, but they prevailed, – and as a consequence the money was stopped. There were no longer British troops in the island, now re-christened Tasmania. All the paraphernalia of home wealth, and home empire, and home influence were withdrawn. Of course there has been a reaction. I do not dare to say that the Tasmanians regret their convicts; but they do regret the attendant expenditure and attendant ceremonies of the convict establishment. The colony had been fostered by extraneous help and not by internal energy. It was easier to see and to feel the meanness in the eyes of the world of this position, than to rise at once to the national effort necessary for success on its withdrawal. The 'Van Diemonians' were all but united in the declaration of their determination that no

more convicts should be sent to them. They are now almost
equally united in their declaration that the cessation of the
coming of the convicts has been their ruin. They think that
England has been hard to them in the measure of justice which
she has meted. There might have been a regiment or at any rate a
company of soldiers left in the island, – a few red jackets if only
to enliven the streets and gladden the eyes of the women. Was it
to be expected that all the money was to be withdrawn at once, –
or if not quite at once with so great rapidity? There still remains,
and will yet remain for a few years, – as I shall explain more at
length in another chapter, – a small subsidy for the expiring
needs of the old establishment; but that is becoming less and less
every year, and the want of the money is felt in every station and
in every shop.

We all know the listlessness and unmanly apathy which has
hitherto been engendered all the world over by government pay.
In England for the last twenty years we have been making great
efforts to cure the evil, but the fact that the efforts have been
found to be necessary is the best proof of the truth of the
assertion. Government cannot get the same work out of its
workmen that is got by private employers. It cannot build a
ship, or manage an estate, or erect a palace with that economy
which a private master can ensure. Six hours of work, dimin-
ished perhaps to five or four as opportunities may allow, takes
the place of the eight hours given by servants employed in
private enterprises. This scope for idleness produces idleness till
it becomes the great blessing of the service that real work is not
exacted. To pretend to do something, – not even to pretend to
do much, – is the gentlemanlike thing. There has been much of
all this in England, but more of it, I think, among Englishmen
employed out of England. The evil is by no means limited to the
clerk, or secretary, or commissioner who feels himself to be a
great man because he has very little to do for his salary, but
extends itself to all those who see and know and envy the great
man. A profuse expenditure of government money in any
community will taint the whole of it with the pervading sin.
Men learn to regard the government as babies regard the nurse, –
and are like the big calf which can only be kept from its
overwrought mother's dugs by some process of disagreeable
expulsion. Personal enterprise and national enterprise are equally

destroyed by it. In Dublin, you are told that Dublin could not thrive if the Lord Lieutenant were withdrawn; and, consequently, Dublin with its Lord Lieutenant does not thrive. Of all food this national mother's milk, when taken beyond the period of infancy, is the most enervating. Van Diemen's Land had the strength of character necessary for the abandonment of it by her own effort. I think myself that she has a constitution sufficiently strong to enable her to live through the consequent crisis, and to walk honestly on her own legs after a period of weakness. In the meantime she feels herself to be sick, and she longs for the unwholesome nourishment which she herself was wise enough to throw away from her.

I need hardly say that the island now called Tasmania lies south of Australia. The port of Launceston, which is the largest town in the northern division of the island, is, at the present rate of steaming, about twenty-five hours distant from the port of Melbourne. The island, with the small adjacent islands belonging to it, is somewhat smaller than Ireland. It comprises nearly seventeen million acres, of which less than a fourth have been alienated from the Crown, – that is, purchased and used by settlers in the colony. A small portion of the vast remaining area is leased by the Crown to squatters, and is depastured, – if I may use a word which I have found to be common in the colonies; but by far the greater proportion of the island is covered by dense unexplored forests of gum trees. It is now divided into eighteen counties, of which five in the west are, as far as I could learn, altogether uninhabited and uninhabitable. Of others only strips of land near the sea or by the side of rivers have been 'taken up'. It is mountainous, the mountains boasting of but moderate altitudes, – 5,000 feet, and the like. It is intersected by many rivers, and watered by many lakes, being in this respect altogether unlike the mainland of Australia. It was discovered in 1642, originally by Abel Jan Tasman, a Dutchman, – as were so many of the Australian pioneers. Tasman, so says the legend, was violently in love with Maria, the daughter of one Van Diemen, who in those days was governor of the Dutch East Indian possessions. Tasman had been sent out on this expedition by Van Diemen, and showed his gratitude and gallantry by the liberal use of his patron's name and that of his patron's daughter in the nomenclature of the places he discovered. The whole country he called Van Diemen's Land. The largest of the adjacent islands which he saw he christened Maria. The lady's name still stands on the maps; but posterity, with a justice which is not customary in such matters, after more than two centuries, in its hatred of a sound which had become connected all over the world with rascaldom, has gone back to the real discoverer, and has created for the colony the name of Tasmania. For many years after Tasman's discovery it was thought to be a part of the continent of New Holland, as Australia was then called. It was not till 1798 that George Bass discovered the straits which still bear his name. In 1803 the island was first occupied on behalf of Great Britain by a party sent from New South Wales, and in 1804 Colonel David Collins was appointed as its first lieutenant-governor, he being at that time subject to the governor of the parent colony. The settlement in Van Diemen's Land was made with the express intention of relieving New South Wales of a portion of its convicts, and specially with a view of sending thither those who had been hitherto stationed at Norfolk Island, – which place had been found to be ill fitted for the purpose. At this time the only, or at least by far the paramount, interest taken by the mother country in the possession of Australia had reference to her convicts. New South Wales had been found to be a place to which convicts could conveniently be sent; but the number which could be safely kept there was not sufficient for the purposes of the home government. Van Diemen's Land might supply the deficiency, and to Van Diemen's Land were despatched a certain proportion of the convicts who crowded and embarrassed the hands of the governor of New South Wales. Two stations were opened, the first on the north and the second on the south side of the island. And thus sprang up two towns, Launceston on the Tamar in the north, and Hobart Town on the Derwent in the south. These are still the chief and, perhaps I may say without offence to various flourishing villages, the only towns in Tasmania; and they are joined together by such a road, 120 miles in length, as is not to be found elsewhere in the Australian colonies. This was, of course, made altogether by convict labour.

From this time, 1804, down to the year 1856, when responsible government began, the history of Van Diemen's

Land is simply the history of a convict establishment. How to manage convicts, how to get work out of them with the least possible chance of escape, how to catch them when they did escape, how to give them liberty when they made no attempt to escape, how to punish them, and how not to punish them, how to make them understand that they were simply beasts of burden reduced to that degree by their own vileness, and how to make them understand at the same time that if under the most difficult circumstances for the exercise of virtue they would cease to be vicious, they might cease also to be beasts of burden, – these were the tasks which were imposed, not only upon the governors and their satellites, not only on all officers military and civilian, not only on the army of gaolers, warders, and such like, which was necessary, but also on every free settler and on every free man in the island. For no one who had cast in his lot with Van Diemen's Land could be free from the taint of the establishment, or unconnected with the advantages which it certainly bestowed.

A double set of horrors is told of the convict establishment of Van Diemen's Land, – of horrors arising from the cruelty of the tyrant gaolers to their prison slaves, and of horrors created by these slaves when they escaped and became bushrangers. It must be borne in mind that almost every squatter was a gaoler, and that almost every servant was a slave. But no tidings that are told through the world exaggerate themselves with so much ease as the tidings of horrors. They who are most shocked at them, women who grow pale at the hearing and almost shriek as the stories are told them, delight to have the stories so told that they may be justified in shrieking. The ball grows as it is rolled, and the pile of wonder is accumulated. But no doubt the work to be done was very nasty work, and there was of necessity much of roughness on both sides. It must be understood that these prisoners in Van Diemen's Land were not to be kept as prisoners are kept in our county gaols and penitentiaries at home. They were to be out at work wherever the present need of work might be. Nor were they to be watched when at work by regular wardens as many of us have seen to be done with gangs of prisoners at Portland, Portsmouth, and elsewhere at home, – so watched that immediate escape, though not perhaps impossible, is very difficult. A portion of the convicts sent to Van Diemen's Land were no doubt locked up from the first, a portion were employed on government works and were probably kept under close though not continued surveillance; – but the majority both of men and women were sent out as servants to the free settlers, who were responsible, if not directly for the safe custody of those entrusted to them, at least for immediate report should any escape. The first preliminaries of escape were easy. A man could run into the bush, and be quit at any rate of the labour of the hour. If he were shepherding sheep, or building fences, or felling timber, during the greater part of the day, no eye unless that of a brother convict was upon him. He could go, and the chances of the world were open to him. But when these first preliminaries were so easy it was of course essential that they should ordinarily be rendered unsuccessful, and that the attempt should be followed by speedy and sharp punishment. The escaped convict was at once hunted, and generally tracked by the facilities which starvation afforded to his pursuers. No one but an escaped convict would feed an escaped convict, and none but they who had established themselves as bushrangers had food either to eat or to give. Even the established bushrangers, who had homes of some sort in the mountain recesses, who were in league with the blacks, and who knew how to take the wild animals, the kangaroos and walliby and opossums, were not unfrequently driven by famine to surrender themselves.

Of course the escapes were numerous, and of course the punishments were severe. And it was not only that the men would escape, but also that when punctual to hours and punctual in receipt of their rations, they would not earn their rations by work. They would not work after such a fashion as to please their masters; –and, as a necessity, the masters had a redress for such occasions. A convict who would only eat rations and never earn them, – and who could not be dismissed as can an ordinary idle servant, – required some treatment more or less severe. The master himself was not allowed to inflict corporal punishment, – but the neighbouring magistrate was entrusted with that power. The magistrate could, on hearing sufficient evidence of wilful idleness or other delinquency, inflict a certain number of lashes. The

thing became so common, of such everyday occurrence, that
very light evidence was soon found to be sufficient. The
neighbouring settler or squatter was probably the friend of the
magistrate, who was a squatter himself; and what better, –
indeed what other evidence could the magistrate have than his
friend's word? The practice became very simple at last. If the
man would not work, or worked amiss, or was held to have
sinned in any way against his master's discipline, he was sent to
the magistrate to be flogged. He himself would be the bearer of
some short note. 'Dear Sir, – Please give the bearer three dozen,
and return him.' The man as a rule would take the note, – and
the three dozen, and would return. A bold spirit would perhaps
run away. Then he would be tracked and dogged and starved,
till he either came back or was brought back, – and the last state
of that man would be worse than the first.

Of course there were horrors. The men who did escape, and
some who did not, committed fresh crimes and underwent fresh
trials, – with very small chance of verdicts in their favour. And
of all crimes murder and attempts to murder seem to have been
most in excess. Men were hung for murder and attempts to
murder and for various other crimes. The hangings were
frequent and gave rise to sharp expostulations. There is a story in
the island that the gaol chaplain at Hobart Town once rem-
onstrated, – not against hanging in general or the number that
were hung, – but as to the inconvenient celerity with which the
ceremony was performed. Thirteen men, he said, could be
comfortably hung at once, but no more. The crowding had been
too great, and he trusted that for the future the accommodation
afforded by the gaol might not be too far stretched. The
hangman was a great and well-paid official. There were flagellators also, generally convicts themselves, promoted to the
honourable employment of flogging their brethren at the different stations. There is still, I am told, an old pensioned hangman
living under protection in the island. The flagellators have
disappeared, some having gone to Victoria as miners, some
having died in their bed, – a reasonable proportion having been
murdered. It may be understood that the flagellators would not
be popular.

Not a few of these forlorn ones did escape and make their way
into the wilderness, living in holes and amidst rocks and

sometimes in habitations built for themselves in the deep recesses of the forests. The names of some of these still live in the memory of old Tasmanians, and some few still live themselves as respectable members of society. There was one Brady, who seems to have possessed himself of half the mountain tops in the island, for, let the traveller go where he will, he will be shown a 'Brady's Look-out'. Brady, I think, was hung at last. And there was one Howe, who had a wonderful career, living with a native girl whom he at last murdered because she was not fleet enough of foot to escape with him, and who was himself at last murdered by a companion. And then there was one Cash, who had a long career as a bushranger, and who now lives in dignified and easy retirement. There is also one Markham, now carrying on business satisfactorily as a gardener, who lived for seven years in a retreat he made for himself in the bush, coming down occasionally and stealing such articles as were essential for him, growing a little wheat on a plot round his cottage, keeping a goat and rearing a few sheep. For seven years the man lived on in this way, all alone, undiscovered, sufficing in all things for himself, – except in regard to those occasional thefts from his nearest neighbour. Then the solitude became too much for him, and he crept down to a neighbour's home, – the squatter from whom he had been accustomed to steal, and finding the mistress of the family, he gave himself up to her in order that the law might do as it would with him. The squatter, who had been the man's prey, was an Irish gentleman, with a tender heart, who felt thankful to the man for not having murdered his wife and children. Having position and influence he interfered on the man's behalf, and the law was lenient and the man was pardoned. The story was told to me by the lady to whom Markham surrendered himself, wild, with long locks, clothed in a sheepskin, haggard with solitude, tired out with absolute independence. Now he is a prosperous grower of apples. What an episode in life for a man to carry about always in his memory!

There was much of murder and robbery; much of hanging and slavery. English settlers to whom convicts were assigned of course learned the sweets of slavery. Their servants were intelligent beasts of burden, who had only to be fed, coerced, and made to work. The slave too was not purchased, and if he died there was no loss. The system of course was bad, as with our present lights we can see plainly enough. But though the system was bad, the men who carried it out did, I think, mainly strive to do so to a good end. Though one hears much of flogging in Van Diemen's Land, one hears still more of the excellence of the service rendered by convicts. Ladies especially are never weary of telling how good and how faithful were the females allotted to them and to their mothers. Indeed it is from the ladies of the colony that one hears the loudest regrets in regard to the good things that have now been lost for ever. And though the ladies are the loudest, men also tell of the convicts by whose labour they were enriched in the old days. Again, on the other hand, the inquirer is constantly startled by the respectability of career and eminent success of many a pardoned convict. Men who came out nominally for life were free and earning large incomes within comparatively few years. Unless a man was reconvicted he was sure to be made free, having at first a ticket of leave, which enabled him to work within a certain district on his own behalf, and then a conditional pardon, which allowed him to go anywhere except to England. In the records of Tasmania, which we have at home, we are told of the cruelty and sufferings inflicted and endured on both sides, of the cruelty of masters and of all that their slaves endured, of the bloodthirsty malignity of bushrangers, and of the evils which they perpetrated on the community. Horrors are always so popular that of course such tales are told the loudest. Enduring good conduct with good results creates no sensational enjoyment, and therefore we hear little or nothing of masters and mistresses so satisfied with the docility of convicts as to find them superior to free servants, or of men who have been sent from England as abject, nameless wretches, who have risen, after a period of penal service, to opulence, respectability, and almost to honour.

When the establishment was first set on foot in Van Diemen's Land, not only were convicts sent out to certain of the settlers as labourers without hire, but the settlers who took them had with each convict a grant of land, – so many acres for each convict taken. The owner of the slave was then bound to feed and clothe the man, but was not required to pay him any wages. That the convicts were sufficiently fed and clad by their employers I have never heard denied. Indeed food was so cheap, – or at least meat was so, – that no deficiency in this respect was probable. Nor, as far as I can learn, were the men overworked. No doubt the amount of labour performed by them daily was less than that ordinarily given by free labourers. But absolute submission was required from them, – that absolute touch-your-hat-and-look-humble submission which to this day is considered necessary among soldiers. They were to give implicit obedience, and masters accustomed to implicit obedience and absolute submission are apt to become arbitrary. And the scourge, when it is in use, recommends itself strongly to those who use it. The system could not but be evil. Then, after some years, wages of £9 per annum were required from the masters for each man, – out of which the men found their own clothes. This was a great improvement in the condition of the convicts, as they were thus enabled to own property and to exercise some of the rights of free men. At the same time they had awarded to them the privilege of leaving their masters if they chose, and of going on to the public works. This was a privilege which was but seldom exercised, as private work and private rations and private discipline were always better than the work and rations and discipline of the public gangs. But it was something for a man who could not endure a master to be able to shake that master's yoke from his neck.

In different parts of the island, as the public works demanded, large stations were built for those employed. There were various of these stations on the route from Launceston to Hobart Town, where the men were kept while they constructed the road. They were built of stone, and the ruins of them are still to be seen on the roadside. Here also resided wardens and gaolers and flagellators, and I fancy that life in the gangs was generally very much worse than life in private service. The streets and roads about Hobart Town were made after this fashion, and many of the public buildings were put up by the convicts. The traveller is astonished at the neatness and excellence of these works in Hobart Town till he learns by degrees what it was that convict labour in old days did for a convict establishment.

And there was a third mode of bestowing the convicts in Tasmania which was, – and indeed is, for it still remains,– the most remarkable of the three. There were men who could neither be sent out as private servants, or even trusted to work in gangs, – men for whom prison was needed. A prison home also was needed for the newcomers, as to whom in the first months of their service solitary confinement and good discipline were a part of the bad bargain they had made for themselves. This prison was after a while established at Port Arthur, a peninsula joined to the mainland by a neck of land only a few yards broad, and has been, I think, in many respects the most remarkable, as it is probably the most picturesque, prison establishment in the world. It is still in operation, as a certain proportion of old English convicts are still in durance, and I shall therefore speak of it in the next chapter. Now it is altogether under colonial control; but it has been so only for a year or two. The transfer was, I think, finally made in 1870, till which time Port Arthur was an imperial establishment. Perhaps no spot on the globe has been the residence during the last sixty years of greater suffering or of guiltier thoughts.

The system of transportation as carried on in Van Diemen's Land no doubt was bad. It was bad to stain with the crime of so many criminals a community which must necessarily be in itself so small. It could never have been hoped that the population of Van Diemen's Land could swallow up so large a body of English criminals as would be sent thither, without becoming a people especially noted for its convict element. And yet it was never intended that Van Diemen's Land should be devoted to convicts, as was Norfolk Island, and as is the little spot of land called Spike Island in the Cove of Cork. And the portioning out of convicts to settlers to be employed as labourers was bad; for it created a taste for slavery which has not yet lost its relish on the palate of many Tasmanians. A certain amount of harshness and bitter suffering was, no doubt, incidental to it. But I do not believe that men became fiends under its working. The fiends came out ready made, from England, and were on the whole treated with no undue severity. Of course there were exceptions, – and the exceptions have reached the public ear much more readily than has the true history. Nevertheless the people rebelled against the system, – or rather repudiated it with such strength, that the government at home was at last forced to give way.

In 1853 Van Diemen's Land ceased to receive convicts, and in 1856, following the example of her elder and younger sisters on the Australian continent, she went to work with a representative government of her own. There had been considerable difference of opinion between the colony and the mother country. The convict establishment was very convenient to us. We all know well how hard of solution is the question of the future disposition of the man against whom a judge has with great facility pronounced a sentence of penal servitude for a certain term of years. Whither shall we send our afflicted brother? Our depôts at home are small and easily crowded. Van Diemen's Land in this respect was convenient, and was at first hardly thought to have a voice loud enough to make itself heard. The governor of the day, Sir William Denison, did what he could to save the thing. But the people were in earnest and they prevailed.

Up to that time the colony had no doubt prospered. Wool, the staple of all the Australian colonies, had been grown with great profit in the island. It was from Van Diemen's Land that the district now called Victoria had been first supplied with sheep. It was found that almost every plant and almost every animal that thrives in England could be acclimatized in an island whose climate is only a little warmer than that of England, and a little more dry. It became known in the East for its breed of horses, for its whale fishery, – which was pre-eminently successful, – for its wheat and oats, and especially for its fruit. It could supply all Australia with fruit if only all Australia could be made to take it. For a time the markets were at any rate good enough to secure wealth. Men in Van Diemen's Land became rich, and both Launceston and Hobart Town were prosperous boroughs. Schools were general, hospitals were established, the institutions of the colony generally were excellent. Van Diemen's Land had not indeed a great reputation. It had a name that seemed to carry a taunt in men's ears. But it was prosperous and fat; and, unless when the bushrangers were in ascendancy, the people were happy. Such was their history up to 1856, when transportation had been abolished and representative government was commenced. Now the Tasmanians declare themselves to be ruined, and are not slow to let a stranger know that the last new name given to the island is that of 'Sleepy Hollow'. When the stranger asks the reason of this ruin, he is told that all the public money has gone with the convicts, and that, – the rabbits have eaten up all the grass. The rabbits, like the sheep, have been imported from Europe, and the rabbits have got ahead of the sheep. 'If it was not that this is Sleepy Hollow,' they say, 'we should stir ourselves and get rid of the rabbits. But it is Sleepy Hollow, and so we don't.'

CHAPTER II

PORT ARTHUR

When it had been decided between the mother country and the colony that transportation to Van Diemen's Land should be at an end, the colonial Houses of Parliament petitioned the Queen that the name might be changed, – so that the convict flavour and the convict odour attached to the old sound might be banished; and the Queen of course assented. Hence has sprung in the catalogue of our colonies the name of Tasmania, as pretty as any that we have, but to my ears somewhat fantastic. In New South Wales, with its enormous area, and in the absence of any sea barriers by which convicts could be hemmed in, the traveller does not at present hear much about convicts. They have wandered away whither they would. Now and then good-natured reference is made, in regard to some lady or gentleman, to the fact that his or her father was 'lagged', and occasionally up in the bush a shepherd may be found who will own to the soft impeachment of having been lagged himself, – though always for some offence which is supposed to have in it more of nobility than depravity. But in Tasmania the records are recent, fresh, and ever present. There is still felt the necessity of adhering to a social rule that no convict, whatever may have been his success, shall be received into society. 'But if he should be a member of the Assembly?' I asked. Well, yes, my informant acknowledged that there would be a difficulty. There are occasions on which a member of the Assembly may almost demand to be entertained, – as a member of the House of Commons has, I imagine, almost a right to dine with the Speaker. It is not only that men and women in Tasmania do not choose to herd with convicts, but that they are on their guard lest it might be supposed that their own existence in the island might be traced back to the career of some criminal relative.

In the meantime, though a new name sweet as a rose has been invented, the odour and the flavour have not as yet quite passed away. A certain number of convicts are at work on the public domain in Hobart Town, but they are always the convicts of the island, – men who have received their sentences for deeds done in Tasmania. At the extreme south-west of the island, – in a peninsula called by the name of Tasman, which is all but an island, – is maintained a station called Port Arthur, and there are at present kept as many as remain of the old English exiles. With them are a portion of the convicts of the island. For those who were sent out from England, England still pays the cost of maintenance, amounting to £36 19s. and 8d. per annum for each man under sentence, and something less for lunatics and paupers. Of these the great majority are now either paupers or lunatics, who would be free were they able to earn their own bread. England also pays, and will, by agreement, continue to pay for some further term of eight or nine years, a lump sum of £6,000 per annum towards the general police expenses, which were commenced on behalf of the mother country. When an English convict, who has had a conditional pardon, is reconvicted, he is maintained at the expense of the colony if reconvicted after a period of six months of freedom; but at the expense of England if within that period. And so the convict system is dying out in Tasmania, and will soon be extinct, and at last the odour and the flavour will be gone.

I visited Port Arthur, and was troubled by many reflections as to the future destiny of so remarkable a place. It is in a direct line not, I believe, above sixty miles from Hobart Town, but it can hardly be reached directly. The way to it is by water, and as there is no traffic to or from the place other than what is carried on by the government for the supply of the establishment, a sailing schooner is sufficient, – and indeed more than sufficiently expensive. In this schooner I was taken under the kind guidance of the premier and attorney-general of the island, who were called upon in the performance of their duties to inspect the place and hear complaints, – if complaints there were. We started at midnight, and as we were told at break of day that we had made only four miles down the bay, I began to fear that the expedition would be long. But the wind at last favoured us, and at about noon we were landed at Tasman's peninsula in Norfolk Bay, and there we found the commandant of the establishment and horses to carry us whither we would. We found also a breakfast at the policeman's house, of which we were very much in want.

Tasman's peninsula, which has been held entire by the Crown for the purposes of the convict establishment, is an irregularly formed piece of land about twenty-five miles long and twelve broad, indented by various bays and creeks of the sea, very hilly, covered with primeval gum-tree forest, and joined on to the island by a very narrow neck of sand. Port Arthur, where are the prisons, is about nine miles from Norfolk Bay; but our first object was to visit the neck, – called Eagle Hawk Neck, – partly for the sake of the scenery, and partly because the neck is guarded by dogs, placed there to prevent the escape of the convicts. I had heard of these dogs before I visited Tasmania, but I had thought that they were mythic. There, however, I found them, to the number of fifteen, chained up in their appointed places at and near the neck. The intention is that they should bark if any escaped prisoner should endeavour to swim at night across the narrow arm of sea which divides the two lands. In former days they used to be employed in hunting the men down. I doubt whether they are now of any service. They are allowed regular rations, one pound of meat and one pound of flour a day per dog; and I found the policemen stationed at the Neck very loud in their assurances that the business could not be carried on without the dogs. The policemen also have rations, – somewhat more than that of the dogs, though of the same kind; and it struck me that to the married men who have families in the neighbourhood, the rationed dogs might be serviceable.

The scenery at this spot is very lovely, as the bright narrow sea runs up between two banks which are wooded down to the river. Then we went farther on, riding our horses where it was practicable to ride, and visited two wonders of the place, – the Blow-Hole, and Tasman's Arch. The Blow-Hole is such a passage cut out by the sea through the rocks as I have known more than one on the west coast of Ireland under the name of puffing-holes. This hole did not puff nor blow when I was there, but we were enabled by the quiescence of the sea to crawl about among the rocks, and enjoyed ourselves more than we should have done had the monster been in full play. Tasman's Arch, a mile farther on, is certainly the grandest piece of rock construction I ever saw. The sea has made its way in through the rocks, forming a large pool or hole, some fifty yards from the outer cliffs, the descent into which is perpendicular all round; and over the aperture stretches an immense natural arch, the supports or side pillars of which are perpendicular. Very few even now visit Tasman's Arch; but when the convict establishment at Port Arthur comes to an end, as come to an end I think it must, no one will ever see the place. Nevertheless it is well worth seeing, as may probably be said of many glories of the earth which are altogether hidden from human eyes.

On the following day we inspected the prisons, and poor-house and lunatic asylum and farm attached to the prisons, – for there is a farm of well-cleared land, – seventy or eighty acres under tillage, if I remember rightly; and there is a railway for bringing down timber and firewood. The whole was in admirable order, and gave at first sight the idea of an industrial establishment conducted on excellent commercial principles. The men made their own shoes and clothes and cheeses, and fed their own pigs, and milked their own cows, and killed their own beef and mutton. There seemed to be no reason why they should not sell their surplus produce and turn in a revenue for the colony. But prisons never do turn in a revenue, and this certainly was no exception to the rule.

I found that there were altogether 506 persons, all males, to be looked after, and that no less than 97 men were employed to look after them. Of these 25 were officers, many of whom were in receipt of good salaries. There was the commandant, and the Protestant chaplain, and the Roman Catholic chaplain, and the doctor, and the doctor's assistant, and the postmaster, forming with their wives and families quite a pleasant little society, utterly beyond reach of the world, but supplied with every comfort, – unless when the wind was so bad that the government schooner could not get round to them. These gentlemen all had houses too. I was hospitably received in one, that of the commandant, which, with its pretty garden and boat-house, and outlook upon the land-locked bay of the sea, made me wish to be commandant myself. There would have been nothing peculiar in all this, except the cleanness and prettiness of the place, were it not that it must apparently all come to an end in a few years, and that the commandant's house, and the other houses, and all the village, and the prisons, and the asylum, and the farm, and the church, will be left deserted, and allowed to fall into ruins. I do not know what other fate can be theirs. Tasmania will not maintain the place for her own prison purposes when there is an end of the English money; – and for other than prison purposes no one will surely go and live in that ultima Thule, lovely as are the bays of the sea, and commodious as may be the buildings.

Of the 506 men to be looked after, 284 belonged to England, and 222 to the colony. Of the 506, 234 only were efficient for work; and of this latter number only 39 were English convicts. It will be understood that the lingering English remnants of transported ruffianism would by this time consist chiefly of old men unfit for work. There were 146 English paupers, – convicts who have served their time, but who would be unable to support themselves if turned out, – and there were ten invalids who would return to their convict work when well. There were also 89 lunatics, of whom only four were still under sentence. With 506 men to be looked after, 97 officers and constables to look after them, and with only 234 men able to do a day's work, it may well be imagined that the place is not self-supporting. Its net cost is, in round numbers, £20,000; of which, in round numbers again, England pays one-half and the colony the other. It was admitted that when the English subsidy was withdrawn, – for in fact England does pay at present £6,000 a year for general expenses over and above her contribution per man to the establishment of Port Arthur, – that when this should be discontinued, Port Arthur must be deserted.

The interest of such an establishment as this of course lies very much in the personal demeanour, in the words, and appearance of the prisoners. A man who has been all his life fighting against law, who has been always controlled but never tamed by law, is interesting, though inconvenient, – as is a tiger. There were some dozen or fifteen men, – perhaps

more, – whom we found inhabiting separate cells, and who
were actually imprisoned. These were the heroes of the place.
There was an Irishman with one eye, named Doherty, who
told us that for forty-two years he had never been a free man
for an hour. He had been transported for mutiny when hardly
more than a boy, – for he had enlisted as a boy, – and had since
that time received nearly 3,000 lashes! In appearance he was a
large man and still powerful, – well to look at in spite of his
eye, lost as he told us through the misery of prison life. But he
said that he was broken at last. If they would only treat him
kindly, he would be as a lamb. But within the last few weeks
he had escaped with three others, and had been brought back
almost starved to death. The record of his prison life was
frightful. He had been always escaping, always rebelling,
always fighting against authority, – and always being flogged.
There had been a whole life of torment such as this; forty-two
years of it; and there he stood, speaking softly, arguing his
case well, and pleading while tears ran down his face for some
kindness, for some mercy in his old age. 'I have tried to
escape, – always to escape,' he said, – 'as a bird does out of a
cage. Is that unnatural, – is that a great crime?' The man's first
offence, that of mutiny, is not one at which the mind revolts. I
did feel for him, and when he spoke of himself as a caged bird,
I should like to have taken him out into the world, and have
given him a month of comfort. He would probably, however,
have knocked my brains out on the first opportunity. I was
assured that he was thoroughly bad, irredeemable, not to be
reached by any kindness, a beast of prey, whose hand was
against every honest man, and against whom it was necessary
that every honest man should raise his hand. Yet he talked so
gently and so well, and argued his own case with such
winning words! He was writing in a book when we entered
his cell, and was engaged on some speculation as to the
tonnage of vessels. 'Just scribbling, sir,' he said, 'to while
away the hours.'

There was another man, also an Irishman, named Ahern,
whose appearance was as revolting as that of Doherty was
prepossessing. He was there for an attempt to murder his
wife, and had been repeatedly re-tried and re-convicted. He
was making shoes when we saw him, and had latterly become

a reformed character. But for years his life had been absolutely
the life of a caged beast, – only with incidents more bestial
than those of any beast. His gaolers seemed to have no trust in
his reformation. He, too, was a large powerful man, and he,
too, will probably remain till he dies either in solitary
confinement or under closest surveillance. In absolute infamy
he was considered to be without a peer in the establishment.
But he talked to us quite freely about his little accident with his
wife.

There was another remarkable man in one of the solitary
cells, whose latter crime had been that of bringing abominable
and false accusations against fellow-prisoners. He talked for
awhile with us on the ordinary topics of the day not disagree-
ably, expressing opinions somewhat averse to lonely existence, and not altogether in favour of the impartiality of those
who attended upon him. But he gave us to understand that,
though he was quite willing to answer questions in a pleasant,
friendly way, it was his intention before we left him to make a
speech. It was not every day that he had such an audience as a
prime minister and an attorney-general, – not to speak of a
solicitor-general from another colony who was with us also,
or of the commandant, or of myself. He made his speech, –
and I must here declare that all the prisoners were allowed to
make speeches if they pleased. He made his speech, – hitching
up his parcel-yellow trousers with his left hand as he threw out
his right with emphatic gesture. I have longed for such ease
and such fluency when, on occasions, I have been called upon
to deliver myself of words upon my legs. It was his object to
show that the effort of his life had been to improve the morals
of the establishment, and that the commandant had repressed
him, actuated solely by a delight in wickedness. And as he
made his charge he pointed to the commandant with denoun-
cing fingers, and we all listened with the gravest attention. I
was wondering whether he thought that he made any impression. I forget that man's name and his crime, but he ought to
have been a republican at home, and should he ever get out
from Port Arthur might still do well to stand for a borough on
anti-monarchical interests.

But of all the men the most singular in his fate was another
Irishman, one Barron, who lived in a little island all alone; and

of all the modes of life into which such a man might fall, surely his was the most wonderful. To the extent of the island he was no prisoner at all, but might wander whither he liked, might go to bed when he pleased, and get up when he pleased, might bathe and catch fish, or cultivate his little flower-garden, – and was in very truth monarch of all he surveyed. Twice a week his rations were brought to him, and in his disposal of them no one interfered with him. But he surveyed nothing but graves. All who died at Port Arthur, whether convicts or free, are buried there, and he has the task of burying them. He digs his graves, not fitfully and by hurried task-work, but with thoughtful precision, – having one always made for a Roman Catholic, and one for a Protestant inmate. In this regularity he was indeed acting against orders, – as there was some prejudice against these ready-made graves; but he went on with his work, and was too valuable in his vocation to incur serious interference. We talked with him for half an hour, and found him to be a sober, thoughtful, suspicious man, quite alive to the material inconveniences of his position, but not in the least afflicted by ghostly fear or sensational tremors. He smiled when we asked whether the graves awed him, – but he shook his head when it was suggested to him that he might grow a few cabbages for his own use. He could eat nothing that grew from such soil. The flowers were very well, but a garden among graves was no garden for vegetables. He had been there for ten years, digging all the graves in absolute solitude without being ill a day. I asked him whether he was happy. No, he was not happy. He wanted to get away and work his passage to America, and begin life afresh, though he was sixty years old. He preferred digging graves and solitude in the island, to the ordinary life of Port Arthur; he desired to remain in the island as long as he was a convict; but he was of opinion that ten years of such work ought to have earned him his freedom. Why he was retained I forget. If I remember rightly, there had been no charge against him during the ten years. 'You have no troubles here,' I said. 'I have great troubles,' he replied, 'when I walk about, thinking of my sins.' There was no hypocrisy about him, nor did he in any way cringe to us. On the contrary, he was quiet, unobtrusive, and moody. There he is still, living among the graves, – still dreaming of some future career in life, when, at last, they who have power over him shall let him go.

Of the able-bodied men the greatest number are at work about the farm, or on the land, or cutting timber, and seem to be subject to no closer surveillance than are ordinary labourers. There is nothing to prevent their escape, – except the fact that they must starve in the bush if they do escape. There is plenty of room for them to starve in the bush even of Tasman's peninsula. Then when they have starved till they can starve no longer, they go back to the damnable torment of a solitary cell. None but spirits so indomitable as that of the man Doherty will dare to repeat the agonies of escape above once or twice.

There was a man named Fisher dying in the hospital, who had been one of those who had lately escaped with Doherty, and had, indeed, arranged the enterprise, and had gotten together the materials to form a canoe to carry them off. Before they started he had been possessed of £10, which, – so the officers said, – he had slowly amassed by selling wines and spirits which he had collected in some skin round his body, such wine and spirits having been administered to him by the doctor's orders, and having been received into the outer skin instead of taken to the comfort of the inner man. Thus, it was supposed, he had sold to the constables and warders, and had so realised £10. Now he was dying, – and looked, indeed, as he lay on his bed, livid, with his eyes protruding from his head, as though he could not live another day. But it was known that he still had three of the ten sovereigns about him. 'Why not take them away?' I asked. 'They are in his mouth, and he would swallow them if he were touched.' Think of the man living, – dying with three sovereigns in his mouth, procured in such a way, for such a purpose, over so long a term of years, – for the man must have been long an invalid to have been able to sell for £10 the wine which he ought to have drunk! What a picture of life, – what a picture of death, – the man clinging to his remnant of useless wealth in such a fashion as that!

In the evening and far on into the night the premier was engaged in listening to the complaints of convicts. Any man who had anything to say was allowed to say it into the ears of the first minister of the crown, – but all of course said uselessly. The complaints of prisoners against their gaolers can hardly be efficacious. So our visit to Port Arthur came to an end, and we went back on the next day to Hobart Town.

The establishment itself has the appearance of a large, well-built, clean village, with various factories, breweries, and the like. There is the church, as I have said, and there are houses enough, both for gentle and simple, to take away the appearance of a prison. The lunatic asylum and that for paupers have no appearance of prisons. Indeed the penitentiary itself, where the working convicts sleep and live, and have their library and their plays and their baths, is not prison-like. There is a long street, with various little nooks and corners, as are to be found in all villages, – and in one of them the cottage in which Smith O'Brien lived as a convict. The place is alive, and the eye soon becomes used to the strange convict garments, consisting of jackets and trousers, of which one side is yellow and the other brown. If it were to be continued, I should be tempted to speak loudly in praise of the management of the establishment. But it is doomed to go, and, as such is the case, one is disposed to doubt the use of increased expenditure.

All those whom I questioned on the subject in Tasmania agreed that Port Arthur must be abandoned in a few years, and that then the remaining convicts must be removed to the neighbourhood of Hobart Town. If this be done there can hardly, I think, be any other fate for the buildings than that they shall stand till they fall. They will fall into the dust, and men will make unfrequent excursions to visit the strange ruins.

CHAPTER III

HER PRESENT CONDITION

It is acknowledged even by all the rival colonies that of all the colonies Tasmania is the prettiest. This is no doubt true of her as a whole, though the scenery of the Hawkesbury in New South Wales is, I think, finer that anything in Tasmania. But it may be said of the small island that, go where you will, the landscape that meets the eye is pleasing, whereas the reverse of this is certainly the rule on the Australian continent. And the climate of Tasmania is by far pleasanter than that of any part of the mainland. There are, one may almost say, no musquitoes. Other pernicious animals certainly do abound, but then they abound also in England. Everything in Tasmania is more English than is England herself. She is full of English fruits, which grow certainly more plentifully and, as regards some, with greater excellence than they do in England. Tasmanian cherries beat those of Kent, – or, as I believe, of all the world, – and have become so common that it is often not worth the owner's while to pull them. Strawberries, raspberries, gooseberries, plums, and apples are in almost equal abundance. I used in early days to think a greengage the best fruit in the world, – but latterly, at home, greengages have lost their flavour for me. I attributed this to age and an altered palate; but in Tasmania I found the greengages as sweet as they used to be thirty years ago. And then the mulberries! There was a lady in Hobart Town who sent us mulberries every day such as I had never eaten before, and as, – I feel sure, – I shall never eat again. Tasmania ought to make jam for all the world, and would do so for all the Australian world were she not prevented by certain tariffs, to which I shall have to allude in the next chapter. Now the Australian world is essentially a jam-consuming world, and but for the tariffs Tasmania could afford to pick, and would make a profit out of, the cherries and raspberries. And this is not the only evil. The Victorians eat a great deal of jam. No one eats more jam than a Victorian miner, – unless it be a Victorian stock-rider. But they eat pumpkin jam flavoured with strawberries, – and call that strawberry jam. The effect of protection all the world over is to force pumpkin jam, under the name of strawberry jam, down the throats of the people.

The Tasmanians in their loyalty are almost English-mad. The very regret which is felt for the loss of English soldiers arises chiefly from the feeling that the uniform of the men was especially English. There is with them all a love of home, which word always means England, – that touches the heart of him who comes to them from the old country. "We do not want to be divided from you. Though we did in sort set up for ourselves, and though we do keep our own house, we still wish to be thought of by Great Britain as a child that is loved. We like to have among us some signs of your power, some emblem of your greatness. A red coat or two in our streets would remind us that we were Englishmen in a way that would please us well. We do not wish to be Americanised in our ways and thoughts. Well, – if we cannot have a red-coated soldier we will at any rate have a mail-guard with a red coat, and a real mail-coach.' And they have the mail-coach running through from Launceston to Hobart Town, and from Hobart Town to Launceston, not in the least like a Cobb's coach, as they are in the other colonies, but built directly after that ancient and most uncomfortable English pattern which we who are old remember, – and they have the coachman and the guard clothed in red, because red has been from time immemorial the royal livery of England.

Launceston is a clean, well-built town, and does most of the importing and exporting business of the island. It is on the north side of the island, and therefore within easy reach from Melbourne, with which port most of the business of Tasmania is done, – exclusive of the export of wool. It has no look of decay, in spite of the evil things that are said, and at any rate appears to prosper. The scenery round Launceston is not equal to that of Hobart Town, but there are one or two very pretty walks, –noticeably those up the hill over the waterfall whence the visitor looks down upon the South Esk, which there is as pretty as the Lynn at Linton.

An English farmer hearing of land giving 60 bushels of oats
to the acre, averaging over 40 lbs. the bushel, would imagine
that the owner of such land ought to do well, – especially if he
knew that the same crop could be raised on the land year after
year. But yet land growing such crops will not give a rent, or
even a profit, to the combined landowner and farmer of 10s.
an acre. The corn has to be sent into Launceston, and will not
fetch when there above 2s. a bushel, – or 16s. a quarter. Now
oats in England, at that weight, range I believe, from 30s. to
34s. a quarter. With us the wages of rural labourers are 11s.,
12s., or 14s. a week, according to the county or district. In the
part of Tasmania of which I am speaking, men were receiving
£30 per annum wages, with rations, consisting of 10 lbs. of
meat, 10 lbs. of flour, 2 lbs. of sugar, and ¼ lb. of tea per
week, worth 7s. a week. They also had cottages if married, or
house-room if single, – and some extra sums of money were
given to them at harvest time, – £3 or £4, – to secure their
services. This altogether, would be worth 20s. or 21s. a week;
whereas living is generally cheaper to the working man in
Tasmania than in England. The result is that the labourers are
able to pay, and as a rule do pay, 6d. a week each for the
schooling of their children. The labourer does well, – but the
farmer makes but a poor profit out of his tilled land. It should
be explained that on the farms which I visited, – and which
belonged to a family of brothers, cousins, and uncles, –
everything was done with the best implements brought out
from England, and that manure was used. Hitherto the use of
manure in tillage is not common in any of the colonies. It is
thought to be more profitable to take what the land will give
and then to leave it for awhile than to carry manure to it.
Gradually, however, they who are most deeply concerned in
agriculture find that there must soon be an end to a system
such as this. In the district of which I am speaking wheat was
subject to rust, which is the great scourge of the Australian
farmer. The price of wheat in Launceston was 4s. 3d. to 4s. 6d.
a bushel; but my friend told me that it would pay him better to
send his wheat to London than to sell it in the colony, and that
he intended to do so.

I found that ordinary day-labourers throughout the colony
were getting 4s. a day without rations, or on an average from

9*s*. to 10*s*. a week with rations and house accommodation. The men without rations would of course be employed with less certainty of duration than those hired as permanent hands with rations. Journeymen carpenters, masons, plasterers, wheelwrights, and the like, were getting 6*s*. 6*d*. a day; domestic men-servants £30 per annum with board and lodging, and female servants about £20. I found also that all provisions were cheaper than in England, or as cheap: bacon 8*d*. a pound; butter 1*s*. to 1*s*. 6*d*.; bread 3 ½*d*. the 2 lb. loaf; beer, brewed in the colony and very good, 2*s*. the gallon; mutton 4*d*. a pound; beef 6*d*.; sugar 4 ½*d*.; coffee 1*s*. 2*d*.; tea 2*s*.; potatoes £3 a ton. I am afraid that domestic details may not be very interesting to general readers, but they may serve to afford to some intending emigrant an idea of the fate which he would meet in Tasmania.

I must say of this colony, as I have and shall say of all the others, that it is a paradise for a working man as compared with England. The working man can here always eat enough food, and always clothe and shelter himself, and can also educate his children. His diet will always comprise as much animal food as he can consume, – and if he be a sober, industrious man he will never find himself long without work. Tasmania is no doubt at present not popular with the young Tasmanian working man, because the search for gold has not hitherto been prosperous in Tasmania. The young men go off to Victoria, though it may be doubtful whether they improve either their comfort or their means by the journey. A miner in Victoria will earn from 7*s*. to 8*s*. a day, – the average wages were 7*s*. 6*d*. when I was at Sandhurst; but to earn that a man must be a miner. He must lose time in going in quest for his work, and cannot always readily find it. And when he has got it, and has learned to be a miner, and is in receipt of 45*s*. a week, he lives hard in order that he may gamble in gold speculation with all that he can save. I think that the labourer in Tasmania has the best of the bargain; but the desire for gold is so strong, and the chances of fortunate speculation are so seductive, that the young men of the island colony are gradually drawn away.

Of males, there were in the island in 1870, in round numbers, 27,000 under twenty years of age, – only 10,800

between twenty and forty, and 11,500 between forty and
sixty. These figures prove that the male population has by far
too great a proportion of old and young for thorough
well-being and a wholesome condition. Of females, there
were 25,000 under twenty, the number of the girls as
compared with that of the boys giving one evidence among
many of the fact that the male progeny of Australia is more
numerous than the female, – a rule which applies to horses,
sheep, and cattle as well as to the human race. Between twenty
and forty there were 12,000 women, who thus beat the men
during that, the strongest, period of life, by 1,200; and
between forty and sixty there were only 7,000 women,
sinking below the the number of men for the same period by
4,500. What becomes of the old women in Tasmania I cannot
say. Between sixty and seventy there are 3,200 men, and only
1,200 women. I cannot suppose that after a certain time of life
the Tasmanian women go to the diggings. I am almost
disposed to think that the statistical tables of the colony show
that ladies in Tasmania do not give correct records as to their
ages. On 31st December, 1870, – and I have no information
corrected up to a later date, – there were altogether in
Tasmania 53,464 males and 47,301 females, – in all 100,765.
Since 1870 the increase has been very slight. In 1853, when
transportation from England ceased, the population was
75,000. The colony, therefore, has not grown as have the
other Australian colonies, – not as Queensland, which began
her career as an independent colony in 1859 with 18,000
inhabitants, and had 115,000 in 1870. But even in Tasmania
there has been a steady increase, though the increase during
the last few years has been small.

The road from Launceston to Hobart Town is as good as
any road in England, and is in appearance exactly like an
English road. It was made throughout by convicts, and was
manifestly made with the intention of being as like an English
road as possible. The makers of it have perfectly succeeded.
When it passes through forest land, – or bush, – the English
traveller would imagine that there was a fox covert on each
side of him. There are hedges too, and the fields are small.
And there are hills on all sides, very like the Irish hills in
County Cork. Indeed it is Ireland rather than England to

which Tasmania may be compared. And, as I have said before, English, – or Irish, – coaches run upon the road; a night mail-coach, with driver and guard in red coats, and a day coach with all the appurtenances after the old fashion. I found their pace when travelling to be about nine miles an hour. We went by the mail-coach as far as Campbelltown, – a place with about 1,600 inhabitants, which returns a member of parliament, and has a municipal council, four or five resident clergymen, a hospital, an agricultural association, and a cricket-club. Quite a place! – as the Americans say. When I asked whether it was prosperous, my local friend shook his head. It ought to be the centre of a flourishing pastoral district. It is the centre of a pastoral district, which is not flourishing, – because of the rabbits. This wicked little prolific brute, introduced from England only a few years ago, has so spread himself about, that hardly a blade of grass is left for the sheep! But why not exterminate him, or at least keep him down? I asked the question with thorough confidence that the energies of man need not succumb to the energies of rabbits. I was told that the matter had gone too far, and that the rabbit had established his dominion. I cannot, however, but imagine that the rabbit could be conquered if Tasmania would really put her shoulder to the wheel.

We passed a place called Melton, at which a pack of hounds was formerly kept, – so called after the hunting metropolis in Leicestershire; and as I looked around I thought that I saw a country well adapted for running a drag. Foxes, if there were foxes, would all be away into the mountains. They used to hunt stags, but I should have thought that the stags would have taken to the hills. But the hunting had belonged to the good old prosperous convict days, and had passed away with other Tasmanian glories. At Bridgewater, within ten miles of Hobart Town, there is a magnificent causeway over the Derwent, about a mile long, which was of course built by convict labour, and which never would, – in Tasmania never could, – have been made without it.

Hobart Town, the capital of the colony, has about 20,000 inhabitants, and is as pleasant a town of the size as any that I know. Nature has done for it very much indeed, and money has done much also. It is beautifully situated, – as regards the water, – placed just at the point where the river becomes sea. It has quays and wharves, at which vessels of small tonnage can lie, in the very heart of the town. Vessels of any tonnage can lie a mile out from its streets. It is surrounded by hills and mountains, from which views can be had which would make the fortune of any district in Europe. Mount Wellington, nearly 5,000 feet high, is just enough of a mountain to give excitement to ladies and gentlemen in middle life. Mount Nelson is less lofty, but perhaps gives the finer prospect of the two. And the air of Hobart Town is perfect air. I was there in February, – the height of summer, – having chosen to go to Tasmania at that time to avoid the great heat of the continent. I found the summer weather of Hobart Town to be delicious. And there were no musquitoes there. I have said something about Australian musquitoes before. They were not so bad as I had expected; but in certain places they had been troublesome, – especially at Melbourne. But I knew nothing of them in Hobart Town. Other living plagues there were plenty in Tasmania, – no doubt introduced, as were the rabbits, with the view of maintaining the general likeness to England. All fruits which are not tropical grow at Hobart Town and in the neighbourhood to perfection. Its cherries and mulberries are the finest I ever saw. Its strawberries, raspberries, apples, and pears are at any rate equal to the best that England produces. Grapes ripen in the open air. Tasmania ought to make jam for all the world, and would make jam for all the Australian world, were it not for Australian tariffs. Tasmanian jams would probably come to England if Tasmania could import Queensland sugar free of duty. As it is, fruit is so plentiful that in many cases it cannot be picked from the trees. It will not pay to pick it!

So much in regard to the gifts bestowed by nature upon the capital of Tasmania. Art, – art in the hands of convicts, – has made it a pretty, clean, well-constructed town, with good streets and handsome buildings. The Government House is, I believe, acknowledged to be the best belonging to any British colony. It stands about a mile from the town, on ground sloping down to the Derwent, – which is here an arm of the sea, and lacks nothing necessary for a perfect English residence. The public offices, town-hall, and law courts are all excellent. The supreme court, as one of the judges took care to tell me, is larger than our Court of Queen's Bench at Westminster. The Houses of Parliament are appropriate and comfortable with every necessary appliance. They are not pretentious, nor can I say that the building devoted to them is handsome. There is a Protestant bishop of course, and a cathedral, – which a stranger, not informed on the subject, would mistake for an old-fashioned English church in a third or fourth rate town. I was told that it is tumbling down; but a very pretty edifice is being erected close by its side. The work is still unfinished and funds are needed. Perhaps a generous reader might send a trifle.

From Hobart Town various expeditions may be made which amply repay the labour. I have already told how I went to Port Arthur. I was very anxious to go to Lake St. Clair but did not succeed. Lake St. Clair is nearly in the middle of the island, – somewhat towards the west, or wilder part of it, – in County Lincoln, and is, I was informed, wonderfully wild and beautiful. It was described to me as another Killarney, but without roads. The beauty, too, I was told, could be well seen only from a boat, and there was no boat then on the lake. I found that I could not compass it without devoting more time than I had to spare, – and I did not see Lake St. Clair. I went up the Derwent to New Norfolk and Fenton Forest, and across from Hobart Town to the Huon River and a township called Franklin, finding the scenery everywhere to be lovely. The fern-tree valleys on the road to Huon are specially so, – and in one of these I was shown the biggest tree I ever saw. I took down the dimensions, and of course lost the note. It was quite hollow, and six or seven people could have sat round a table and dined within it. It was a gum-tree, bigger I imagine in girth, though not so tall as that which I described as having been found in Victoria, near the road from Woods Point to Melbourne. The River Huon is a dark, black, broad stream, running under hanging bushes, – very silent and clear, putting me in mind of the river in Evangeline.

On the Upper Derwent, in the neighbourhood of New Norfolk, where the River Plenty joins the Derwent, there are the so-called Salmon Ponds. Now these salmon ponds are a matter of intense interest in Tasmania, and very much skill

and true energy have been expended, – and no slight amount
of money also, – in efforts to introduce our river fish,
especially the trout and salmon, into Tasmanian waters. In
reference to trout the success has been perfect. The quantity in
the rivers is already sufficient to justify the letting of fishing
licences at 20s. a year, and men who know how to fly-fish can
get excellent sport. I have seen trout six and seven pound
weight, and have eaten I think better trout in Tasmania than
ever I did in England. In regard to salmon I can only say that
there has as yet been no success. No one has as yet caught a
Tasmanian salmon, though there are stories about of salmon
having been seen. The man who catches the first salmon will
be entitled to £30 reward.*

Mr. Allport, of Hobart Town, a gentleman who has taken
pains with the subject, and who thoroughly understands it, is
confident of success. He gave me reasons to show how it is
that the salmon should take much longer than the trout to
establish themselves, and to prove that there was as yet no
reason for a faint heart on this great matter. Mr. Allport's
enthusiasm was catching, and I found myself ready to swear,
after hearing him, that there must be salmon. Some other
great scientific authority has declared, – thinks I believe that
he has proved, – that it is impossible that there should be a
salmon in Tasmania. It is a great question. I myself, in my
ignorance, lean to Mr. Allport's side altogether, because I
had the advantage of knowing Mr. Allport. I was only told
of the adverse great authority. But the trout are a fact. I ate
them again and again, with great satisfaction. I do not doubt
that before long, with true Australian fecundity, they will
swarm in Tasmanian rivers.

In this part of the Island, – the part of which New Norfolk
is the centre, about twenty-four miles up the Derwent from
Hobart Town, – hops have lately been introduced with
success. They grow with great luxuriance, and bear heavily.
It is, indeed, hard to find anything that will not flourish in
Tasmania, – except wheat, which seems in the Australian
colonies generally to be of all the crops the most hazardous.

---

* Since these words were first published the first salmon has, I am informed,
been caught, and the reward given.

Everywhere one hears of rust. The stalk becomes hard, red, and thick under the influence of the sun, and then the grain is either not produced at all, or is a withered, shrivelled atom, giving no flour. Respecting the hops, I asked whether that at any rate was not a profitable enterprise. It would be, I was told, but for the damnable Victorian tariffs which had been invented with the primary object of ruining Tasmania, – of bringing her so low that, to escape absolute ruin, she should be forced to annex herself to her big and cruel sister. That is the Tasmanian creed, and it is one altogether unfounded on facts. It must be understood that Victoria is the natural market for Tasmanian produce. Setting wool aside, which almost as a matter of course goes to England, and which constitutes above a third of the total exports from the colony, we find that nearly three-fourths of its surplus produce is shipped for Victoria. This is done in the teeth of the terrible Victorian tariffs, and we may therefore be sure that the proportion would be much greater, and the produce sent very much more extensive, if the Victorian markets were open. Permission to sell her produce in Melbourne is the one thing necessary to ensure prosperity to Tasmania. This refers to almost everything she produces, – to flour, wheat, oats, barley, fruit, jam, vegetables, cheese, butter, hides, and horses. I always take delight in reminding a Victorian, – who is a jam-loving creature, – that he is obliged to eat pumpkin jam, a filthy mixture just flavoured with fruit, because of the tariff by which he protects the fruit-grower of Victoria, – who after all can't grow fruit. I know that this will bring down wrath on my head, because fruit is grown in Victoria, – very fine fruit, which I have seen and eaten. And how shall I be believed when with the same breath I warm my fingers and cool them, – when in the same paragraph I declare that the fruit is grown and not grown? Money and care no doubt will produce fruit in Victoria, – but even Victorian shearers and Victorian miners cannot afford to eat jam made from costly fruits. Over in Tasmania fruit is rotting, – fruit as fine as any that the world can produce, – because it is thought expedient to protect the Victorian raspberry. Oh, my Victorian friend, deluging your unfortunate inwards with pumpkin trash, it grieves me to think that the madness of this protection will not make itself

apparent to you, till your taste will have been polluted and
your digestion gone! You will, I fear, never live to learn what
comforts, what luxuries, what ample bounties the rich world
will give to him who will go out freely and buy what he wants
in the cheap markets, – or how great, how fiendish, how
unnatural is the injury done by him who won't let others go
out and buy! In the meanwhile Tasmania sits pining because
she cannot sell her fruit, – cannot sell her hops.

Wool is at present the staple of this colony, – as of all the
others. But pastoral interests do not prosper here as they do in
the four great colonies on the continent. Although comparatively so small a portion of the land has been bought from the
Crown, – less than four million out of a total of nearly
seventeen million acres, – very few flocks are pastured on runs
leased from the Crown. There are altogether in Tasmania
1,350,000 sheep; and of these all but about 100,000 are
pastured on purchased lands. In 1870 the sum derived by the
colony from leases was only £7,210. In 1853 it amounted to
very nearly £30,000. No doubt this has been caused by the sale
of lands which had before been let; but the fact shows that it
has not been found expedient to take up new lands for pastoral
purposes, nor is it worth the wool-grower's while to do so.
By far the greatest portion of the island is unfit even for
pastoral purposes, – is too rough, too inaccessible, too rocky,
and too heavily timbered. The grasses used for wool are not
there, or if there cannot be reached.

I must not misuse the colony by omitting to say a word of
her gold-fields. She has gold-fields, – especially that at Fingal.
I believe I shall hardly be wrong in saying that there is no other
to which it is necessary to call special attention. But even on
the Fingal gold-digging, very much has not yet been done.
The young men of Tasmania who run to gold-rushes seek
their fortunes beyond the island, Nevertheless, gold that pays
has been found in the north-eastern part of the colony, and it
may be that even yet Tasmanian rushes will come into
fashion.

The form of government in Tasmania is very much the
same as in the other colonies. There is a 'Legislative Council'
or Upper House, and an 'Assembly', which is the Lower
House. The governor of course is king, and is politically

irresponsible. The Council is elected, and goes out by rot-
ation, each man sitting for six years. The Assembly is elected
for three years. In the latter manhood suffrage is the rule, – it
being necessary that a man should be twenty-one years old,
and have resided for a certain number of months in his district.
For the Legislative Council there is a property qualification.
Votes are of course taken by ballot. The chambers were not
sitting when I was in Tasmania, and I was informed that they
do not sit on an average above two months in the year.
Legislation in the colony is undemonstrative and unexciting.
But I think that a quiet common sense prevails which makes it
unnecessary that a Tasmanian should blush when he compares
the legislative doings in his parliament with the work of any
other colony.

It strikes an Englishman with surprise to find repeated in so
small a community as that of Tasmania all the fashions of
government with which he has been familiar at home, but
which, while he has acknowledged them to be good and
serviceable for their required purposes, he has felt to be
complex and almost confused, – and which he has known to
have been reached not by concerted plan, but by happy
accident, or rather by that arranging of circumstances which
circumstances effect for themselves, when the intentions of
men in regard to them are honest and high-minded. When a
ministry at home is in a minority on any important subject, –
any subject as to which the ministry has pledged itself, – the
ministers resign in a body, and the Queen, at the advice of the
outgoing premier, sends for that premier's chief political
enemy. If that enemy, on assuming power, finds that the
majority which brought him there will not support him while
he is there, he – goes to the country. A new House of
Commons is elected, and as that House may have a bias this
way or that, this or that political chieftain becomes the
Queen's adviser. The system is complex, and very difficult to
be understood by foreigners. Even Americans find it difficult
of comprehension. We call it constitutional, but it is written
nowhere. There is no law compelling the beaten minister to
resign. There is no law compelling the monarch to send for a
perhaps unpalatable politician. There is no standard by which
the importance of measures can be measured, – so that a man

may say, On this measure a beaten minister will retire; but in regard to that measure a ministry, though beaten, may hold its ground. But by those who attend to politics at home the working of the thing is understood, and the system has become constitutional. No minister could live who would put himself into direct opposition to it, let his genius and statesmanship be what they might. Nor could any sovereign oppose it, and continue to be a sovereign in England. The system is supported by no law, but by a general feeling which is stronger than all laws, – and that general feeling of what is expedient makes, and builds up, and alters from time to time the political arrangement of public matters which we call our constitution. We understand, not accurately indeed, but after some fashion, this slow growth, and gradually self-arranging political machinery among ourselves at home who are an old people. But it is very singular that the same system should have been adopted with complacency, – almost without thought, – by our democratic children. The Australian colonies claim to govern themselves in everything, to make what laws they please, to have what public ministers they choose, to spend what money they think right, – to be bound to the mother country only by their loyalty to the Crown. They do choose their own ministers, and give them what name they like. In one colony they have a colonial secretary, in another a chief secretary. In one colony it is reckoned that this secretary must be, and in another that he only may be, the head of the government. One colony delights to call its minister the premier, another taboos the name altogether. One colony has seven cabinet ministers, another six, another five. Tasmania has only four, one of whom has neither portfolio nor salary. In these matters they independently make their own arrangements. But the system under which ministers go out and come in, dissolve parliament, and live upon majorities, – under which the governor is advised by the retiring chieftain to send for the then popular rising star, – even though he, the governor, should think the then popular rising star to be the most inefficient and dangerous man in the colony, – is the exact copy of our political constitutional system at home.

The revenue in Tasmania amounts to about £220,000 a year, and the expenditure has been a little higher. I do not give the exact sum, because the figures before me will be an old story

before this is published. The public debt amounts to
£1,328,000, which includes a sum of £400,000 advanced to the
Launceston and Deloraine Railway. The taxation only just
exceeds £2 a head, and cannot therefore be regarded as heavy.
There is a separate land fund, which is burdened with expenses
incident to the land. The amounts received for sale and leases
of crown lands are expended on the land or on public works,
so that no absolute revenue is thus received.

CHAPTER IV

FUTURE PROSPECTS

That Tasmania is going gradually to the mischief seems to be the fixed opinion of Tasmanian politicians generally. That such a belief as to one's country should not be accompanied by any personal act evincing despair, has been the case in all national panics. English country gentlemen have very often been sure of England's ruin; but I have never heard of the country gentleman who, in consequence of his belief, sold his estate and went to live elsewhere. Speculative creeds either in politics or religion seldom prove their sincerity by altered conduct. Modern prophets have more than once or twice named some quick-coming date on which the world would end; but the prophets have made their investments and taken their leases seemingly in anticipation of a long course of future years. So it is in Tasmania. Even they who are most unhappy as to the state of things live on comfortably amidst the approaching ruin. What the stranger sees of life in the island is very comfortable. The houses are well built, and are kept in good order. The public offices are clean, spacious, and commodious. The public garden is large, and, for so small a place, well kept and handsome. The inns are fairly good, as also are the shops. I here speak both of Hobart Town and Launceston, the only two towns in the colony. Hobart Town in round numbers has 20,000 inhabitants, and Launceston 11,000. But they have the appearance of large and thriving cities much more than have towns with a similar population in England. Nevertheless, the Tasmanians acknowledge it to be the fact that Tasmania is going to the mischief.

The loudest grumblers declare that the ruin is to be found rifest in the rural districts, among the country folk and poor people. Hobart Town, they say, is kept alive by visitors who flock to it for the summer months from the other colonies; and

Launceston has whatever relics of prosperous trade the island still possesses. The people in the rural districts, they say, are generally so poor that they can with difficulty live. I have, however, already stated how infinitely superior is the condition of the Tasmanian labourer to that of his brother at home in England.

No doubt, however, there are grounds for grumbling; or it might be more just to say that there is cause for apprehension. Though Tasmania is as yet only seventy years old, as a country inhabited by white men, and, being still in its early youth, it should be yearly laying up new blood and new bone in the shape of increased population. It is not doing so. For some years past there has been no increase of which the colony can boast. During four years, from 1866 to 1870, the total increase was 403. As 340 emigrants, chiefly German, were brought in to the colony in 1870 by a system of bounties, – a number so small as to show that the effort was a failure, – it must be acknowledged that those immediate attractions which give increased population to a young colony have departed from it. And the grumblers are justified also by the condition of trade generally. In 1861 the eight chief articles exported from Tasmania were as follows, –

Wool	Value	£326,000
Wheat		82,000
Oats		81,000
Sperm Oil		59,000
Timber		55,000
Fruit (including jams)		50,000
Horses		42,000
Flour		39,000
		£734,000

In 1870 the amounts were altered as follows, –

Wool	£246,000
Wheat	15,000
Oats	56,000
Sperm Oil	33,000
Timber	37,000
Fruit (including jams)	84,000

| Horses | . | . | . | . | . | . | . | . | . | 5,000 |
| Flour | . | . | . | . | . | . | . | . | . | 11,000 |

$$£487,000$$

These figures show a decrease in every article except fruit; a total decrease of £247,000, – or in round numbers, about one-third, – and a decrease of £120,000 in corn and flour alone. No doubt for so small a community such a falling off is very serious, and justifies apprehensions. Such a diminution in the supply of wheat would lead to the fear that the colony would soon fail to feed itself with flour and grain, did we not know that the exportation of these articles from Tasmania had been stopped by the Victorian tariffs. As long as Victoria charges 9d. a hundredweight on the importation of all grain, Tasmania will be shut out from the market to which she has hitherto been able to sell her produce other than wool.

In regard to wool, which is still the staple of the colony, and as to which the above figures show the greatest decrease, the circumstances admit of a certain amount of explanation. The weight of the wool exported in 1870 was as great as that produced in 1861, – indeed, something greater; and the fall in the figures is due to the depreciation in value, – which, as all persons interested in the Australian colonies are aware, has again risen very greatly since the crop of 1870 was sold. And, again, the time of shearing, which varies according to the circumstances of the year, threw over a portion of the wool of 1870 to the sales of 1871. It appears that in 1868 the amount of Tasmanian wool sold was 6,136,426 lbs.; in 1869, 5,607,083 lbs.; and in 1870, only 4,146,913 lbs. The great difference apparent between 1868 and 1870 was caused by the later shearing of the latter year, and therefore does not show, as it might seem to do, any serious decay in the pastoral interest of the colony.

In respect to the other articles enumerated, – especially in regard to cereal produce, – there is evidence of decay where especially there should be increasing life; and it is of extreme importance that they who are interested not only in this colony, but in the Australian colonies generally, should inquire and understand how it has come to pass that in a land so gifted as

Tasmania, – in a land more fitted by climate for English emigrants than, I believe, any other on the face of the earth, – in a land that might flow with milk and honey, in a country possessing harbours, rivers, and roads, – things should already be going from bad to worse, instead of from good to better. The convict system no doubt brought with it much of evil for which it must answer, – as also many advantages with which it should be credited. The profuse expenditure of government money, and the use of what may be called slave labour, no doubt had a tendency to paralyze the energies of the settlers. The condition produced was unwholesome, and such unwholesomeness clings long. But the Tasmanians themselves understood this, and got rid of the thing. The convict flavour is quickly passing away from them; and though a certain lack of vitality among some classes may still be due to the condition of a convict settlement as I have endeavoured to describe it, Tasmania will gradually throw off that disease as New South Wales has already done. But there are other diseases which she cannot throw off, – or rather there is another cause for disease of which she cannot rid herself, – as long as the existing unnatural position of the Australasian colonies towards each other in regard to commerce remains unaltered. I will state here the populations of the colonies roughly:–

Victoria	750,000 souls
New South Wales	500,000 "
South Australia	185,000 "
Queensland	120,000 "
Tasmania	100,000 "
Western Australia	25,000 "
New Zealand	250,000 "

Putting aside New Zealand, which, however, is quite as much interested in the matter as the others, – we find that they are like so many English counties, or, as the area is very large, like so many American states, contiguous to each other, speaking the same language, having the same or similar interests, connected in and out by joint properties, joint families, and joint names, attached to the same mother country, having nothing but a name to mark their borders. There is indeed no such dissimilarity of interests as between Lancashire and Wiltshire, for wool is the staple produce of each of them. There is no such cause of disruption as between the Southern and Northern States of America, – no dissimilarity of character as between the Eastern and Western States. They are at least as much one people as are the inhabitants of the dominion of Canada. They are much more one people than were the various German nationalities who had found it to be impossible not to bind themselves together by a customs union, even before Prussia had bound them together politically. They are all English, – and not a law can be passed by them without the assent of an English minister or his deputy. And yet they levy customs duties among each other as do the various nations of Europe, – or rather as did the various nations of Europe before the principles of free-trade had been efficacious in liberating a single branch of commerce.

It is not my purpose here to discuss free trade, or to attempt to prove its beneficent action. I am content in my humble way to point out that people who reject free trade must be content to eat pumpkin mixture and call it strawberry jam. Those of my readers who are still in favour of protecting home industry by duties on imported goods will not be converted by me. In regard to the great majority of my countrymen I may take it for granted that on this matter we are of one opinion. The question here is not one of free trade, – but of free trade between the Australian colonies, which may be accompanied by any amount of protection by them all against the outside world. It is as though we should have discussed the expediency of border customs between Lancashire and Yorkshire at a time in which we levied duties on silks from France and Italy. There was a question among us then, – a much vexed question, – as to the imposition of duties on foreign articles; but no man would have been listened to for a moment who would have proposed border customs between our counties at home. Such a man would have been simply insane. The man who should do so in America with regard to the different states would be equally so. The German Zollverein showed what was the feeling of Germany generally in the matter. But the Australian colonies still act against each other as though they were separate nations.

And they are forbidden by the English law as it at present stands to do otherwise – though the English government has more than once offered to the colonies its sanction for the abolition of the absurdity in the gross. As the law stands at present any British colony, and therefore any one of the Australias, may levy what taxes and what customs duties it thinks fit to levy; but it cannot levy differential duties. New South Wales for instance may put what duty it shall please on sugar, – but it cannot receive Queensland sugar free of duty and charge a duty on sugar from the Mauritius or from Cuba. And yet there is no more than a nominal border-line between the two colonies, the two places being as closely joined as any English counties. Victoria may receive wheat free from all the world; but she cannot receive wheat free from South Australia, with which she borders as Yorkshire does with Lancashire, unless she receive it free also from all the world. The law has been so fixed in order that no dependency of Great Britain should be able to sin against that free-trade policy by which England professes to regulate her dealings with foreign countries. Differential duties may, no doubt, be levied with the express view of injuring the trade of an especial country; and if England binds herself not to commit the injury, it is intelligible that she should bind her dependent colonies to the same extent.

But England has in point of fact abandoned the principle in regard to intercolonial trade, – not because it is felt that the principle is not as applicable to the colonies as to England, but on the conviction that Australia in regard to trade must and should be regarded as one whole, – as is the Canadian dominion, as are the United states, as were the German kingdoms when Germany was politically divided. A reference to the population of the colonies, to their geographical position and affinities, to their joint interests, to their real oneness as a people, convinces the merest tyro in political economy of the absurdity of border duties between them, – almost equally of the absurdity of duties levied from port to port. On the 15th July, 1870, the Secretary of State for the Colonies wrote the following circular to the different Australian governors:

'SIR– I think it important to ensure that the governors of the Australian colonies should not misunderstand the views of Her Majesty's government with regard to intercolonial free trade.

'The different colonies of Australia are at present, in respect of their customs duties, in the position of separate and independent countries. So long as they remain in that relation, a law which authorised the importation of goods from one colony to another on any other terms than those applicable to the imports from any foreign country would be open, in the view of Her Majesty's government, to the objection of principle which attaches to differential duties.

'But Her Majesty's government would not object to the establishment of a complete customs union between the Australian colonies, whether embracing two or more contiguous colonies, or, – which would be preferable, – the whole Australian continent with its adjacent islands. If any negotiations should be set on foot with this object you are at liberty to give them your cordial support.

(Signed) 'KIMBERLEY.'

I cannot think that any one will read this without agreeing with Lord Kimberley, though most who do so would express their agreement in stronger terms, as to the present condition of Australian customs duties than it would suit a Secretary of State to use. But this proposition on the part of Lord Kimberley altogether abandons the question as to differential duties between the colonies. If there were an Australian customs union New South Wales would get Queensland sugar free of duty, but might still charge what duty it pleased on Cuban sugar. Victoria would import free wine from New South Wales, – which she does largely, – and free wine from South Australia, and free hops from Tasmania; but would still put what duties she pleased on French wines, and Chilian wheat, and English hops. And this permission would be given, not because English statesmen have gone back in their opinion about differential duties, – but because the maintenance of hostile trade interests between communities so bound together as are these colonies is a worse evil than the semblance of differential duties which would thus be allowed to exist.

But the colonies are not ready for a customs union. Three of them, Tasmania, South Australia, and New Zealand, have expressed a general concurrence, – others a qualified concurrence. Victoria is the greatest sinner in the matter, – being for the time wedded to protection in all its deformity. In the meantime permission has been asked by certain of the colonies, – and notably by Tasmania, on whose behalf the matter has been argued with great vigour by her minister, Mr. Wilson, – that they should be allowed to arrange their intercolonial customs without reference to the duties charged on extra-colonial articles, – and that they should be permitted to do this, as a measure paving the way to a customs union. This permission has been refused them, and I must acknowledge that in the correspondence which has taken place on the subject I think that the Tasmanian statesman gets the better of Downing Street. I give in an Appendix, No. 3, – as they are too long for insertion in the text, – Lord Kimberley's circular dispatch on the subject, dated 13th July, 1871; and Mr. Wilson's memorandum in answer to it.

We cannot prevent the colonists from entertaining protect-ionist principles, – cannot go back to a condition of things which would enable the mother country to dictate to the colonies on the subject. Universal suffrage undoubtedly assists protection. The fabricator of any article sees that a tax on that article when imported will force the world around him to use the article home-made, and that then his peculiar labour will be fostered and protected. If foreign boots be made dear by a tax, the local bootmaker can get 5s. a pair for making boots; but if foreign boots be sold cheap, he cannot get above 3s. 6d. The Victorian farmer, – a very small man usually, – thinks that he cannot grow wheat and live if wheat from Adelaide be admitted to the markets on the same terms as his own wheat. Men learn so much quickly. The lesson is acquired on the first aspect of the matter. The consequent evil results to these shallow pupils in having to pay double for goods which they consume and do not produce, requires a deeper insight into matters, and an insight accompanied by some calculation, before it produces a conviction. At home, in England, the working man is certainly not superior in intelligence to his Australian brother, but he is subjected in his political instincts and inquiries to higher, and I must say, to more honest influences. I cannot bring myself to believe that he is generally made to understand great political truths, but he is made to believe that this or that politician is a safe political guide, and he votes accordingly. And on one subject, which is to him of all the most important, – the subject of food, – he has been made to understand that free trade means a cheap loaf. In

Australia food is plentiful, and the labourer feels comparatively little solicitude on this subject. Each man wishes to protect from competition that which he himself makes. The Victorian, in his wisdom, desires to give nothing out of his store to any fellow-labourer from South Australia or from Tasmania, – at any rate to give as little as possible. He therefore is a protectionist, – and the would-be minister of the day is a protectionist because he wants the labourer's vote.

It is thus that protection has become rife, and we cannot cure the evil suddenly by any order to be given, or by any permission to be refused. The ordinary educated traveller in the colonies, – getting into the society which will fall naturally in his way, – will find that almost every person he meets is opposed to protection. But everybody will tell him at the same time that protection cannot be abolished. The voters like it, and the voters are omnipotent. There is a variation in the feeling in the various colonies, – but this is the general state of the colonial mind on the subject. If it be so, it should, I think, be the object of governments at home to develop as far as possible all operations which will tend in the first place to create intercolonial free trade. The existing state of things has the double evil, – the first natural evil of impeding trade and of impoverishing everybody concerned; and the further evil of fostering rivalries and hostilities between people who are in fact one and the same. That a general customs union would, of all steps in the right direction, be the greatest and the wisest there can hardly be a doubt. To me it seems to be almost equally clear that any measure tending to abolish customs duties between the colonies would be a step towards a customs union. Let New South Wales be enabled to take free sugar from Queensland, and Queensland will take fruit on the same terms from New South Wales. The condition of the colonies makes it obvious that there should be no customs levied between them.

Poor little Tasmania is straining every nerve to obtain the privilege of sending her produce for the consumption of her sister colonies, especially of Victoria, without which privilege she cannot continue to exist. The value of the exports from any country are, or should be, but small in comparison with the value of the produce consumed at home, – but the smaller the country is, the more certain is the ruin entailed upon it by prohibition from selling its goods in an outside market.

Its condition becomes such as that would be of a small wheat-growing English county debarred from selling its wheat beyond its own confines. The richness of its own produce would become its own greatest burden. Industry and energy would naturally disappear. A large population with diverse employments producing all, or nearly all, that it wants, can live in such a condition, though the life would be a bad life, – but a small community would be as were Robinson Crusoe and his man Friday, wanting almost all that man requires, though overladen with much plenty.

There is a remedy for the injury which Tasmania now suffers, – but it is a remedy which she cannot adopt without soreness of heart, without dishonour, without self-annihilation. She can become a part of Victoria, and then the Victorian markets will be open to her. Let her implore Victoria to take her, and then she will be able to sell her wheat and her oats, her fruit and her jam, her hops and her horses at Melbourne. 'You had better do it,' the Victorian says to the Tasmanian. 'It will come at last.'

Men in Tasmania are beginning to feel that perhaps they had better do it, though the idea is odious to them. It is impossible that this island ever should be amalgamated with the big continental colony on equal terms. Were the arrangement made on seemingly equitable terms, on terms fixed in accordance with the population, Tasmania would send to the Victorian legislature one Tasmanian for every eight Victorians, – or thereabouts; and the men so sent would have to remain in Melbourne for eight or nine months of parliamentary work. This small minority would be almost voiceless among their louder brethren, and it would soon come to pass that Tasmanians would not go there. Tasmania would be represented by Victorians, to whom she would now have to pay the salaries which Victorian legislators now receive. Hobart Town would no longer be a seat of government. Some judge would come there on periodical visits as often as Victorian generosity would permit, and the judge would be Victorian. The little colony would be handed over, bound hand and foot, to her strong-fisted sister, and there would be the end of all her glories. The reader will perhaps feel that these are simply sentimental objections, and will say that the material advantages to be gained would more than compensate them. But sentimental grievances are of all grievances the heaviest to bear, and the material advantages are only those which the colony has a right to expect without any sacrifice of her honour.

Such a change of things would be detrimental not only to Tasmania, but to all Australia generally. I have suggested in a former paragraph that a general federal union of these colonies into one nationality will take place sooner or later. Such I believe to be the opinion of almost all who have thought upon the subject. But nothing will tend so much to delay this result as the special greatness and superiority in population and wealth of any one colony. The big colony will think twice before it will admit the little colony to equal terms with it. There was much generosity on foot when Virginia and New York united themselves with Rhode Island, and a great patriotic idea was urgent in the breasts of great patriots. Among the Australian colonies each colony recognises with astonishing accuracy its own position in wealth and population. Victoria is even now much the biggest. Were Tasmania to become a part of Victoria, I fear that the difficulty of forming, first, a customs union and then a political federal union, would become greater even than it is at present.

It is to be presumed that such amalgamation could not be effected without the consent of the government at home, and that the matter is one as to which a Secretary of State would feel himself justified in refusing his consent on the ground of general policy. If there is to be an Australian as well as Canadian dominion, or rather a union of states, – for such must be the condition rather than the other, – it will be more easily effected with many than with a few. Before that day shall arrive, there will probably be a northern colony in Queensland, and a further division from New South Wales in the direction of the big rivers. And there will be a northern territory in that which is all now called South Australia, with a capital at Port Darwin. I trust that the fairest and prettiest and pleasantest of all the colonies will not then have been absorbed, so that the name of Tasmania shall be absent from the roll of Australian States.